THE

DESIGN

OF

POETRY

New York

THE
DESIGN
OF
POETRY

By

CHARLES B. WHEELER

THE OHIO STATE UNIVERSITY

W · W · NORTON & COMPANY · INC ·

Contents

Preface

This book is a general introduction to poetry. It begins, as both logic and custom dictate, with certain fundamental questions about the nature of poetry, to which I have tried to supply more complete and more carefully reasoned answers than one normally finds in a book of this sort. My first chapter presents poetry as a special way of using language, within the context of other uses of language. The second chapter takes up the qualities of language which this use brings into being, and the third moves on to consider the inner life or purposiveness of the creative act which we know as a poem. A group of six chapters then deals with various typical poetic designs, including metrical and stanzaic forms, and the last chapter sets forth the principles of interpretation which follow from the view of poetry thus presented. The result is a systematic analytical essay that minimizes the importance of mere information about poetry and concentrates instead on the task of developing insight into it, so that the reader may free himself as soon as possible from dependence on outside helps.

My aim in writing has been to satisfy the needs of two separate but not necessarily different audiences: the one composed of students enrolled in undergraduate college courses, the other of literate adults, whatever their status, whose reading had stimulated their curiosity and suggested to them the value of answering these questions about poetry. Certainly no formal prerequisite is as important as the reader's genuine interest. I have therefore tried to write something which is self-contained, with its own commentary and illustrations, usable both inside and outside of the classroom. Because I am not addressing fellow specialists, I have played down the merely technical side of my subject, I have avoided documentary notes, and I have modernized the spelling and punctuation in some of the quotations of older poetry when it seemed appropriate to do so.

The approach to poetry which I have taken might be broadly characterized as linguistic. That is, I agree entirely with Mallarmé's often-quoted remark to Degas that poems are made with words, and I have tried to work out the consequences of this truth here. My approach might also be characterized as formalistic or analytical, in the modern tradition of "close reading" or *explication de texte*. But the chronic fault of all theories which locate poetry in the objective form of language *per se* is that they cannot explain why it should be there. Nor, correlatively, can they provide any rationale for the process of getting it out. What does one explicate a poem *for?* If a poem is only so much poetry, and poetry itself is distinguished only by possessing certain qualities to a greater degree than nonpoetic language does, no generic lines can be drawn around them, and the activities of the critic and the poet are equally mysterious. My answer has been to reverse the direction of that approach by taking the poem as not just the primary locus of poetry but indeed the very cause of its existence. Poetry is a special use of language, and it is made by the act of writing a poem: this is what my concept of "design" comes to.

I am well aware that there is nothing really new in this concept. As those best qualified to know can most easily tell, it is rooted very thoroughly in the literary criticism of the past 200 years. But my book is in no sense a compendium or even a selection of critical doctrines from this area; rather, it is an attempt to devise an independent theory of poetry, and it should be judged by its own accomplishments, not by what its antecedents may have been. My specific borrowings from other critics are very few. I took the distinction between positive and negative theories of poetic diction in Chapter 1 from F. W. Bateson's *English Poetry and the English Language*, the concept of inductive and deductive design in Chapter 7 from Donald A. Stauffer's *The Nature of Poetry*. The treatment of the clothes-symbolism in *King Lear* in Chapter 2 owes something to Robert B. Heilman, though the actual analysis is entirely my own. My ideas on meter were clarified by a reading of John Thompson's *The Founding of English Metre*. I was not able to read *Poetic Meter and Poetic Form*, by Paul Fussell, Jr., until after completing Chapters 8 and 9, but I am pleased to see that we have come to many similar conclusions. I should like to acknowledge here a general debt to the linguistic studies of Ferdinand de Saussure and the members of the Prague Circle (the latter as made accessible by Paul Garvin and Victor Erlich), the Chicago neo-Aristotelians (though I cannot follow them in all respects), Owen Barfield's *Poetic Diction*, and—not that anyone could fail to see his influence on this book —the greatest critic of all: Samuel Taylor Coleridge.

I also owe much to my colleagues and to the opportunity which I have had in teaching the introductory course in poetry at The Ohio State University. I have been able to test my ideas in that most stimulating environment, the classroom, and in fraternal association with other scholars. Professors Claude M. Simpson, Jr., and Richard D. Altick have contributed helpful information. At a critical early stage in the preparation of this book my manuscript was read by Professors Robert M. Estrich and Albert J. Kuhn, who gave themselves unselfishly to the task and whose comments were of immense value. Finally and above all I should like to thank Professor Oliver W. Ferguson of Duke University, who has read every word of the manuscript and made a great many wise and pertinent suggestions. He is not, of course, to be blamed for the faults remaining in the book, which are my responsibility alone, but I should like him to receive credit with myself for its better qualities. In a very real sense his support has made this work possible.

1 ·
What Is Poetry?

The purloined letter, in Edgar Allan Poe's short story, would never have been recovered if M. Dupin had not entered the case, for he alone was capable of understanding the tactics which the thief had used to baffle the police. These tactics were, in part, to display the letter openly, where it was sure to be seen by anyone searching the apartment. Convinced that an object of such value would necessarily be hidden, the police did not bother to examine what was in front of them all the time.

Perhaps it is not straining at a point to claim that we enjoy the story because, as well as identifying ourselves with M. Dupin and sharing in his triumph, we also sympathize with the police in their bafflement. We too would have made the same mistakes. Poe's story has something valid to say about human psychology in general, about a tendency which we all show when called upon to find something of especial importance: we overlook the obvious. Certainly this is true for most persons beginning the study of poetry. Nothing could be more natural than to assume that an art whose value is traditionally ranked so very high should be rare, difficult, and hidden. Since poetry needs to be studied, it must hold secrets from the uninitiated, and in particular the secret of its very nature—the answer to the question, What is poetry?—must lie well concealed behind the words that the reader sees when he looks at a poem. Yet at that moment the printed page itself is telling him the answer; the one basic truth about poetry which cannot be kept a secret confronts him directly. It is not what the words are saying, but simply the fact that they are there. Poetry is an art of words.

This basic truth is indeed obvious enough, once it has been pointed out. The reader's sense of discovery may be tempered, however, by a feeling that his task has now only begun. If the Paris police had found the purloined letter, they would have accomplished their mission. Recognizing that poetry is an art of words is merely the first step in the study of poetry, and a step that does not seem to point very clearly in any one direction. Nevertheless, its implications are enormous. This chapter will attempt to explore them and will outline the definition of poetry that follows as a logical consequence.

Being an art of words, poetry is different from an art of patterns and colors (painting), or an art of sounds (music), or an art of three-dimensional forms (sculpture). Each of the arts, as further examples would continue to show, is characterized by the use of a distinctive medium or combination of media. More than that, each art is confined to the medium which it uses. A composer who wants to write music has no choice but to use sounds, however much he may want to use modeling clay or water colors—or even nothing at all. The significance of this observation lies in what it suggests about the relationship between each of the arts and its medium, a relationship so close that the term "medium" is not only inadequate to express it but misleading as well. A work of art is not a translation or rendering into perceptible form of something else that exists in its own right. The symphony is what we hear; the painting is what we see; the poem is what we read. Take the words of the poem away, and everything else goes with them. That is, words are not just the vehicle for poetry: poetry *is* words.

If poetry is words, then it must be something that language alone makes possible. Not all poets have themselves believed this, for the opposite point of view, the "Platonic," has had many advocates. Shelley was one of the most eloquent. According to his *Defence of Poetry*, poetry transcends language, always escaping complete expression in words; it is a spiritual or ideal quality like "order" or "beauty" or "truth," favoring at times with its evanescent visitations all aspects of human life and by no means limited to the compositions in language called poems. Shelley is very persuasive, and there is much in his essay that compels agreement. Yet his theory, when followed consistently, leads to a complete dead end for the critic or reader. The effect of defining poetry in terms of qualities not related exclusively to language (an effect that Shelley himself saw and welcomed) is to make it impossible to distinguish between a poem and anything else sharing the same qualities. Ordinarily we would regard it a figure of speech to call a suspension bridge a "poem in steel," but if we define poetry as order and beauty, for example, we must regard the phrase as literal, and then presumably go on to call Shelley's "Ode to the West Wind" a "poem in words"—which sounds rather queer. Whatever poems and bridges may have in common, they are normally treated as being profoundly different. To upset the verdict of common sense here would create far more problems than it would solve. If the bridge and the poem are both essentially "poems," what are we to make of the fact that one will get you across a river and the other will not? There must be a means for discriminating between them on the basis of essential characteristics peculiar to each.

As for the transcendence of poetry, which is the other half of the Platonic doctrine, it is a notion especially congenial to the poet, who is always comparing the poem he thinks himself capable of writing with the poem he did write, to the disadvantage of the latter. The finished poem may indeed be a mere shadow of the original conception in the poet's mind, but all that the readers have or ever will have is what lies on the printed page; for better or worse that is poetry to them. They will be lucky to do justice to this, without worrying about the poetry still hovering in the empyrean that the poet strove to capture and missed.

These words that make up poetry are physical objects

—black marks on white paper and vibrations of the air—but they are also significant elements of human experience. Hence the analogy with the other arts cannot be carried further. The notes of the scale or the sounds they represent are quite without musical value by themselves, nor is there any real value inherent in the painter's pigments or the sculptor's stone. The words used by the poet, however, have independent meanings; they are all in the dictionary. They have these meanings because they have been put to certain uses, because human beings have for many years conversed, argued, corresponded, reasoned, joked, cursed, speculated, named, sung, and hoped with them. Each word epitomizes a bit of cultural history and carries with it, as the token of its association with the human mind, a set of connotations. Of necessity this is all reduced to the barest outline in the dictionary, but that book is still our best witness that language is not a neutral and indifferent material, like plaster, simply waiting to be cast into any mold and always fresh for every new use.

It follows, therefore, that another basic truth must be admitted: not only is poetry an art of language, but poetry (more generally, all literature) is the only art that works habitually with second-hand materials. Although poets may now and then create new words or new combinations (one thinks of Hopkins' "wanwood leafmeal"), they exercise this privilege rather seldom and for the most part draw their vocabulary from the same source used by everybody else who speaks a given language. The words appearing in poetry can also be found in inventories, telephone conversations, laundry lists, final examinations, and numerous other contexts just as unexciting as these. And they appear *at the same time*. This fact is worth emphasizing because it means that poetry is in direct competition with other uses of language.* The words the poet uses are characteristically enriched by human associations, but this enrichment is not a matter of past history entirely: it is also a continuing process, affect-

* That is, poetry competes with other uses of language for materials (words), but not in its aim. For the latter point, see pages 14 and 23, following.

ing words through their involvement with the mundane affairs of contemporary life.

Again an exception has to be made, this time for poets who have agreed that ordinary language is in competition with poetry, but who have deplored or resisted this fact. During the eighteenth century in England it was widely held that poetry requires a special language, a "poetic diction." The classic statement of this theory is Thomas Gray's, "The language of the age is never the language of poetry." The objection was on the grounds that poetry is an art of exalted thoughts and refined sentiments, conveying what is generally true and not what is local or circumstantial. The theory had both a negative and a positive aspect. Negatively some words were proscribed because they were "low" (thus Samuel Johnson objected to Shakespeare's use of the word "knife" in a speech of Macbeth's because the effect of the passage is weakened "by the name of an instrument used by butchers and cooks in the meanest employments"). Positively, some words were recommended because they were inherently poetic, or as a statement attributed to Oliver Goldsmith puts it: "There are certain words in every language particularly adapted to the poetical expression; some from the image or idea they convey to the imagination; and some from the effect they have upon the ear." The theory of poetic diction cannot be dismissed quite as Shelley's theory of transcendent qualities was dismissed, since it actually affected the way poets in this period wrote. Their work cannot be read with sympathetic understanding unless one takes into account what they were trying to accomplish. Nevertheless, the best poetry of the period tends to be that which is least marked by poetic diction, and the poetry which followed the current theory most faithfully is on the whole very bad indeed. (When Wordsworth, more than a generation later, tried to substitute a diametrically opposite theory of his own, having to do with "the real language of men," he succeeded no better.) This is not the place to speculate why, but it does seem as though a priori theories of composition, which set out rules for what all poets must or must not do, affect poetry harmfully, and in

more or less exact ratio to their strictness. Even if such theories had worked better, they would have accounted for
only a small portion of the poetry which a modern reader
wants to master. He has to look for something more com-
prehensive, something that will apply to the poems of
Wyatt, Donne, Dryden, Tennyson, and Yeats as well as to
those of Collins, Gray, Thomson, and Pope.

It is not necessary yet to investigate these different poetic idioms for what they have in common—enough that
they are all legitimately called poetic. The verdict of tradition is sufficient. At this point the only thing necessary is to
realize that they could not all have been formed by the same
selection of language. Poetry is not a special kind of language. It is, rather, a special way in which language is used.

In order to prepare for seeing what is distinctive in this
use of language and what qualities poetry possesses as a result of it, something must now be said about language as a
whole, and its other uses must be described in their relation
to poetry. The diagram on the opposite page is a way of
doing all this visually, through a schematic picture of the relationships. In the remainder of this chapter, it will be explained part by part, but since it is both schematic and
pictorial, the explanation will have to carry some warnings
against the distortions that it introduces.

SPEECH

Nothing about man is more remarkable than his power
of speech. Although many animals have a repertory of noises
by which they express themselves and communicate with
one another for various purposes, only man has become able
to use these noises as a means of freeing himself from the
tyranny of his environment. There is no need to speculate
about whether animals think, remember, imagine, or have
self-consciousness, since the important point is that as far as
vocal behavior is concerned they cannot do anything but
respond to situations immediately confronting them—and
there are severe limits on the number and kinds of situations

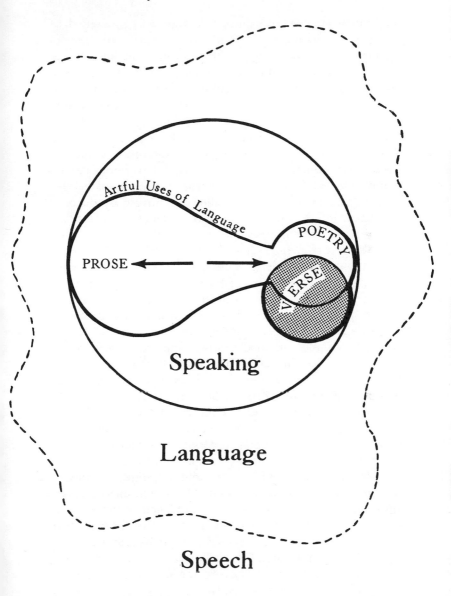

Artful Uses of Language

PROSE ←——→ POETRY

VERSE

Speaking

Language

Speech

that they can even recognize. A dog who succeeded in forming a generalized notion that postmen are hateful (though there is no reason to believe that such an achievement is possible) would still have no means of indicating so until a postman actually appeared and gave him something to bark at. On the other hand, man, if he wishes, can create an entire world of non-present things. This great communal achievement of the human race has nothing necessarily to do with man's having vocal organs, or with their adaptability to the production of a wide variety of patterned noises, though we have no better term for it than "speech." Instead, it is a matter of man's ability to invest these noises with meaning irrespective of circumstances, to *refer* to things, to give the noises content.

Not less than his opposable thumb or his large cranial capacity, man's power of speech has been of incalculable service in the development of his race. Thanks to speech he can manipulate his environment in the abstract, using tokens of purely nominal value, which are capable of being either held in reserve or freely circulated and which have systematic relationships with one another. Speech in this sense is like money: various coins and bits of paper have been stamped with a conventional mark indicating their worth (which is seldom the worth of the metal or paper itself), and they are used to buy and sell things which would be too cumbersome to exchange directly, as well as to store up the value of these things. The contents of a person's wallet, or (even more abstractly) the figures in his bank account, can stand for the equivalent in farms, buildings, ships, machinery, and all variety of concrete goods. These bits of money or figures in a book are not isolated phenomena but parts of a system: ten dimes are just as good as a dollar bill, and their being round and shiny instead of crisp and green has nothing to do with the case. The analogy with money does not tell the whole truth about speech, but it does tell something that is absolutely fundamental.

Speech is not a part of the diagram; it is the paper on which the diagram is printed, the ground for everything else. Speech is manifested in the existence of particular languages, but speech itself, in the most general sense of that term, is best considered as the potentiality of having any language at all.

LANGUAGE

The area enclosed by the dotted line stands for any particular language, in this case English. Two things are represented by this part of the diagram. (1) The dotted line is meant to suggest that a language is an abstraction rather than a concrete entity. English is real enough, to be sure, but there is nothing that one can put his finger on and say, "This is English—it's right here." English is both more than and less than what is printed in books or spoken by English-speaking persons. In order to demonstrate the existence and the nature of English, one would have to point to these partial manifestations, but the total of all manifestations would still not provide the thing itself. (2) The irregular shape of the area is meant to suggest that a language is not static, but that, like a living organism, it constantly changes, advancing and retreating at different rates on different portions of its periphery, adding and sloughing off, adapting to new circumstances, altering in its relationships with kindred languages. In spite of these processes, a language as a whole remains much the same year after year, and only when the scale of time is considerably enlarged can any net effect of the changes be seen.

What separates one language from another most obviously is the fact that they have different sets of signs for referring to more or less the same set of things. So we tend to think of the English language as being represented by the contents of the English dictionary. But English also has rules for modifying words and for combining them into larger units, that is, into organized utterances. These rules may be collectively termed the "grammar" of the language, and they are quite as important as its vocabulary, though they are less conspicuous. By various methods of analysis linguists have succeeded in discovering and codifying many of these rules. Whether they will ever complete the job is doubtful. This will in no way affect the use of English, however, since in the first place the rules of grammar are implicit in the way people speak: that is their mode of existence and their location. The rules are not derived from books but from the speech of other persons using English, nor is it ever necessary to be conscious of a rule as such in order to obey it.

SPEAKING

Language, as it is being considered here, is like the game of chess; it has words (pieces) and a set of rules. But the pieces and the rules do not of themselves play the game—it takes people to do that—and *a* game of chess that two of these people might play is not the same thing as *the* game of chess. For example, player "A" might defeat player "B" in a particular series of fifteen moves; but we would not then conclude that the game of chess requires these pieces, these rules, and these fifteen moves. There are millions of possible games, all different, of which this was only one. The problem, such as it is, comes from the ambiguity of the word "game." So that a similar ambiguity in this discussion of language can be avoided, the word "language" is understood as referring to the total system of vocabulary and grammar within which and in accordance with which individual speech acts take place. The application or concrete embodiment of language, the sum of speech acts themselves, is here called "speaking." It is what people do with the language that they have. The diagram merely places speaking within the boundaries of language, though the relationships between the two are more complex than that and certainly have nothing to do with space, which is the only dimension suggested there.

Speaking includes what exists in print as well as what is said orally. There are differences between oral and written language, but they are not germane here. If "speaking," like "speech," tends to suggest oral language only, its use can be defended on the ground that it helps to correct an opposite tendency that we all have to think of language as essentially something written. Writing is inessential: many languages of remarkable complexity are in use among people who do not have and never have had any system for writing down what they say. Most of the various systems that do exist are cumbersome and inconsistent, and the particular one being used in this book is notoriously one of the poorest of all.

VERSE

The area included under this term is the only exception to the general principle on which the diagram is constructed, since verse is both a use of language and a kind of language. As a kind of language, verse can be easily defined: it is the metrical arrangement of words. Quite often verse is accompanied by rime and one of the many stanza forms, but these are not essential to it. The only feature absolutely required is the occurrence of stressed syllables according to a regular pattern. These regular stresses of verse are immediately distinctive. Being so unlike the irregular stresses found in everyday speech and in prose, they mark verse off, even to the untrained ear, as belonging in a category of its own. If necessary, the characteristics of verse can be measured and demonstrated, so that to call a given selection of language "verse" is a judgment of fact and not an opinion or an evaluation. Chapter 8 will take up the question of verse in greater detail.

In the diagram, "verse" is shaded in order to make clear its exceptional status. The diagram further shows that the areas of poetry and verse do not wholly coincide. The reason why poetry lies partially outside the area of verse is that some poetry is not written in metrical language. That is the so-called "free verse," which was developed and popularized during the early years of this century by poets of the vers libre movement, and which is still being written, though modern poets seem to be going back more and more to the traditional meters. Most readers know free verse through the work of such pioneers as Amy Lowell, Carl Sandburg, Hilda Doolittle, William Carlos Williams, Ezra Pound, E. E. Cummings—and of course Walt Whitman, who antedated the movement as such. The case for accepting free verse as legitimate poetry has long been won; the only difficulty now is the phrase "free verse" itself, which is illogical in terms of the definition of verse proposed here, since verse is just the thing that this unmetrical poetry is free from. "Verse-free poetry" would be much better. But it is too late by several decades to do anything about that.

Poetry, whether in verse form or not, will be discussed separately in this chapter. What remains is an area of verse outside the area of poetry. Here verse is still a kind of language—i.e., metrical language—but it is also a particular artful use of language that is no less distinctive in its own fashion when properly understood. It conveys much proverbial wisdom:

> Red sky at morning, sailors take warning;
> Red sky at night, sailors' delight.

It is often a way of assisting the memory:

> Thirty days has September,
> April, June, and November. . . .

It brightens many occasions with the harmless little stanzas printed on greeting cards, like

> Though wanderings me from you divide,
> In thought you're always by my side;
> The world does not contain another
> So near and dear to me as Mother.

And it is especially familiar as a vehicle for advertising messages on radio and television, such as

> Murphy's beer, Murphy's beer,
> Brings you happiness and cheer;

> See it sparkle, see it foam,
> Take a case of Murphy's home.

This language raises no serious questions on its own part; everyone appreciates it for what it is. The difficulty appears when such examples as the four above are placed next to certain other examples which may also come to mind:

> Full fathom five thy father lies,
> Of his bones are coral made. . . .

> A sweet disorder in the dress
> Kindles in clothes a wantonness. . . .

> Tyger! Tyger! burning bright
> In the forests of the night,
> What immortal hand or eye
> Could frame thy fearful symmetry?

> Polyphiloprogenitive
> The sapient sutlers of the Lord
> Drift across the window-panes.
> In the beginning was the Word.

These lines, roughly parallel in form with the examples of verse, are obviously different from them, too. But exactly how they are different is not so obvious. Although the subjects are not the same, the two sets of examples—as sets—do not differ from each other in subject matter any more strikingly than some of the individual examples within either set differ from others in the same set. There is as much distance between beer and mothers as between beer and tigers. Is it that the second set is better than the first? No doubt. It would be hard to believe otherwise after recognizing in these lines the shaping genius of Shakespeare, Herrick, Blake, and Eliot. Yet however justified the presumption of value for the second set may be, the comparison is meaning-less unless it is made clear on what ground these latter are to be preferred. We have to ask, better *what?*

The way out of this impasse is to recognize and give due weight to the purpose for which all of the first set were written. They exist because they serve a human need to re-member things or convey traditional sentiments or increase the sale of products, and as far as anyone can tell that is their only excuse for being. They may have aesthetic quali-ties, but it would be idle to spend any time considering this possibility in view of the overriding importance of their use. On the other hand, the examples in the second set are not, as far as anyone can tell, aiming at a definite goal. They seem to have no use. If the commercial for Murphy's beer was written to sell beer, what was Blake's "The Tyger" written to sell? The appropriate reaction to hearing the beer commercial is to go out and do what it says: buy a case of Murphy's. What is the appropriate reaction to reading Blake's "The Tyger"? Going to the zoo? One can imagine the advertising agency responsible for the Murphy account deciding to discard the jingle because it was not producing results, but what standards would allow anyone to deter-mine whether Blake's poem should be discarded? Not the same ones, surely. The point is this: it does no harm to assert, following the normal instinct to make value judg-ments, that Blake's poem is better than the beer commercial, but we do not want to be put in the position of having to say that the beer commercial might have been as good as the poem if it had only been better written. They are just not comparable. *There is no way to write a beer commercial as a poem.* It does not matter how splendid the language is; the moment an author adopts as his purpose that of getting his audience to do something, he has made his language subor-dinate or instrumental to that end, and the only real merit it can have is effectiveness. We judge it, as we must, by look-ing away from the composition and out into the external world. The distinction between verse and poetry is a generic one and not a matter of gradation or refinement. The fact that both sets of examples here are written in metrical language ("verse" in the first of its two senses) indicates nothing about their essential natures.

Verse in the second sense is therefore the art of composition in metrical language for the purpose of achieving some definite external goal. This goal can be described or specified in every case, and in no case does it yield precedence to other features of the composition, all of which are strictly subordinate to it. Since poetry and verse are radically different uses of language, they do not really compete. A preference for one over the other would be about as meaningless as a preference for smoking expensive cigars over going bareheaded in the rain—it is impossible to imagine any situation in which the two activities or the two uses of language might present themselves as genuine alternatives.

The series of questions about Blake's "The Tyger" and the beer commercial, above, was rather obviously contrived for the sake of making a point. This procedure did no damage to the commercial, but it may have misrepresented the poem somewhat. Certainly it oversimplified the case. It is not true that poets write poems without considering how readers will react to them, or that the ability to produce a certain reaction is not an important requisite for the success of a poem. Granted that Blake did not write his poem in order to sell tigers, we could still say that he wrote it in order to sell awe, if the one word "awe" were allowed to stand for the very complicated attitude that Blake manifests, and encourages in us, toward the marvelous paradoxes of creation. Yet there is no way to *carry out* Blake's poem, as it were. Blake has so arranged things that the reader looks around him in vain for anything to do. If he wants to buy the awe that Blake has to sell—and the jarring inappropriateness of this commercial language is itself a good argument for preserving the distinction—how else can he do so than by carefully and sympathetically attending to the words of the poem, savoring its meanings, pondering its implications? The aim of the poem is outward to the reader only for the sake of capturing him and bringing him back to the poem itself.

This distinction leaves bad poetry out of account, as it must. Although no statistics are obtainable, one can assume that bad poetry is at least as common as verse, since it is regularly printed in periodicals with a general circulation, forms the entire output of many small presses and obscure magazines, and fills the desk drawers of uncounted amateur poets who have strong feelings about life and love but lack the skill to do them justice. Such poetry is bad because it fails to reach the level of good poetry to which it painfully aspires, not because it fails to rise above the level of the beer commercial. If it were good it would be so in the way that poetry is good and not in the way that verse is good. Being bad, it is still bad poetry.

PROSE

As the line which encloses the three of them indicates, prose, like poetry and verse, is an artful use of language. "Artful" means consciously managed for effect, having a stylistic tradition, requiring to be learned. On this basis prose is distinguished from everyday language, which surrounds it and which furnishes its linguistic material. Everyday language is not artful but natural. Once having begun to learn it from hearing it spoken around us, we do not need to apply ourselves deliberately to the job of learning: the process seems to be almost automatic. Given the inborn equipment to do it with, everybody learns everyday language, and having learned it they use it spontaneously, without giving any particular attention to the job of fitting what they want to say to how it should be said. Like the fabled centipede who found that he could not move at all if he stopped to think about which foot went first, human beings manage everyday language well mainly on condition that they ignore the problems of self-expression.

When circumstances force them to attempt prose, it is much different. The kind of mental cramp that often seizes people when they sit down in front of a sheet of blank paper testifies to the artificiality of the situation. At such times people who are normally fluent often become inarticulate, and to others accustomed to hearing them speak, what they write seems uncharacteristic. Yet artless language can be written; for example, a boy writing home from summer camp might produce this:

> Dear Mom—
>   I am fine and there are lots of freinds here. We found a snake in our tent. The cookies are all gone. The counsler killed it so don't worry.
>   Love,
>   Bobby

This is a communication, but hardly a letter. Consider also the following typical occurrences: a wife calls up her husband at the office and says, "We'll just have to tell the Simpsons some other time—I can't get a sitter for Friday, and besides Ann still had a degree of fever this morning"; a golfer shouts, "Fore!"; a filling-station attendant says, "Check your oil and water?"; and an absent-minded professor writes on his desk calendar, "Don't forget to return themes." Are they using prose, any more than Bobby was when he wrote home? The question seems idle. In fact, it is never asked, and this is not because we assume all along that the vehicle of everyday communication is prose but because we assume that this vehicle does not have or require a special name. To call these examples "prose" would entail finding another name for the language in which this book is being written, if only as a nominal reward to the author for having filled so many wastebaskets with rejected drafts.

There is some historical reason for emphasizing this distinction, because prose is always a late and sophisticated development of language. By the time that the first prose writers appear on the scene, the first poets are already legendary, and the first users of everyday language are forever lost in the darkness surrounding the infancy of the human race. Furthermore, prose is always evolving and changing, subject to fashions in style just as poetry is, whereas everyday language, if it can even be said to have a "style," is much more conservative. Nothing in the last fifty years has happened to the language we speak that is as revolutionary as the changes wrought in literary prose because of the efforts of James Joyce and Ernest Hemingway. The mention of these particular names (and others could be added) suggests also how diversified prose can be, even within the same period. Everyday language is relatively homogeneous, relatively static.

Not all prose, to be sure, is literary prose, nor does prose necessarily have to be written down or composed on paper. These reservations are important, but less so than the guiding principle of this section, that prose and poetry do not between them exhaust the possibilities of language. What prose is written for—the end or ends toward which this artful use of non-metrical language is directed—will be discussed in the following section.

POETRY

Three mistakes commonly made in defining poetry are to define it by (1) subject matter, (2) form, or (3) mode of apprehension. The first two of these can be dealt with very briefly. The main reason why neither the subject matter of poetry nor its form (verse form, choice of words, or verbal structure) can be used as a basis for a definition is that poets have written on too wide a range of subjects and in too many different forms. In such a variety it is impossible to find the set of common characteristics a definition would require, nor is there any reason to believe that new subjects and forms cannot always be added to those existing, regardless of precedent. The definition in terms of subject matter is particularly vulnerable because it implies that all a poet has to do is choose a "poetic" subject if he wants to write a poem. This is simply not true. It makes no difference whether one conceives of the subject narrowly or broadly —whether, for example, the subject of Burns's familiar poem is said to be a louse on a lady's bonnet or (at the other extreme) the spectacle of human vanity—as long as the subject is abstracted from the totality of the poem and considered per se it will fail to show any characteristics that could not as well be adapted to prose. When a poem from a foreign language is translated into English prose, as sometimes happens, it is the subject matter that remains more or less intact and the poetry that disappears.

The third kind of definition requires more extended scrutiny. By "mode of apprehension" is meant something in the way the poet's conception works, something in the way his mind meets the external world and transmutes the mere raw stuff of the senses. This mental operation has been characterized as primitive and magical—even when it takes place in a civilized society—because of being a throwback to much earlier times, when man was not prevented by the accumulation of his own artifacts from meeting nature face to face, when his capacity for wonder had not been enfeebled by too long an acquaintance with trivialities nor his spiritual palate jaded by overstimulation. The typical mode of thought then was synthesis, not analysis. Ideas were grand and simple; human sensibility was not split between thinking and feeling, but both were organically combined; language was concrete, not abstract. Instead of drab scientific truth, men had myth: the very names that they gave to things were poetry. In our own age, the argument goes, the poet is best able to recapture this earlier state, while the rest of us are mainly dependent upon him for whatever glimpses of celestial light we can obtain.

This notion is one product of civilized man's long romance with the idea of the noble savage. Whether it is true or not, no one can say. Although there are still primitive cultures, there are no surviving primitive languages (if indeed there ever was such a thing as a primitive language). Judgments made upon one culture from the point of view of another are always susceptible to bias, and the bias can as easily be favorable to the alien culture as unfavorable. What is really needed is some way to penetrate into the primitive mind from the outside, yet allowing it to remain primitive—a task as hopeless as that of trying to see whether the light goes out inside the refrigerator when the door is closed, for the very conditions under which the experiment must be performed destroy all chances of its success. Still, there are theoretical objections to the picture of a society whose language was naturally poetic, whose daily life was filled with the vivid apprehension of the numinous. How could these people have been conscious of speaking poetry if they never spoke anything but poetry? As in the story of King Midas, who turned all he touched to gold, the conferring of identical value on everything destroys value itself. If all is poetic, nothing is poetic. We are entitled to suspect that the "poetry" that outsiders find in these mostly imaginary reconstructions of primitive life comes from the same source and has about the same right to be taken seriously as the "quaintness" that American tourists find in flea-bitten native villages where their buses stop long enough to allow a few photographs of pigs in the street and citizens dozing under sombreros. It is fairly certain that the natives do not think of themselves as quaint, or even as natives, for that matter. Tourists and readers of this bent find the qualities they are looking for, and naturally these are never in short supply, but the qualities are not inherent in the objects of view, being created entirely by the social or cultural perspective.

The chief objection to defining poetry in terms of mode of apprehension, however, is that it makes poetry a way of thinking rather than a way of writing. If poetry were only thinking, all sorts of mute inglorious Miltons would qualify as poets. Poetic apprehension is private and inaccessible, an interior psychological phenomenon. Should it be successfully put into words, we still have to ask why *these* words embody *this* apprehension. Thus a definition that is to be of any help to a reader facing a page on which poetry is printed has to begin with the language he sees— for it is all he sees—and there is no use skipping back behind the language to some hypothetical state of mind that supposedly explains everything. Moreover the definition ends with what he sees, because the qualities of poetry must be in the language, or as far as he is concerned they are nowhere at all. Since they are in the language, nothing further is needed to account for them, and whether the poet himself had to view the world after a certain fashion in order to put them there is, for this purpose, quite irrelevant.

Poetry is a way of writing, a distinctive use of language. All that needs to be determined now in order to complete the definition is the nature of this use. It will have to be something common to all the examples of language that we call poetry, and it will have to be something appropriate to language as language. (Cutting words out of newspapers and pasting them onto lampshades would not qualify, being a decorative or visual use of language.) Although this is not a requirement of equal importance, it ought also to be something that can be related in an intelligible way to other uses of language. The diagram on page 7 attempts to answer all three requirements, the last one perhaps more successfully than the others. Of the artful uses of language pictured there, if we take the diagram at its face value, poetry would seem to be distinguished mainly by its opposition to prose. This distinction has the advantage of reflecting popular usage, which has no term for everyday language comparable to the terms "poetry" and "prose," and which therefore tends to create the impression that nothing else exists. While not necessarily to be trusted, popular usage may still embody an essential aspect of truth, and in this case despite the fact that both poetry and prose have already been located within a larger context, these terms (and even more so the adjectives "poetic" and "prosaic") call attention to a polarity in the uses of language that is somehow of final importance. After all, poetry not only shares its vocabulary with everyday language, but it also finds the very tone and rhythms of the latter sometimes worth borrowing, e.g.:

For God's sake hold your tongue, and let me love

or

He disappeared in the dead of winter

or

>Well! If the Bard was weather-wise, who made
>The grand old ballad of Sir Patrick Spence. . . .

But poetry is in permanent and total opposition to prose.

These two uses of language are not only, or merely, different. As the diagram indicates, they are related: their difference involves whatever is fundamental to the nature of each, and neither of them can be defined except in terms which have at least implicit reference to the other. (How poetry might have been defined for the reader in an earlier society, where the art of prose had not yet been developed enough to permit such an opposition, is something that does not concern us, since our own society is long past that stage.) The diagram allows a kind of narrow isthmus between poetry and prose in order to keep a visual symbol of their connection and to suggest that some migration back and forth is possible, but its narrowness also shows that they occupy little or no common ground.

This radical separation of poetry and prose is important because without it the notion of degree tends to creep in. The objection to degree is not so much that it permits the blending together of poetry and prose at some middle point as that it also permits the establishment, at least theoretically, of an absolute point at each extreme, where poetry and prose are, in their respective ways, both "pure." Since there is no practical means of determining when this ideal purity has been reached, it might be thought that the notion of purity is harmless, but the existence of the notion tends to cast suspicion upon all actual poetry, only a very small part of which (but which part?) could by any definition fulfill the ideal. If one of his main objects in reading poetry is to test it for purity, the reader will be unable to give adequate attention to its other qualities, and he will inevitably devalue or discard a great many otherwise inoffensive works just because they do not further his preoccupation. It is surely an odd approach to poetry to begin with a concept that excludes most of what normally passes under this name, even if the exclusions are afterwards readmitted under some kind of waiver. It is far better to resist introducing a judgment of value like "purity" into the definition of poetry, and instead to concentrate on finding a ground for the definition in fact. This must be general, so as to include all poetry (the bad as well as the good), and also sharply specific, so as to differentiate all poetry from all prose.

In the diagram this ground is represented by two arrows. The arrows indicate polarity of force. The axis upon which the arrows lie could be labeled "purpose," for it is in respect to purpose that poetry and prose diverge. Stated in the baldest possible way, the distinction is this: the purpose of prose is to be useful, to serve something, whereas the purpose of poetry is to be of no use, to serve nothing. Prose is an instrument; poetry is an end in itself.

Let us take care to remember that all these comments apply to *language*, for reasons outlined earlier in the chapter. They are not intended to offer anything more than sketchy hints as to why people write poetry or prose or why people read one or the other. And they are not intended to indicate relative value. Since poetry and prose are trying to do opposite things, they cannot be judged as though they were in competition with each other.

The distinction between poetry and prose is very similar to that between poetry and verse. In both cases there is a fundamental difference in the purpose for which the language is used, and in both cases the non-poetic use of language has for its purpose something external to the language itself. But while the use of language called "verse" is simply utilitarian, the use called "prose" is more complex. Some prose compositions are themselves, as wholes, utilitarian, in the same fashion as the beer commercial quoted earlier and the verses on the greeting card. Examples of these would be the directions printed on a can of sardines, a news story in the daily paper, a textbook presenting a subject for study, the constitution and bylaws of a society, a promissory note, a political speech, a biography in *Who's Who*, and a book of etiquette. They are all artful uses of language. But they are not works of art. Rather, they are instruments for recording and conveying information or for moving people to action. The only reason for their existence is the results they can produce. Other prose compositions, however, use language artfully for ends which are not in any way practical and which cannot clearly be separated from the compositions themselves. These are short stories, novels, essays, and plays—all of them normally included in the concept of belles-lettres. The test applied to Blake's "The Tyger" is also applicable to them and yields the same results. There is no way for the reader to carry out, obey, or fulfill a novel like Melville's *Moby-Dick*, any more than for him to do the same to Blake's poem, because the novel is not an invitation to action or a set of instructions. It is complete in itself, and though it has a great many affiliations with the outside world of real places, events, and persons, it does not require that the reader leave the novel behind him and turn to the outside world in order to respond to the novel properly. The reader keeps coming back to the novel itself, as he does to the poem. It is final and irreducible. And yet it is not a poem.

The answer to the puzzle lies in the function of language in these prose compositions. Early in this chapter it was said that a work of art is not a translation or rendering into perceptible form of something else that exists in its own right. This is just as true of a novel as it is of a poem, in the sense that language alone makes possible their existence. If the words had never been put to paper, there would have been neither novel nor poem. There are no alternatives open to a novelist: he *must* use language, and after he has used it this language stands for all time and without exception as the novel that he wrote. However, he is using it with a different purpose in mind than the poet, for the novelist has a story to tell. Or if the term "story" seems too naïve, we can say that the novelist attempts to create a quasi-real world of human actions, thoughts, and feelings into which the reader can imaginatively project himself—which amounts to the same thing. The story is created by language, but the story and the language are not identical. This duality, inherent in the novel, is absent in the poem.

The story—or let us call it here the "substance" of a prose fiction—can usually be further analyzed into constituent parts, such as plot, character, setting, theme, and so forth. It makes perfectly good sense to abstract these parts from the totality which they help create and to consider them separately. For example, D. H. Lawrence's short story "The Prussian Officer" presents with great vividness and power the story of an officer who finds himself irresistibly drawn to persecute an enlisted man serving as his orderly, and who brings about, through his obsession, the destruction of them both. The officer's behavior, which looks at first like mere gratuitous cruelty, as the story progresses reveals itself to have causes and to be something more complex: a mixture of both love and hate. This ambivalent feeling in the officer, and the enlisted man's struggle to preserve some vestige of his integrity in the face of it, are matters of the greatest interest to anyone who has read the story. The reader is under no compulsion to do anything further than read the story in order to carry out the author's intention, which by then is adequately realized, but most readers will find the relationship between these two men so interesting and so widely suggestive that they will want to continue thinking about it, and perhaps make comparisons between it and the similarly obsessional relationships presented in stories like Poe's "The Tell-Tale Heart" and Conrad's "The Secret Sharer." The point is not only that such acts of abstraction and comparison can be made, but also that they are felt by everyone to be normal and appropriate. And when they are made, the language of the stories—the exact words that the authors put down on paper—does not always have to be consulted. The language used by the authors has created entities with an existence of their own.

The discussion of a poem must be carried on with the language of the poem in full and constant view. Browning's "My Last Duchess" could well be compared with the short stories mentioned above, since it also deals with an ambivalent and obsessional relationship between two persons, in this case a wealthy connoisseur of art and his young wife. But references to the poem have to be made in the poem's own terms. Any abstraction from the poem, like a summary of its "plot," omits the values that make the composition a poem. Consider the well-known passage:

> . . . This grew; I gave commands;
> Then all smiles stopped together. . . .

The effect here depends to a considerable extent on the vagueness of "commands" and the chilling finality of "Then all smiles stopped together," together with the strong aura of power communicated by the three short, stabbing clauses—a controlled power that is so sure of itself as to be able to risk understatement. What happened to the Duchess? We do not know, exactly, and are not meant to know. (When Browning himself was interrogated on the point, he refused to give a definite answer.) The values in this passage have very little to do with the event in the story which it conveys in this oblique fashion—we would certainly be no better off if we knew what "really" happened to the Duchess—and very much to do with *these* words; they would be quite lacking in

> . . . This grew; my orders followed,
> And put an end to her smiling. . . .

—or in any other possible rewording of the matter. Yet there is not a single speech in any of the three short stories referred to above that has to be preserved verbatim, nor any single passage of description or narration either—not because the stories are badly written, but because the language in them functions as prose rather than as poetry.

One of the themes that could be abstracted from "My Last Duchess" is that of life versus art. This theme can also be found in Yeats's "Sailing to Byzantium" and Keats's "Ode on a Grecian Urn." If one attempted to discuss the three poems in relation to this theme, as one could discuss the three short stories in relation to the theme of obsession, it would quickly become apparent that the real values in the poems reside much less in the theme per se than in the language used to embody it. The fact that the poems all come out, in their several fashions, for art as superior to life, means very little in itself. Basic to all three is the judgment that art is permanent and changeless. But have we not already had that judgment well enough expressed for us in the saying, *ars longa, vita brevis?* And also by Longfellow in

> Art is long, and Time is fleeting,
>   And our hearts, though stout and brave,
> Still, like muffled drums, are beating
>   Funeral marches to the grave.

What we want are such things as Yeats's explosive "That is no country for old men . . ." and the subtle blend of nostalgia and disgust in his "sensual music," or Keats's enigmatic "Thou still unravish'd bride of quietness," and the felicity of his line, "More happy love! more happy, happy love!" which contains three very ordinary words transfigured by their context and by the repetitions which push the language itself to the verge of satiety as it strives to make real the feeling of creatures whose capacity for pleasure is never sated because they are frozen in the attitudes of perpetual expectation. The Latin phrase and the stanza from "The Psalm of Life" are no less true, but they are infinitely less interesting. When objections are raised to the proposition "Beauty is truth, truth beauty" in the last stanza of Keats's ode, it is not the idea as such that is usually criticized but the fact that the idea is stated in the form of a philosophical platitude. These three words, merely as words, are neither better nor worse than "more happy love." In the poem, however, they become an unassimilated abstraction, contrasting awkwardly with the vividly concrete language around them; they are thoughts translated into words, rather than thoughts and words as an integral unity.

The real test of poetry is the test of translation. To translate or "carry over" a poem from one language into another in such a manner that it will retain in the second language the same qualities that it had in the original is a

task that is everywhere conceded to be impossible. The best
that a translator can hope for—and he will only rarely be
able to achieve this—is the creation of an independent poem
in the second language, with its own poetic qualities, that
will more or less parallel the original. FitzGerald's *Rubáiyát*
and Pope's *Iliad* are works of this kind. There is no theoretical reason why poetry should be untranslatable; the definition given in this chapter does not preclude the finding of
exact equivalents in another language. Yet it never seems to
happen. Most readers of any experience learn to take this
fact into account when exploring a foreign literature in
translation. Prose, on the other hand, translates very well.
To be sure, not every nuance and every connotation can
be carried over into the second language, even by a skilled
translator. But it simply does not make a great deal of
difference, where prose is concerned. For all ordinary purposes, a reasonably good translation of a work in prose is as
good as the original. This is never true of poetry.

   In the translation of prose, what is much more important than verbatim rendering, and what is fortunately much
more possible to attain, is an accurate reproduction of the
original author's style. To translate Faulkner into French
would be unthinkable if in the process he came out sounding like La Rochefoucauld; it would be worth a great deal
of infidelity to his exact wording to avoid this outcome. To
some extent what is involved here is the relative looseness or
approximateness of prose, as compared with the exactness of
poetry. Whether the looseness causes a piece of writing to
be prose, or the fact that it is prose causes the looseness (in
the sense that our awareness of how it is intended encourages us to give it less detailed attention than we would
give to poetry) is a difficult question to settle. It remains
true that entire sections of most novels could be rewritten
in different language without noticeably changing the nature of the whole, if the same over-all style were maintained. Some novelists, especially Flaubert, have agonized at
every stage over the *mot juste*, but they never get an
amount of attention that is commensurate with their own
labor. Though the novelist may fashion his language as care-

fully as if he were writing a poem, the reader is going to read the novel as a novel anyway.

From the writer's point of view the difference was well stated by Yeats: "The correction of prose . . . is endless, a poem comes right with a click like a closing box." This "click" no doubt refers to the writer's subjective awareness of having achieved a form of language that perfectly suits his purpose, or, to use a term that will be defined at length in the next chapter, a perfectly "appropriate" language. From the reader's point of view, no purpose can be discerned separately from the language itself: there are not two things but one. Even in prose of the kind just described —that is, what might be called belletristic prose as contrasted with utilitarian prose—this unity is lacking. The composition as a whole may have the same kind of intrinsic purpose that a poem does, but the language of the composition is a vehicle or means of conveyance, related functionally to the substance of the composition.

The English critic T. E. Hulme called poetry "a pedestrian taking you over the ground" and prose "a train which delivers you at a destination." The connotations of "pedestrian" are a little unfortunate, but this definition very justly differentiates the intrinsic purpose of poetry from the extrinsic purpose of prose. In reading a poem, as Coleridge put it, the reader is carried forward "by the pleasurable activity of mind excited by the attractions of the journey itself." In reading a prose composition, he is traveling to get somewhere. Another form of the same pregnant analogy is Paul Valéry's statement that poetry is to prose as dancing is to walking. Being so radically differentiated in the way they use language, it is no wonder that poetry and prose repel each other in the fashion suggested by the diagram. Let us notice, however, that in repelling each other they are doing the opposite of trying to supplant or abolish each other. Poetry and prose are quite willing to tolerate each other's existence at long range. Indeed, it has already been hinted earlier in this chapter that the distinctiveness, which is as much as to say the very existence, of any particular use of language may depend upon its contrast with other uses, and the contrast between prose and poetry, being the sharpest one of all, may well be the most functional and the one most needful to preserve.

The definition of poetry advanced in this chapter contains four major elements: (1) poetry is language, (2) poetry is a use of language rather than a kind of language, (3) poetry is artful, not natural, and (4) poetry aims at the fulfillment of a purpose intrinsic to the language itself. How these elements might be combined into a final and exact formula is a problem of little importance now. There is nothing magical about any definition as such; by itself this one will open no doors that were not at least partly ajar. It will be helpful in the understanding of poetry only if the reader has followed the process of argument and analysis that produced it, in which case he has done all that is really needed.

In this inevitably roundabout way we come once again to the question with which the chapter began. A language is a system of verbal signs by means of which humans can communicate with one another; one of its outstanding features is that these signs have content, refer to the world of experience, stand for things. Ordinarily this is the feature of greatest use, and everyday language functions in the main as a way of transaction: to pass something on from one person to the next. Its content is what matters. We must now think of language in poetry as having somehow escaped the servitude under which language toils in everyday life. It is as though language had long nourished an ambition to be, itself, the subject of the transaction rather than the means, as though somehow this were a goal which the inherent logic of its nature made desirable, despite the fact that by far the greatest proportion of language, however it is measured, continues without any appearance of strain to function referentially, as indicated above. Poetry is language that asserts itself. It keeps saying, in effect, "Look at me! Here I am!" It has no function other than to be what it is. It delivers no messages that can be separated and valued in their own right. It is not an alternative way of saying something, but the only way.

Poetry is refractory, opaque, durable. Using materials selected from the verbal traffic of everyday life, poetry manages to secure for them exemption from the common fate of language. It is not even defeated by our lack of complete understanding; it knows, so to speak, that our habit is to take the contents if we can and then throw away the package. Thus it prevents this easy transaction by perpetually withholding some undefinable remainder of its meaning, forcing us to come back to the language itself again and again. And when we do so, with full attention to the texture as well as the import of what we read, we discover that even the areas of meaning supposedly familiar appear fresh and new, miraculously reanimated. This experience is freely available; it is not reserved for the few. But it demands as a primary condition that we respect the inherent right of language to aim at a state of virtual autonomy. Having placed ourselves within the charmed circle, we can share in the feeling of achievement, even though we are in some sense the victims. For language is a human achievement, and poetry is language triumphant.

2 ·

The Qualities
of Poetry

When Matthew Arnold proposed his famous "touchstones," brief passages taken from some of the ancient and modern classics, his aim was to suggest how the quality of greatness in poetry might be identified. Being assured in advance that X, the touchstone, was great, the reader had only to determine whether Y, the sample under consideration, did or did not resemble it. Obviously there are many weaknesses in such a method, one of the chief being the fact that a reader who was capable of interpreting its results correctly would probably not have needed the touchstone in the first place. But it was an honorable attempt on Arnold's part to bypass theoretical discussion and to place the main responsibility where in any case it must eventually rest, on the reader's direct intuition. Arnold recognized that great poetry has distinctive qualities which can best be shown by pointing. They are *there*.

We cannot follow Arnold by abandoning theoretical discussion and analysis altogether. It is now opportune, however, to put the definition given in Chapter 1 to some kind of formal test. Poetry was defined as the effect of a certain cause, namely, the artful use of language as an end in itself. The most appropriate test would be to confront poetry directly in selections from actual poems; if the definition of poetry is sound, then one should be able to work backward from the effect, the poetry, to the cause. In other words, instead of accepting on faith and as a matter of general principle that a given passage is poetry because it must have been so intended, one should be able, by examining it in context, to identify the specific forces at work that made it what it is. In order not to prejudice the attempt, let us take two touchstones that Arnold himself would never have chosen:

> Pray you, undo this button. . . .

and the following, written some 400 years afterward,

> I have measured out my life with coffee spoons. . . .

These touchstones invite explanation. They have no obvious poetic qualities, as Arnold's tend to have, which might engage the reader's attention and persuade him that an investigation of their cause is unnecessary. Many readers will be convinced that they are poetry only if it can be shown that they are not prosaic interludes or momentary descents from the level on which their authors customarily operate, but are instead absolutely of a piece with the larger poetic contexts where they occur.

The first touchstone comes from Shakespeare's *King Lear*. In the final scene the tragedy reaches its climax with this speech delivered by Lear over the body of Cordelia, the beloved daughter whom he had once so brutally rejected:

> And my poor fool is hang'd! No, no, no life!
> Why should a dog, a horse, a rat, have life,
> And thou no breath at all? Thou'lt come no more,
> Never, never, never, never, never!
> Pray you, undo this button. Thank you, sir.
> Do you see this? Look on her, look, her lips,
> Look there, look there!
> > [*Dies*]

The speech is incoherent because Lear is torn by powerful conflicting emotions. The five repetitions of "never" express the ultimate pitch of Lear's despair; the passage beginning "Do you see this?" a brief moment of irrational hope. The two opposite emotions are deeply characteristic of Lear, the extremist. They are separated by a neutral space, an interlude of everyday concern with a button. The *dramatic* effect here is one of pathos, a vein in which Shakespeare was always supreme, and the pathos is caused by the contrast in both tone and subject matter between the line selected for our attention and those surrounding it. But the *poetic* effect is something else again and comes from causes that remain to be explored.

The origin of the catastrophe goes back to the first scene in the play, where Lear announces his decision to "divest" himself of the burdens of rule by giving away his kingdom to his three daughters. His scheme runs into trouble at once because he mistakes the outward garb of filial love in the dissembling speeches of Goneril and Regan for its true substance and correspondingly fails to see the true substance in Cordelia's unadorned reply. The "plaited cunning" of the evil daughters is indeed unfolded in time, but first Cordelia, who has done nothing "to dismantle/ So many folds of favor" except to be herself, is cast off by her father, and the disastrous consequences almost immediately begin.

Lear's error is by no means solely the mistaking of appearance for reality. For Shakespeare's own audience, familiar with the official doctrine of monarchy at that time, it must have been also the notion that a king can take it upon himself to give away the prerogatives and functions of an office to which he is born and which he exercises upon divine authority. Kingship is not a cloak to be assumed and removed at will. Furthermore, a king cannot have only the benefits of his position, as Lear wishes: to keep the title and honors of a king without any of the duties they entail. In this light his gift is seen to be an act of supreme selfishness. Lear's fate is then to be really disrobed, reduced to "a poor, bare, forked animal," the lowest common denominator of humankind.

Lear's public self-exposure helps set in motion a train of concealments and countermeasures. Kent, who dared to speak frankly to his sovereign, disguises himself in order to rejoin Lear and serve him. In the parallel plot, Edgar, the legitimate son of Gloucester, flees for his life on the discovery that his father has turned against him and adopts the manner and appearance of a lunatic beggar. Lear himself, after having been repulsed in turn by Goneril and Regan, goes out "unbonneted" into the gathering storm. The rest of Lear's ordeal takes place outdoors, where he is unprotected from the fury of the elements, or in chance temporary shelter of the rudest sort. The storm occasions his speech:

> Poor naked wretches, wheresoe'er you are,
> That bide the pelting of this pitiless storm,
> How shall your houseless heads and unfed sides,
> Your loop'd and window'd raggedness, defend you
> From seasons such as these? O! I have ta'en
> Too little care of this! Take physic, Pomp;
> Expose thyself to feel what wretches feel,
> That thou mayst shake the superflux to them,
> And show the Heavens more just.

The experience which is driving him to the brink of madness is also humanizing him. After hearing Edgar's (necessarily) fictitious account of himself, Lear decides that Edgar is the only type of natural and unaffected man because he wears no silk, leather, wool, or other borrowed covering, and in a frenzy of sympathy Lear tears at his own clothes: "Off, off, you lendings! Come, unbutton here." At his final appearance as a madman, Lear enters "fantastically dressed" (according to the traditional stage direction) with rank, worthless weeds plucked from the fields. Lear is eventually rescued by the French forces under Cordelia, and in the last scene of Act IV—an interlude of calm and sanity between the mental violence preceding it and the physical violence to come—he is introduced lying upon a bed asleep, with soft music playing in the room and his daughter preparing to welcome him back to her love. All passion is spent. Appropriately for one who has at last returned to a kind of human wholeness and normality, Lear has been arrayed in fresh garments.

Clothing, both actually and symbolically through images in language, is one way in which the meaning of *King Lear* is presented, one focus for the complex system of ideas in the play. Scarcely a third of the instances where clothing or the lack of clothing enters into the texture of the play have been mentioned here. The reader who is interested might enjoy finding the rest for himself. At any rate we are now prepared to understand more fully Lear's last speech. With the repeated "never," Lear feels rising in him once more the *hysterica passio*, a physical sensation of choking brought on by intense emotion, and asks one of the bystanders to help him get relief by loosening his clothing. (His hands are not free because he is holding or embracing the body of Cordelia.) He asks not as a king but as a man, for a human favor. The last thing done for him is the smallest possible thing, yet in these circumstances the only possible thing. There is no stage direction here, but the service to Lear is almost certainly done by Kent, his most devoted follower. All distinctions of rank have passed from the King's mind. His "Thank you, sir," is addressed to Kent, whom he fails to recognize, as one man to another.

This button and the act of undoing it concentrate at a single point all the multiple significance of clothing in the play—as disguise, as outward show, as means of distinguishing ranks and degrees of men, as artificial covering, as protection against the vicissitudes of the world, and as constraining force. If the phrase is one of the "topmost peaks of poetry," as A. C. Bradley claimed, it is so because the button has been transmuted from a humble domestic or personal convenience into something like a symbol of our common humanity. Man is a clothed animal, after all; civilization is not optional but necessary. The abuses of office, the vices of concealment, and all the other products of the artifice with which man has complicated his existence cannot be simply ruled out of order or wished away. They have to be faced and conquered. *Responsibility*, which both Lear and Gloucester at first so grievously lacked, is the remedy, and this means, among other things, accepting the limits of the human condition and working humbly within them as well as one can. Waiting on the outside, always, is nature—not the impersonal forces that Lear madly apostrophized during the storm, for they are ethically neutral, but the natural anarchy of appetites which man has inherited from his animal past.

The system of contextual relationships in *King Lear*, merely sketched above, has given to "button" most of the significance that it now has. Yet the button remains, somewhat paradoxically it may seem, still an ordinary button, specific and unmistakable. If the individuality of the button were wholly dissolved in the symbolic significance, the point of this episode in the drama would go with it; the button must contrast with the other circumstances at this moment. The object itself and the word used to refer to it are both second-hand. Buttons are part of our daily life. Shakespeare has not discovered a poetic word; he has created one.

The other words in this phrase also take on the quality of poetry, though their appropriateness, like their symbolic value, is less immediately striking. We can note the absence of the personal pronoun "I" in the request, which helps make the phrase concise, direct, and expressive of Lear's new humility. While it is and must be simple in its diction, the phrase could not be simplified further without making it sound peremptory or damaging its gravity and candor (compare "Pray, undo this button"). As is also fitting, the meter of Shakespeare's line is unobtrusive. And the demonstrative "this" serves to focus one's attention on the button as a specific and particular object, again underlining the drastic change in scope which Lear's concerns have undergone during the five acts of the play: a kingdom reduced to a button—indeed, a life reduced to a button.

The hero of T. S. Eliot's "The Love Song of J. Alfred Prufrock" is also a man in whose life clothing plays an important role, even to the composition of his surname (Prufrock), and the poem through which he speaks shows from beginning to end his morbid fear of exposing his private self to the outside world. He has good reason to fear exposure, being hollow. Unlike Lear, who "but slenderly" knew himself at first and who won his way through suffering and madness to a dramatically convincing realization of his own nature, Prufrock knows himself very well indeed, and though there is a fluctuating line of dramatic tension in the poem, the conclusion toward which the poem moves is not a tragic climax. What Prufrock achieves in the end might be called the exhaustion of alternatives: he is forced to look at himself and at his future as they must be, to face without hope the essential emptiness of his life. On the way to this conclusion Prufrock's vivid imagination discovers various methods of expressing his self-knowledge through images; one of them occurs in the following passage:

> For I have known them all already, known them all:—
> Have known the evenings, mornings, afternoons,
> I have measured out my life with coffee spoons;
> I know the voices dying with a dying fall
> Beneath the music from a farther room.
>   So how should I presume?

"Coffee spoons," like "button," is an ordinary domestic term. If it has more than usual value here, if it is not mainly functional but worthy of careful and repeated attention for its own sake—that is, if it is not prose but poetry—this extra quality must somehow have been given to it by the way it is used in Eliot's poem.

The most striking quality of the whole line is the sudden rise in dramatic intensity that it carries. It has the air of being a key statement, the finality of truth. That it is a man judging himself here intensifies the effect. Yet at the same time these words are poles apart from Lear's "O! I have ta'en/ Too little care of this," or any other such expressions of tragic self-knowledge, because the incongruity, the disparity in size and importance between life and coffee spoons, prohibits us from taking Prufrock very seriously. Although parts of the line are incongruous, the line itself fits in quite well with the poem as a whole, where the same device of ironic juxtaposition is used again and again to help create the picture of Prufrock as a slightly absurd figure—

not a Lear, no, nor a Hamlet, either. Not even his irresolution attains a tragic stature.

"Coffee spoons" is both a synecdoche and a symbol: a fragment selected from the whole complicated apparatus of conventional social behavior and used to stand for that whole, for what we loosely call "society." Why Eliot made this particular selection, instead of perhaps "visiting cards" or "patent-leather shoes," needs to be considered. What he apparently wanted to do here was to emphasize the idea of measurement. Prufrock is a man who is growing older without getting anywhere, and the means are always at hand by which to measure this lack of progress. His life is nothing but a succession of appointments, of routine social engagements—all form and no content. His entertainment is without pleasure, his closeness without intimacy, his activity without work. Yet it is not an unbearable life, even for one who realizes what it is; were it not for hints that a world of high adventure and real involvement with fellow human beings lies potentially all around him, Prufrock would no doubt be well satisfied. His meditations on his condition tend themselves to take on the dreamlike inconsequence of the life to which they refer. So the line

> I have measured out my life with coffee spoons

is effectively incongruous by reason of its sudden thrust, its decisiveness and sharp particularity. Life is not normally measured by coffee spoons—the statement is nonsensical taken at face value—but Prufrock's is. The spooning of sugar into coffee and the circumstances attendant on this act symbolize his life: the precise measurement (for the sake of taste, not nutrition), the circular stirring motion (which gets nowhere), and then the vague sweet substance (sugar is "refined") melting silently away, to the accompaniment of voices over the clink of silver on china—the voices of people who talk through musical performances, who nibble every possible subject (even the heroic Michelangelo) down to the same dimensions of triviality, whose language stifles genuine communication by its sheer abundance, who, for Prufrock, seem always to be passing some obscure but damning verdict on him, the exact outlines of which he cannot quite grasp. And it is all to be repeated: yesterday, today, tomorrow—so many identical portions of time scooped out, dissolving, and gone without a trace.

The line is effective by reason of its organization as well as its symbolic content. "Coffee spoons" and "measured out" are exactly right, as any attempt to substitute other phrases for them would show, but the actual order of the sentence is also exactly right. Compare

> With coffee spoons I've measured out my life.

The quality of this is much different (partly, of course, because of the colloquial "I've" instead of the measured and sober "I have"). The ending with "life" is bright and hard; it should be instead rather dolorous, a dying fall. The absurdity which the incongruous content of the original line produces is strongly reinforced by the descent from "life" to "coffee spoons." The line should point downward; putting "life" at the end makes it point upward. Prufrock's mind habitually moves toward anticlimax:

> There will be time to murder and create,
> And time for all the works and days of hands
> That lift and drop a question on your plate. . . .

Coleridge defined the difference between prose and poetry as that between "words in their best order" and "the best words in the best order"; though he did not say what he would have called "the best words in a poor order," they would obviously be inferior poetry, and it is more than possible that without an artistically proper order they would not even be the best words.

The preceding brief analysis of the touchstones from Shakespeare and Eliot is intended to demonstrate at least the major features of the process by which they became poetry in the contexts where they occur. It is not intended to *prove* that they are poetry. There is no logical necessity to any conclusion reached about a work of art, and even the best argument finally has to end up in the air, because art is a matter of direct experience. Instead of the logician's "Q.E.D.," the critic's last word is, "Well, that's how it strikes me, and I hope you see it the same way." If the reader is now convinced that the two lines are poetry, that is an outcome of his deepened understanding of the lines themselves. The causes of poetry work within poetic contexts and not within critical analyses. Hence Arnold was at least partially right in trying to emphasize the direct experience of poetry. But he was misled by the aura or atmosphere his touchstones possess into thinking that their poetic qualities are somehow inherent in them, instead of coming from our unconscious recollection of their larger contexts. What would "Absent thee from felicity a while" mean to anyone who had never read *Hamlet?* And how much does it mean to someone who has!

The definition in Chapter 1 promised to cover bad poetry as well as good, but so far the only poetry actually discussed has been good poetry. This practice can be excused on the ground that only good poetry adequately rewards discussion. If there were no such thing as good poetry, nobody would talk about poetry at all. A more serious problem is the fact that the term "poetry" itself has been employed throughout in a normative manner, as though it stood both for a way of using language and for a certain degree of excellence in its use, for a certain achievement. The two best arguments against defining poetry according to degree can be paraphrased from the first chapter: (1) if only good poetry is "poetry," there is no term left for bad poetry—it certainly is not prose, nor can it be called "verse" without confusing the proper use of that term; (2) if language becomes poetry only when it is good enough, where is the line that it has to cross to become so, who draws the line, what qualities of language does it concern, and how does one tell when the line has been crossed? The definition of poetry according to use avoids all these difficulties. For language merely to be poetry, regardless of merit, the requirement is simple: just the poet's visible determination to use language as an end in itself. How very little this achieves can well be imagined—indeed, it does not have to be imagined, for it can be seen in print. Again, however, the practice of discussions like the present one is to concentrate on poetry which exceeds this minimal requirement, poetry which vindicates the author's intention by possessing qualities that make careful study of it worth while. These qualities can be isolated and discussed in a general way, with regard to their occurrence in good poetry of various kinds. They are, in a sense, the answer to the question, What is poetry like? The answer to this question will occupy the remainder of the chapter. It will be safe to assume that these qualities are mostly absent from bad poetry, though the authors of bad poems presumably strove to achieve them, and that in concentrating further on good poetry we are not undermining the definition of poetry in Chapter 1 but rather adding an indispensable supplement to it. Chapter 1 had to do with the process; Chapter 2 from here onward has to do with the product.

The qualities of poetry are as numerous as the critic wishes to make them: it is intense, memorable, significant, vivid, complex, precise, evocative, inspiring, musical . . . and so on to the limit of his ingenuity or the reader's patience. But if the best critical term is the one which discriminates most exactly, it is evident that very few or none of the above list will do, since these qualities are often found in language outside of poetry. We are looking for qualities especially characteristic of poetry alone. These are not likely to be numerous. This chapter will concentrate on three of them, called (somewhat arbitrarily, of course) *immediacy*, *appropriateness*, and *resonance*, and discussed in that order.

IMMEDIACY

It is a general law of human psychology that the mind attempts to make its operations, through correct learning and the selective giving of attention, as automatic as possible. Its aim would seem to be that of conserving psychic energy. This process can be called "automatization." The term suggests long rows of machines in a factory whirring away without human supervision and turning out finished parts onto an endless moving belt, or perhaps the quasi-human equivalent of the machine—the robot, the zombie, or the electronic computer. In spite of these rather alarming connotations, the term is a very useful one. It aptly characterizes the way in which most persons perform most of their daily tasks, such as tying shoes, brushing teeth, stopping for traffic lights, unlocking doors, signing letters, and dusting shelves. There is no reason to think about these things, to give them any but the most perfunctory attention. They are not intrinsically interesting, and once learned they can be performed better if higher mental processes do not attempt to take over the role of habit.

Automatization applies not only to routine actions but also to areas of the total field of perception, varying in accordance with the degree of conscious attention given to those areas. Here the relative nature of automatization is most evident: lacking any absolute standard (since human beings are not really machines), all we can say is that something is automatized in respect to something else which is not. This relationship is best imagined in terms of space, as though the human consciousness at any given moment were a stage in a theater on which many objects were arranged for view, some of them up front near the footlights where they more or less monopolize attention, and the rest (the majority) arranged at various distances toward the rear of the stage where they are unobtrusive or even nearly invisible. We shall also have to imagine that these relationships are temporary and can easily be changed. How far back a certain object is on this stage is determined by what happens to be in front of it at the time. A familiar example can be brought to the aid of the analogy: the case of a high-school student who shuts himself up in his room to "study" with the radio going full blast at his elbow. Parents are given to complaining about the practice, on the ground that no one could possibly get anything out of a book under such conditions. Sons and daughters, however, argue that they are really paying attention to the book and just like to have the radio going as a means of filling up the silence that otherwise would be more oppressive and distracting than any noise. In other words, they need a background for the language of the book, and their minds are too restless to be content with surroundings that seem to them like a mere vacuum. It depends on the individual person, of course. Someone who could not automatize the sound of popular music can read attentively for hours on end without being especially aware of the ticking of a clock in the room, the noise of traffic outside, or the hum of an air conditioner. He is helped by the fact that these sensations are monotonously regular. Let the clock develop an extra systole, the traffic be interrupted by a sudden clash of fenders, or the air conditioner stop running, and the relative situation will be quite reversed. Urban people who spend a night in the country are kept awake by the chirping of crickets, whereas at home the roar of the city sends them right off to sleep. Familiarity, habit, custom—all work toward the automatization of experience.

We are also dealing here with another fundamental law of human psychology, one whose operation is so intricately mingled with the conservation of psychic energy that the two can hardly be separated, even in theory. It may be called the law of contrast. It rules that nothing can exist as a distinct entity in human consciousness unless it is different from its surroundings. The extreme case is that of the hypothetical person who has had to wear blue spectacles night and day ever since birth and, as a result, instead of seeing everything as blue, cannot see blue at all. Or to take a more credible case, suppose that someone attended a formal dinner dressed in oily dungarees and ate most of the meal with his fingers, leaning on the table. Why would he be so conspicuous? Because he was out of place, because his dress and manner contrasted so strongly with those of the other guests. In a waterfront dive he would be conspicuous if he did not dress and eat that way. Nudist camps are said to require visitors to disrobe before entering, not in order to ensure that they too will be embarrassed but to ensure that no one will be embarrassed, for nudity (at least as a state of mind) depends upon some persons being clothed while others are not, and fully dressed visitors strolling around the camp would disturb its inhabitants by their suggestive attire. There cannot be a foreground without a background to provide contrast. Thus the automatization of a large part of our lives is a prerequisite to our giving the proper attention to the relatively smaller portion which really counts. The quality of something that deserves and gets this attention is termed "immediacy."

One commonly automatized activity is the everyday use of language. The prose use is also automatized (though not always to the same degree) because the function of prose is to serve some end extrinsic to the language itself. So to speak, we read *through* prose; we want it to be transparent and not to get in the way of the message it is communicating, the subject matter it conveys. Prose is like an ideal servant (in the almost mythical days when there were such things as butlers, valets, and footmen—say, Edwardian England): quite colorless as a person and with no private life worth mentioning, but unsurpassed at getting things done; the kind who materialized at one's elbow with a "You called, sir?" and then after a few murmured "Very well"s apparently vanished into the woodwork. He was just as valuable for his unobtrusiveness as for his practical abilities. If, on the other hand, he had been assertive as a person— banging doors, whistling, cracking jokes, attempting to make conversation—no amount of efficiency could have atoned for this fault. Poetry is a bad servant: always claiming our attention, never getting anything done, insisting on keeping us company. Far from remaining in the background and performing tasks in an automatized manner, it always thrusts itself forward, trying to get as close to us as possible and to fill the entire stage of our consciousness.

Immediacy varies according to the skill and attentiveness of the reader. Even the best poetry is not coercive for someone whose ignorance of or indifference toward the genre keeps him from giving it a proper chance. Then, too, even the best reader of the best poem has trouble sustaining immediacy at a high level if the poem is a long one. This phenomenon has been noticed by many critics, among them Edgar Allan Poe, who held that there is no such thing as a long poem (it is "a flat contradiction in terms") simply because the psychological effect of poetry, being intense, is necessarily transient. But Poe was thinking only of that will-o'-the-wisp, absolute or "pure" poetry. Coleridge, whose thinking on the subject was, as usual, both clearer and more profound, also held that a long poem could not be all poetry, but he did not feel that this kept it from being a poem. The unpoetic stretches, he claimed, had at least one of the characteristics of poetry, "the property of exciting a more continuous and equal attention than the language of prose aims at, whether colloquial or written." That is, the valleys between the peaks of poetry are still functional and harmonious with the whole because they are still immediate relative to the general effects of prose and of ordinary language with which readers are all acquainted, as well as immediate relative to the automatized background of consciousness at the particular time of reading. Even the most utilitarian passages in a long poem, the least appetizing layers of connective tissue, are qualitatively different from prose. If the reader treats them otherwise than as a kind of poetry, he does so at his peril.

APPROPRIATENESS

The second quality of poetry does not require such an elaborate definition; "appropriateness" is used in its ordinary sense of two things fitting together, being especially suited or belonging peculiarly to each other. It is thus a relational term. If the appropriateness of poetic language is considered as the relation between the words and what they say, appropriateness is an absolute quality. In poetry there are no alternative ways of saying the same thing. This fact was brought out earlier during the discussion of prose and poetry in Chapter 1, when the problem was how to discriminate between the two uses of language, and also during the discussion of the line from "Prufrock" in this chapter. The problem now seems to be something else: given the appropriateness of poetic language, as defined here, what further can be said about it? The language and its subject matter or content are inseparable—and that is all. Can any kind of wedge, even temporarily, be driven between the language and its content so as to give at least a glimpse of them as separate entities and permit some appreciation of how the original language functions in embodying the poet's intention? Luckily it can, by the use of a technique already familiar. One discovers the value of what a poet says by trying alternative wordings, other ways of saying the "same" thing. What results is *not* the "same," naturally, and by the distance between this result and what the poet actually wrote some gauge of the value of the original can be obtained. The words we substitute are words that he might have used, but chose not to. The poet's choice has negative as well as positive implications. The answer to why he chose what he did is implied in the answer to why he rejected everything else.

Many readers will protest: "How do you know that he rejected everything else? And is it even possible for a poet to consider every alternative in the English language every time a particular word, whatever it may be, is used?" The answer is that we do not know such a thing, even in the case of poets who left working drafts behind them, although such documents are still very helpful in illuminating the process of composition. We do not need to know such a thing because we *assume* it: what actually happened is irrelevant. The poet may have written his poem thoughtlessly or even by accident. This technique is not a reconstruction of how poems are written; rather, it is a way of organizing the critical analysis of poetic language for the sake of readers who want to do more than just take the poem as a *fait accompli*. Whether the poet could have considered every alternative is no more relevant than whether he did. In any case, he committed himself.

The first example will be the line from *Hamlet* selected as a touchstone by Arnold: "Absent thee from felicity a while." It occurs near the end of the final scene, as Hamlet, already dying, has wrested away from Horatio the cup with its remnant of poison, which the latter in his despair had attempted to drink. Suppose that the line is rewritten to

Refrain from suicide a year or two

or

Delay your trip to heaven for my sake.

All kinds of things are wrong here. Both "refrain" and "delay" lack the regretful connotations of "absent," which are necessary in order to underline the fact that Horatio, by not killing himself, will be missing something desirable (felicity) and continuing to put up with the pain of this harsh world. The alternative words connote not doing something, whereas "absent" connotes not being somewhere and thus further supports the contrast between places: this world and whatever lies beyond it. "Suicide" is too clinical a word. "A year or two" introduces a specific time not in the original line; the limit requested is however long it takes Horatio to clear Hamlet's name, which is the only proper limit, since Horatio has no other reason for continuing to live. "For my sake" is redundant, as the larger context makes clear. And "trip to heaven" is inferior to "felicity" because "trip" sounds like a weekend in the mountains. A trip is something one comes back from. Besides, the phrase destroys a very significant ambiguity in the original: does Hamlet really mean heaven (as a suicide, Horatio would be dying in a state of mortal sin), or does he mean only a blessed release from life? The great question as to what lies beyond, the nature of "The undiscovered country from whose bourn/ No traveller returns, . . ." which haunted Hamlet earlier in the play, may still be unresolved in his mind at the close, and if so it makes the end of this perplexed and daring intelligence all the more characteristic.

The substitutions for the line in *Hamlet* came near to travesty, and so it was easy to demolish them. In the process, however, some insight was gained into the rightness of Shakespeare's own words, which is the sole object of this technique. A more significant test now would be to alter only one word in a poem, if possible some innocuous functional word like a preposition, to see whether the same kind of result follows. Our example can be a short poem of Robert Herrick's:

UPON JULIA WEEPING

She by the River sat, and sitting there,
She wept, and made it deeper by a tear.

In this charming pastoral vignette, so natural and yet so carefully stylized, every detail counts. Not all details are equally important, to be sure, but none of them is merely decorative. The metrical and grammatical inversion of "She by the River sat" avoids the flatness of "She sat by the River," for a short poem has to make its effects quickly. The main character is emphasized by the strong accent placed upon "She," and the appearance of "by the River" out of its normal position suggests that where the main character happened to be sitting is of more than normal interest. The rest of the line, "and sitting there," may look at first like an unnecessary repetition. But it indicates that she must have been there for some time (which is not indicated by the simple past tense "sat"), or at least that there was a delay in time between her sitting down and her weeping. She did not rush outdoors and burst into tears. The stillness of the scene, its pictorial or even monumental quality, is thus emphasized, and we are some way along toward understanding many other things as well. We know that she is the kind of person who seeks privacy in times of emotional stress, who by preference seeks it in nature rather than in manmade surroundings, and who responds to the particular influence of the river (it may once have been a trysting place for her). She weeps, in part, because she is where she is. She is young, young enough to weep at a loss, but old enough both to control her tears and to hide them. It is a loss in love, surely, that she weeps for—the whole tradition of romance in Western culture, into which this poem unmistakably fits, enforces this interpretation.* But it is not a love poem in the usual sense, because the author is not personally involved in it; he is an observer, sympathetically noting it down from some distance in space and also from some distance of age. Now suppose that his second line had been almost imperceptibly different:

She wept, and made it deeper with a tear.

Is "with" inferior to "by"? "With" indicates agency—the thing that made the river deeper. Since her tear did in fact (or fancy) make the river deeper, there is no objection yet. "By" indicates agency also, but it also indicates amount. Herrick chose "by" and thus cast his vote for amount over agency; nevertheless we can pretend that the issue is still undecided and review the evidence for making one or the other decision ourselves.

Long before this point most readers will have begun speculating about the significance of the river. The tendency is to read it as symbolic, perhaps symbolic of the totality of human sorrow, the river of all human tears. There is no way to prove that the river either is or is not symbolic, but some weight must be given to the fact that it will work just as well in the poem if it is an ordinary literal river (a quiet, winding stream, by the way, and nothing as grand as the Mississippi or the lower Thames). Anyhow, "with a tear" means that she added her sorrow, small though it was, to the river, which thereby became deeper. But "by a tear"

---

* Some readers will probably find this argument as to the cause of Julia's sorrow unconvincing. Why does it have to be love? Why can it not be some other kind of emotionally affecting experience, perhaps even the beauty of her surroundings? The best answer to the hypothesis about "some other kind" of experience is that this is an elliptical poem, not a vague one. The kind of experience is meant to be specifically understood, because everything else in the poem is quite specific. And only love, among the possible specific causes of Julia's sorrow, is so well understood by all readers that the author can safely leave it to their imaginations to supply. Had the cause been something like the beauty of the landscape, Herrick would have had to write a different poem than this one.

means that she added her sorrow to the river, which became deeper just to that extent and that alone. How deep was the river afterwards? One tear deeper. The individual human grief is very small compared with the totality into which it merges and disappears, *but it still makes a measurable difference*. It is not too insignificant to count. The poem artfully escapes the danger of minimizing Julia while it escapes sentimentality by placing her grief in perspective. If the revised line were adopted, this perspective would be lost and with it any clear sense of the human value of Julia's grief; instead of a poem which maintained a precise balance between conflicting attitudes, we would have one that was morally indifferent. There is no doubt about which line to prefer.

The effect of substitutions for other words in the poem would be no less damaging; for example, "a River" for "the River," "cried" for "wept," "lay" or "stood" or "leaned" or "crouched" or "slumped" for "sat," and so on. Even the rhythm is important:

> She sat by the River, and as she sat
> She wept one tear.

—"and that was that" might well conclude the descent to triviality.

The point of dwelling so long on Herrick's poem is not that it is uniquely vulnerable to emendation but that it is typically so. Two further examples may help. The sestet of Wordsworth's sonnet "Composed Upon Westminster Bridge" begins

> Never did sun more beautifully steep
> In his first splendour, valley, rock, or hill. . . .

"Steep" connotes quiet warmth, complete penetration, soaking. If "sweep"—which rimes properly and also makes good sense—were substituted, it would bring in an opposite set of connotations having to do with a kind of majestic and overwhelming motion. The latter is a very accurate way of describing what the sun seems to do to the surface of the earth. But not here. Wordsworth's whole sonnet is focused on a moment of cessation, of calm, of freedom and reduced tension, as the passer-by himself stops to watch the city in its arrested life. "Steep" is the word appropriate to all this, whereas "sweep" would introduce an idea not only alien but actually hostile to the poem. Yeats's "The Second Coming" ends with these famous lines:

> And what rough beast, its hour come round at last,
> Slouches towards Bethlehem to be born?

Everything appalling about this half-human, half-bestial image, which the thought of an imminent catastrophic turn in world history awakens in Yeats's vision, is summed up by the verb "slouches," with its connotations of crude power, of menacing purpose, of contempt for public opinion, of vulgar and baggy indolence. This is the apotheosis of the gangster—Antichrist with a hangover. Here the poet is not conveying a certain kind of action only (as in "steeps" versus "sweeps"), but also a certain kind of human character which that action typifies. The added dimension of symbolism, where the meaning of a word is a thing that itself means something, makes the job of analyzing the value of such a word much more difficult, the paraphrase more subjective and approximate. Yet the appropriateness of a word like "slouches" can be shown quite easily through the inappropriateness of substitutes:

> Shuffles towards Bethlehem to be born
> Swaggers . . .
> Slithers . . .
> Shambles . . .
> Stumbles . . .

That appropriateness is a quality of word order as much as it is a quality of words themselves was illustrated in an earlier context with the touchstone from Eliot's "Prufrock." Another example would be the well-known opening line of Frost's "Mending Wall":

> Something there is that doesn't love a wall

rewritten to

> There is something that doesn't love a wall.

The revision removes the poetry from Frost's line, in part by removing the verse. It becomes flat, declarative, prosaic. The expletive construction "There is . . . ," so common in prose, takes an undeservedly prominent position at the beginning of the line. The statement seems preliminary to a direct answer: there is something that doesn't love a wall, and it is—. But in the poem Frost never does say what it is; he is trying, among other things, to depreciate the kind of person who thinks in formulas and behaves by rote, who lacks the imagination to speculate about causes, either efficient or final—who as it were has fences in his mind. That is, a ritualist. The disruption of normal word order in Frost's version, putting the complement ahead of the grammatical subject, emphasizes "Something" and in so doing gives it a specially mysterious quality. Both Frost and the reader know very well what this force is, but it suits the ironic role that the author creates for himself in the poem to make it mysterious. The author's deviousness is also reflected in the roundabout syntax of "Something there is that doesn't . . ." instead of "Something doesn't. . . ." As a myth maker, he wants to combat the tyranny of habit which rules over language (cf. the neighbor's straightforward "Good fences make good neighbors") as over men's other activities, and he likes doing it so well that he repeats the line, unchanged, later in the poem. No stone was ever held to stone more firmly than these eight words are bound together by poetic appropriateness.

As all of the foregoing examples show, the technique of substitution quickly gets the reader involved with the process of poetry. He becomes a participant in the act of writing

and shares the author's view of the author's intentions. It is
clear that the reasons why a certain word is good cannot be
found by considering that word in isolation but must be
sought in the whole artistic structure where it occurs. The
question one must constantly ask is "Why?" Why is
"slouches" a good word in Yeats's "The Second Coming?"
The reader who replies, "Because it creates an ominous
mood, it sounds threatening," has only begun to give an answer. How does it create an ominous mood? Why is an
ominous mood desirable? How can we defend the assumption that Yeats did not write "slouches" by mistake in place
of "slithers"? The poem itself, and nothing less than the
whole poem, tells us.* Since the author's intentions are communicated by the poem and not by any separate or external
means, they are immanent in the words he uses—some
would want to say "concealed"—and they do not reveal
themselves to superficial reading. Poetry demands a degree
of attention commensurate with what it has to offer.

The discovery of what poetry has to offer is the best
answer to those persons who complain about what they call
"tearing a poem apart" or "analyzing all the beauty out of
it." They can fairly be asked to produce what *they* get out
of a poem for purposes of comparison. Or if poetry is too
mysterious even to be discussed in rational terms, then critics and readers of whatever persuasion had better shut up
shop and go home. In fact, poetry never turns out to be
quite as fragile a blossom as these persons claim. A really
good poem will outlive all commentaries. Herrick's delicate
couplet was not blighted by having been analyzed, and
surely it is not unreasonable to hope that for many readers
it will have been strengthened and enhanced. What kind of
reading of a poem is it that is spoiled by the discovery of
what the poet is trying to say?

The technique of substitution is not the normal way of
reading poetry, however. Once the principle of appropri-

* The author's own substitutions, when they can be recovered,
are often very illuminating. In the first published version of "The
Second Coming," line 17 read: "Wind shadows of the indignant desert
birds." Yeats later changed "Wind" to "Reel." The reader might
consult a text of the full poem to find out why.

ateness is understood, the reader does not have to rediscover it in this fashion again and again. He can save the technique for use where it seems to be particularly needed, and the remainder of the time he can read with the heightened sensitivity and attention that he has learned with its help.

RESONANCE

This third and final quality of poetry is one that has already been demonstrated in the discussions of "button" and "coffee spoons": the capacity of poetry to concentrate and hold multiple meanings, to invest otherwise simple denotative words with far-reaching connotations, to make the ordinary in language extraordinary. There would be some point in calling this quality "meaningfulness," which is a clear and literal (though awkward) term, except that the metaphor implicit in "resonance" is needed to convey some idea of the parallel in effect between poetry and music that every reader has noticed. This is not the effect of pure sound, but rather of a complex union of sound and sense. The resonance of poetry is the activation of meanings. Since most of these meanings are connotations lying at some distance from the denotative center of the words, they are analogous to the overtones of musical notes. As they recede farther from the center, as more and more remote areas of our experience are wakened into life, the overtones become faint, ambiguous, even slightly dissonant. Upon them the richness and characteristic timbre of poetry, as of music, depends. Without them both music and poetry would be bare and uninteresting. The resonance of poetry is again like music in that it touches us at once and deeply; though it depends on cognition, it seems almost a direct sensation. The physical symptoms have been variously described, since different persons react in different ways. Few of us are like A. E. Housman, who claimed that he did not dare think of a line of poetry while he was shaving, lest his skin bristle and so stop the action of his razor, or like Emily Dickinson, who said, "If I feel physically as if the top of my head were taken off, I know *that* is poetry." But neither the manner nor the intensity of the reaction is necessarily an index to its genuineness, and it would be a great mistake to identify poetry only by the sensations it evokes. Too many irrelevant factors can be involved. For one thing, a reader whose limited experience of poetry has prevented him from developing a sufficiently discriminating ear may be misled by mere grandiloquence, just as the similarly inexperienced listener to music may not be able at first to hear any difference, in respect to beautiful noise, between the 1812 Overture of Tchaikovsky and the Coriolanus Overture of Beethoven. We need to remember that the sensations, whatever they may be, are the result and not the cause of resonance, and that our attention ought not to be diverted from the poetry itself to the prickling of our skin or the watering of our eyes, which considered only as such are physiological curiosities. The value is in the poetry, not in the reaction to it.

A few concrete examples will do better than any further attempt at abstract definition to indicate the nature of resonance and the variety of its manifestations. We find the quality in Shakespeare's

> Not mine own fears, nor the prophetic soul
> Of the wide world dreaming on things to come,
> Can yet the lease of my true love control,
> Suppos'd as forfeit to a cónfin'd doom . . .

and in Wordsworth's

> There was a time when meadow, grove, and stream,
> The earth, and every common sight,
> 　　To me did seem
> 　Apparelled in celestial light,
> The glory and the freshness of a dream.

Coming as they do at the end of *Paradise Lost*, the following lines are charged with the full weight of meaning developed through the whole of Milton's epic:

Some natural tears they dropp'd, but wip'd them soon;
The World was all before them, where to choose
Their place of rest, and Providence their guide:
They hand in hand with wandring steps and slow,
Through Eden took their solitary way.

And in a slighter poem, Herrick's "Corinna's Going A-Maying," the conclusion has a similar function:

So when or you or I are made
A fable, song, or fleeting shade;
All love, all liking, all delight
Lies drown'd with us in endless night.
Then while time serves, and we are but decaying;
Come, my Corinna, come, let's go a-Maying.

Not all resonant poetry, by any means, is elegiac in tone. It can have the joyous and almost pell-mell excitement of Hopkins'

I caught this morning morning's minion, kingdom of daylight's dauphin, dapple-dawn-drawn Falcon,
in his riding . . .

or the barbaric splendor of Wallace Stevens'

Supple and turbulent, a ring of men
Shall chant in orgy on a summer morn
Their boisterous devotion to the sun . . .

or the ice-cold precision and finality of Pope's

See how the world its veterans rewards!
A youth of frolics, an old age of cards,
Fair to no purpose, artful to no end,
Young without lovers, old without a friend,
A fop their passion, but their prize a sot,
Alive, ridiculous, and dead, forgot!

Nor is it necessary to restrict the sense of "meaning" only to verbal meanings. One very legitimate form of resonance is that which places a fictional person vividly before the mind's eye and encourages our bringing to focus upon it the understanding of character developed through our own experience of fellow human beings. Such is the deftly ironic observation made by Chaucer about his Sergeant of the Law, whose self-importance is noted by

> And yet he semed bisier than he was.

These eight words do more to deepen our understanding of the man than volumes of objective description would. Resonance may be found in an odd and memorable image, like Emily Dickinson's

> After great pain, a formal feeling comes—
> The Nerves sit ceremonious, like Tombs—

in Marvell's pleasant conceit,

> . . . a green thought in a green shade . . .

or in Tennyson's

> Now lies the Earth all Danaë to the stars . . .

in which it is hard to say what is more remarkable: the amount of natural description and classical myth compressed into these words, or the perfect interpenetration of the two. And resonance may also be found in lines the reader hardly understands at all, the very mysteriousness of which is powerfully evocative, such as Yeats's

> Marbles of the dancing floor
> Break bitter furies of complexity,
> Those images that yet
> Fresh images beget,
> That dolphin-torn, that gong-tormented sea.

Poetry, according to Keats, "should strike the Reader as a wording of his own highest thoughts, and appear almost a Remembrance." One of the things the reader feels in many of the lines just quoted is a quality of intimacy or nearness quite out of proportion to his actual familiarity with them; they seem to be telling him of something that he already knew, they arouse echoes within the deepest recesses of his nature, they are unique (as he is well aware) and yet unaccountably nostalgic, with a good deal of the psychological aura of *déjà vu*. "I have been *here* before," he feels. How this happens he cannot say, for he was not otherwise conscious of knowing what he now sees before him. One school of thought would propose the operation of racial memory, or perhaps some kind of innate mental disposition, but the best explanation is much less arcane: it is that human beings in general share the same basic concerns and that they can recognize in poetry their own unarticulated attitudes toward these concerns, especially when clarified and enhanced by a poet's skill in language. The resonance of poetry is in part a response to one of the themes that people always have "on their minds"—birth, death, love, seedtime and harvest, the pageant of nature—because these events are woven into the very conditions of human life. Resonance could therefore be analyzed into two components, one which results from the fact that poetry gives voice to our inmost personal feelings and attitudes, and the other from the fact that it puts us in touch with the feelings and attitudes of people around us—those long dead as well as those now living, for poetry transcends time no less than space. Hence the psychic enlargement which the best poetry affords. It is in poetry that we can hear, if properly attuned, "the still, sad music of humanity." Yet there is nothing automatically effective in these universal themes, as the awkward attempts of many bad poets demonstrate. Our common experience can greatly enhance the resonance of poetry, but by itself it cannot create it. Great themes, flatly stated, are great platitudes. We do not find, nor should we find, anything stirring in the thought that death humbles everyone—until a poet writes

The glories of our blood and state
  Are shadows, not substantial things;
There is no armour against fate;
  Death lays his icy hand on kings:
    Scepter and crown
    Must tumble down,
And in the dust be equal made
With the poor crooked scythe and spade.

The concept of resonance is worth further exploration, but the reader himself should undertake that job, since in the end it is what poetry means to him that counts, and his own reading will never be truly his own until he stops looking at poetry through the eyes of others. At the least he should not make the mistake of thinking that he has learned anything of importance when he has simply added the term "resonance" to his critical vocabulary and mastered some definition of it, even a definition less approximate than the one offered here. The same thing is true of the concepts of immediacy and appropriateness. These are all tools, and they are of value only insofar as they can be usefully employed. Their object is to further the understanding of poetry by giving insight into its nature; if they are helpful in doing this, they have accomplished all they can. The reader should progress, by their means, to the point where he no longer has any need for such tools.

What an approach to poetry through its qualities can and cannot do becomes especially clear when one reverses direction, so to speak, and instead of getting the qualities from the poetry tries to get the poetry from the qualities— that is, to use them synthetically—in this case by adding together immediacy, appropriateness, and resonance. But how to begin? Imagine the predicament of someone who sets out merely to look for words with appropriateness. Unless he has some idea of what the words are to be appropriate to, every word in the dictionary is equally eligible. Appropriateness does not exist in a void. The only way he can find it is by giving up the notion of discovering and exploiting qualities inherent in isolated words, and by turning instead to the consideration of how words may be used: i.e., by writing a poem. If the qualities are then discovered to be present in the language after he has written the poem, it will be because the poem has created them. The dictionary contains all the words in the English language, but none of the poetry.

This concluding point brings the second chapter once more to the definition of poetry as a use of language. Not a selection, but a use. Poetry does not result from uncorking certain bottles and decanting them in certain proportions into a beaker (or a well-wrought urn), where they are stirred and blended into a compound of guaranteed efficacy. It is not a matter of picking out and assembling the sweetest sugar-plums from the grocery store of language, nor a matter of rummaging through works already written and arranging a bouquet of the choicest poetic flowers, which then become one's own offering to the Muse. Poetry is the process of taking what is, poetically speaking, non-existent, and making it exist as poetry. It is a conjurer's trick. If it were not, if poetry could really be written by recipe, then poetry would be a great deal more common than it is—and inevitably a great deal less valuable. Poetry is an act, a gamble, a raid on the unknown, a miracle of faith. People who will not believe intensely that it can be done find it impossible to do. People who try it because they think they ought to, succeed in writing works which no one will read unless he must. To suppose that we are doing anything worth while when we gratify ourselves with the contemplation of poetic ideas (usually dreadful commonplaces about life with a capital "L") is sheer self-delusion, just as it would be to suppose that a soldier is acquitting himself properly in battle if he sits in a trench and thinks heroic thoughts. But the need to be up and doing is not the whole story. What one does and how one does it still count. Here is where all rules and directions fail, since a poet must first write something before he can tell whether it is what he should have written, and his final composition is the result of a series of experiments which have the improbable task of discovering the conditions for their own success. The sum of these conditions is the poem itself. Here is not only the locus of poetry but its source. Qualities of language do not make poetry, though they are integrally involved with it: poetry is made by poems.

3·

The Poem
as Design

In the folklore of American married life no incident is more typical or more thoroughly stylized in its details than the midnight raid on the icebox. Countless repetitions of this pattern in the media of popular entertainment have made us all familiar with it. Like the forgotten wedding anniversary, the domineering mother-in-law, and the wife who hears burglars downstairs, it somehow escapes the question of whether anything like that ever really happens. We know that it must happen; we believe in it. Hence the incident, in all important respects fully shaped and guarded by tradition, might seem to offer very little for a poet to work with, especially if he sets any value on being original. One piece of evidence against this supposition is the following short poem by William Carlos Williams:

THIS IS JUST TO SAY

I have eaten
the plums
that were in
the icebox

and which
you were probably
saving
for breakfast

Forgive me
they were delicious
so sweet
and so cold

It is obvious that this poem has avoided with complete success the platitudes inherent in its subject matter. There may be a certain amount of whimsy in it, but there is no folksiness, no winking and nudging, no trading on predictable cosy responses. The freshness we find here derives in part from the way Williams has stripped his subject, almost ruthlessly, down to the single aspect of the single action. Everything else is implied. Also, rather than a generalized or typical version of the subject, we have here a version that is quite particular, even a bit odd. Only one of the many husbands who have raided iceboxes could have written this. The attitudes the reader brings to the reading of the poem have to be revised in the light of his acquaintance with the person speaking, and the folklore of married life, on which the poem depends, recedes into the background; the foreground is taken over by the poem itself.

The form of "This Is Just to Say" could not be simpler. The poem is composed of two declarative sentences, without punctuation, arranged vertically into three stanzas. Its thirteen lines (the title must be counted as integral with the poem) do not depart from the diction or the word-order of ordinary language. The relative clauses in the first and second stanzas are a little awkward and overexplicit, as they might be in an extemporized note, and the divisions of the lines are what might well have resulted from the writer's having been forced to use a narrow slip of paper for his message—perhaps one torn from a note pad. The stanzas, as stanzas, owe their existence to some minimal influence of literary tradition, yet they also coincide with natural breaks in the flow of thought. The only rhetorical device of any consequence is the parallelism in the last two lines. The "just" in the title seems quite appropriate to these modest results.

As a matter of fact, the chief obstacle to the acceptance

of this poem, for most readers, is its simplicity and naturalness. These are not always disarming qualities. In the
present case they tend to frustrate the reader's effort to find
some kind of handle by which he can grasp the poem and
start coming to terms with it. Indeed, he may have difficulty
believing that it is a poem. What is poetic about it? Perhaps
it is all some kind of hoax, and there is even less here than
meets the eye.

Doubts of this kind are perfectly legitimate, and if the
reader feels them he should be encouraged to give them full
expression. Pretending that they do not (or should not)
exist will not cause them to go away. The important thing is
to use them constructively as a means of gaining insight into
the general problems which they signalize, to resolve them
not for this case only but for all cases where they might
arise.

The first step, however, is temporarily to suspend these
doubts, since as long as they are active they stand in the
way of their own proof or disproof. The composition has to
be read *as something* in order to be read at all. The reader
must be willing to commit himself, to give the composition
a chance, to accept it as though it were what it pretends to
be. In this case the reader must take Williams' poem seriously as a poem at least until further reading compels a
modification of his judgment. There is no risk: the true
nature of the work will be revealed quickly enough by the
failure of attempts to read it as a poem, if it is not one; if it
is a poem these attempts will continue with more and more
obvious success.

"Taking seriously" does not mean "taking as serious";
it means taking the poem on its own terms, or accepting as
provisionally adequate the rules the poem itself sets up.
These rules are always implicit (in this respect they are
very similar to the rules of grammar discussed in Chapter
1). For example, nowhere in a sonnet does one find the
statement, "This poem must end at fourteen lines," and yet
the poem obeys that injunction faithfully. It is difficult to
imagine what a poem which explicitly acknowledged the
rules governing its form would look like, and even more

difficult to imagine how such a poem could provide a satisfying artistic experience for the reader. The use of the sonnet as an illustration here may seem to complicate the problem somewhat, since the rule governing the length of the
sonnet, whether implicit or not, comes from outside the
poem. In undertaking to write a sonnet, a poet agrees to
abide by the traditions of that form; he has no freedom in
the matter. But from the reader's point of view the main
fact is that the author imposed the rule upon himself.
Where it came from is irrelevant. If on reading the poem he
finds that it ends abruptly, with a sense of incompleteness,
or that it seems unduly stretched out, the excuse that the
poem is too short or long because the author was writing a
sonnet merely aggravates the offense, since it indicates that
the faults of the poem are deliberate and not accidental.
And the nature of the rule is of no more concern to the
reader than its origin. The author may decree for himself
that every other word in his poem be a monosyllable. There
is nothing either good or bad in this rule as such, though it
does sound a little peculiar. "Let me see the poem," says the
reader, "and then I can tell you whether he should have followed the rule." Like the other arts, poetry is pragmatic,
not theoretical. The final test of anything in art is whether
or not it works. The result justifies the rule, rather than vice
versa.

This conclusion is not meant to deny all value to such
traditional forms as the sonnet, but only to make clear that
there is no value in these forms per se. A bad poem could
very well be a good sonnet, for a "good" sonnet is merely a
poem of fourteen lines in iambic pentameter following one
of the traditional patterns of rime. A good poem in sonnet
form is a poem that succeeds in making these—and other—
formal characteristics seem inevitably and uniquely suited
to it. As Coleridge said, "nothing can permanently please,
which does not contain in itself the reason why it is so, and
not otherwise."

The aesthetic function of the sonnet form per se is as
testimony to an act of affiliation by which a given poet

places himself alongside Petrarch, Shakespeare, Donne, Milton, and others who have used the same form, inviting comparison with them on the basis of such things as subject matter, tone, and style in general. This is true whether the poet tries to write something obviously traditional in manner, or whether he uses the sonnet form as a point of departure (perhaps because its associations contrast ironically with some aspects of his subject matter, as in E. E. Cummings' " 'next to of course god america i," which is a satire on the rhetoric and attitudes of patriotism). The reason the sonnet form has been virtually abandoned by modern poets is that they have nothing to gain by this affiliation. They can write fourteen-line poems as well as the general run of poets ever could, even though they may not be quite the equals of the great masters, but they have different kinds of things to say and so must find different and more appropriate forms.

Since Williams' poem does not belong to any recognizable tradition like that of the sonnet, it cannot be easily catalogued, and the reader's approach to it is necessarily tentative. Before he discovers whether the implicit rules of the poem are worth obeying he must discover what the rules are. To do this, he frames a general hypothesis: he assumes that everything he sees in the poem belongs just where it is and as it is—that the poem perfectly fulfills the conditions which the author set up for it. On this basis the reader builds a tentative conclusion about the purpose of the poem as a whole. This conclusion is then tested carefully against the poem itself. If in order to retain the conclusion about the whole poem he finds that he must do violence to the sense of its parts, this is a warning that the conclusion is defective. The first decision must be revised in the light of this additional knowledge, then tested again, until the accumulation of experimental data points steadily to one interpretative pattern. But at no time is the reader dealing with anything like certainty; his choice is always from among a number of probabilities, and his conclusion itself is only a probability supported by inference. Its best guarantee is the care with which the process is carried out, and its reward is the enlightenment brought by full participation in the design of the poem, renewed and reinforced as further readings of the poem occur.

"Design" is the key word in this chapter and in this book. It was chosen on purpose for its ambiguity: it can stand both for the poet's intention and for his execution of that intention, for his plan and for the structure he builds in accordance with that plan. Thus, in the latter sense, the design of the poem is a pattern of words arranged just so on the page—not, however, for the pattern as such, as would be the case with a crossword puzzle or an acrostic, but for the meanings which the words convey when so arranged. Hence "design" can be roughly synonymous with "form." In its other sense, as intention, "design" may have rather sinister connotations. We do not like to hear that anyone has designs upon us; we at once become defensive. Yet it remains true that all good poems have designs upon their readers: they are pieces of strategy developed—designed— to produce certain effects. What keeps them from being objectionable on that account is the fact that the reader must become an accomplice to the poet's design in order for it to work. He will not be significantly affected if he does not participate.

A poem is like an invitation or proposal. This truth is attractively illustrated in the following poem by Wallace Stevens, which is worth quoting not only because it is a good example of design itself, but also because it offers an allegory of the way in which a poet ensnares his audience:

THE PLOT AGAINST THE GIANT

First Girl

When this yokel comes maundering,
Whetting his hacker,
I shall run before him,
Diffusing the civilest odors
Out of geraniums and unsmelled flowers.
It will check him.

Second Girl

I shall run before him,
Arching cloths besprinkled with colors
As small as fish-eggs.
The threads
Will abash him.

Third Girl

Oh, la . . . le pauvre!
I shall run before him,
With a curious puffing.
He will bend his ear then.
I shall whisper
Heavenly labials in a world of gutturals.
It will undo him.

The giant is boorish, uncivil, dangerous—a Caliban, a "natural" man, perhaps a symbol for the public as the artist privately sees it. He can be checked or abashed by odors or colors, respectively, but these stratagems do not offer complete solutions, and the reasons why have to do as much with the attitudes of the two girls as with the stratagems themselves. The first girl is contemptuous, the second self-righteous. But the third girl is sympathetic, and we are meant to understand that her stratagem will produce the permanent, and therefore the best, result. The "world of gutturals" is the world of ordinary language, ugly and utilitarian, all that the giant has ever heard; the "heavenly labials" are poetry, which exists by and in its contrast with the other. Poetry is the civilizing force, but it cannot simply be displayed to an audience in order to have this result: the audience must be enticed to it and implicated in it, the words must be offered out of affection, the giant must cooperate in his own undoing.

It does not necessarily follow from this that when the poet sits down to write he always has an end in mind that he knows exactly how to achieve, and still less that he always succeeds in what he intends, even with the help of the reader. For the poet the act of writing is also an act of discovery. But, to repeat, the initial assumption a reader must make is that the poem has an over-all design adequate to account for everything he sees before him and that this design carries implicit within it the rules governing the subordinate parts of the poem. For example, one might ask why Williams' "This Is Just to Say" could not have had as its conclusion a fourth stanza:

I will try
to control myself
a little better
from now on

It is no use answering that the additional stanza is improper because it was written by someone other than the original poet. That is a matter of fact, but fact is not in question now and purpose is. Williams was certainly capable of writing those words. Why didn't he? The answer must take into account the character of the two persons created for us in the poem: the man and his wife. The man whom we see in the first thirteen lines is neither contrite nor humble. It is hard to believe that he would change his attitude as abruptly as he would have had to do if the poem contained the additional stanza. He is confessing to a misdeed, but his state of mind, as evidenced by the reminiscent "so sweet/ and so cold," is more on the pleasure of the experience than on the offense as such, and not at all on the possibility of reforming himself. He is looking backward rather than forward. No woman who would be mollified and amused by a poem ending "so sweet/ and so cold"—we must assume that the poem succeeds in its ostensible aim—would be anything but annoyed by the irrelevant descent to the topic of reform, especially since the promise which seems to have been extorted from her husband by his consciousness of having done wrong follows so closely upon his celebration of the deed. He does not sound very trustworthy. If he is only going to try to control himself a "little better," why bother? The added stanza not only jeopardizes the epigrammatic effect of the original poem, it begins to bring the husband's sincerity under the suspicion that always develops when an excuse is carried on too long.

A simpler way of answering the question would be to say that the added stanza is inconsistent with the rest of the poem. And what establishes the standards of consistency here? Nothing other than the first thirteen lines. It is in terms of what has already been written that the fourth stanza is found inadmissible. In fulfilling itself, the design of the poem has brought into being a set of implicit rules according to which all possibilities are judged and because of which the addition must be ruled out. We do not know what was in Williams' mind when he wrote the poem, but we know the poem that he wrote; if it is what he intended to write (and there is no reason to doubt this), then we can surmise accurately enough why he did not write this additional stanza.

The reader can test the force of the poem's inherent purposiveness by making other emendations. (This technique was demonstrated earlier in Chapter 2.) For example, he could substitute "I have consumed the plums" for "I have eaten the plums." Food is "consumed" by animals, by fire, and by human beings in statistical aggregations (e.g., "consumption of fluid milk was up by 30%"), but not by human beings otherwise—unless an author wants the very special humorous effect that pedantic terms can produce. That kind of humor is utterly foreign to the tone of this poem, however. Or the last stanza might be written thus:

Forgive me
they were delicious
so sweet
so nutritious

It is hard to take "nutritious" seriously (can she really be worried about his diet?), and if it is taken humorously the poem is again marred by an inappropriate tone. It sounds almost as though he were mocking her. The main problem here, though, is the rime. Rime, which is good in many other poems, is bad in this one. "Delicious—nutritious" overpowers the rest of the poem—its immediacy is too great. There is nothing in the two words themselves that justifies their being thrust so aggressively at the reader. And the poem has made a rule that rime will not be permitted, in the only way that a poem can make any rule: by obeying it. In other words, the first two stanzas demonstrate that Williams intended to write a poem without rime. The sudden introduction of a rime at the end of the poem must be interpreted as a violation of this self-imposed rule, or (and this is the only alternative) as the creation of a further, and superior, rule that rime will be allowed to enter under certain conditions and for a certain purpose. If this purpose is the addition of emphasis, we can only say that the rime adds far too much emphasis and that the poem would be better off without it. What other purpose the rime could have had is not apparent. Finding no justification for the rime, the reader must conclude that it is a blemish on the poem. Here, as before, his evidence is entirely drawn from the poem itself.

Emendations like these are useful for demonstrating a point, but they are not the sort of thing that the reader normally encounters. Instead, he finds a poem that was written by one person only and that bears no evidence of alteration; presumably it is just what the poet wanted it to be. When in such a case the reader sees an apparent defect of design, his critical intelligence and sensitivity are put to a severer test. The best general procedure then is for him to exercise great caution in concluding that the design is defective, for the trouble may well be his own failure to see beneath the surface to the poet's deeper intentions or the failure of his own imagination to keep pace with that of the poet. A famous example of apparent inadvertence in a poem is the third stanza of William Blake's "The Tyger," which as we now have it reads

And what shoulder, and what art,
Could twist the sinews of thy heart?
And when thy heart began to beat,
What dread hand? and what dread feet?

A surviving manuscript in Blake's handwriting suggests that he originally intended to begin the next stanza with

> Could fetch it from the furnace deep

—which would have completed the construction by giving the nouns "hand" and "feet" a predicate. But he then deleted the passage containing this line, leaving "What dread hand? and what dread feet?" dangling. The stanza immediately following begins with a new sentence. The readiest explanation for this is that Blake did not notice that he had robbed his question of the predicate necessary for its completeness. Yet Blake's heavily altered manuscript drafts indicate, if anything, that he was taking great pains to get the poem just right. Furthermore, "Could fetch it from the furnace deep" appears only once, in the rough draft which seems to have been his first attempt at composing this poem. Blake would have had to make the mistake not once but several times. How could the poet have overlooked so consistently what every reader of the poem notices the first time he sees it?

We do Blake more credit by assuming that he left the construction dangling for reasons that will prove sufficient when we find out what they are. Otherwise we are judging the poem in terms of what we would have done had we been Blake, rather than in terms of what Blake may have tried to do. The procedure has already been described: in order to find out what the author tried to do, the reader first assumes that he did it (that the poem is the complete realization of his artistic design). From this completed design, the poem, the reader works backward to the author's purposes or reasons. These purposes should form a harmonious structure; if in order to account for some feature of the poem the reader has to hypothesize a purpose conflicting with the others, then something is wrong. And something is especially wrong if the reader can imagine no purpose at all. But before he is entitled to that conclusion, he has some homework to do.

When the reader takes up "The Tyger" again, this

time without preconceptions, he notices that every four-line stanza is a complete unit and that no sentence runs over from one stanza into another. Completion of "What dread hand? and what dread feet?" would require at least one such run-over, and hence would violate this rule that the poem establishes. It could have been done, but at a cost to the consistency of the poem's design. Blake may not have wanted to pay that cost. The next question is whether the failure to complete this sentence did not damage the design even more. Here is where the reader must make an effort to overcome his own prejudice against careless grammar, in order to imagine how what is usually a defect could in some circumstances be an advantage. One must assume that Blake was aware of the problem as he meditated his poem, though his awareness may have been more of the "feel" of the thing than of the exact pros and cons which emerge from someone else's deliberate analysis. What could Blake have wanted?

Surely he had no expectation of deceiving the reader into taking a fragment as a sentence merely because it is punctuated as a sentence. Suppose, rather, that he hoped the reader would see it as a fragment, and that the breaking-off (technically, an aposiopesis) would convey a sense of the poet's awe at the creative energy that could fashion a beast at once so terrible and so beautiful as the tiger. In effect, Blake would be saying: (1) "The very thought of this creative energy momentarily overpowers me and forces an interruption in my own creative process"; and (2) "The imperfect sentence accurately mirrors, in its imperfection, my own weak and conjectural knowledge of divine creativity." The first of these intentions could be called dramatic, the second substantive. And it might be argued that there is a third intention, a rhetorical one, which could be stated thus: "I will astonish the reader with my boldness in leaving this unfinished construction right in the middle of my poem, and at the same time make it impossible for him to accept the poem complacently or automatically." Of course we shall never know what Blake was really thinking. These inevitably awkward paraphrases of his intentions, however, are supported by the fact that each of them can explain why the poem is the way it is. Three independently adequate solutions to the puzzle of Blake's intentions do not necessarily add up to anything more than one solution, since it is possible that Blake had only one intention, but the fact that three of them can be found virtually eliminates the chance that Blake erred in this stanza of "The Tyger." We are at liberty still to disapprove of his tactics and to dislike the result, but we can no longer readily charge him with carelessness.

In taking a poem seriously, the reader is doing nothing more than what the poet would have wanted him to do. If it is a good poem it ought to make sense on its own terms and not require waivers, codicils, exceptions, or special licenses. Does any author in fact set out to write a poem that has to be apologized for? Quite the contrary. He hopes very much that what he writes will stand firmly on its own feet, and if he is at all prudent he does not count on the reader's supplying a rationalization for what he himself could not rationalize.

The critical lesson to be learned from Blake's "The Tyger" is that design may often be found even where it seems to be lacking. Yet the poems which fail in respect to design are surely more numerous than those which succeed, human nature and ability being what they are. These failures fall into three general categories: (1) poems in which the design remains opaque despite the reader's best efforts—he cannot tell what the poet was trying to do; (2) poems in which the reader can tell what the poet was trying to do, but must conclude that it was not worth doing (poems which in one sense are the victims of their own success); and (3) poems in which the poet's design is evident but somehow did not get properly carried out—what the poet was trying to do would have been worth doing if he had only done it. The first two groups present relatively uncomplicated problems; it is mainly the last one that needs attention here. This group includes a whole host of poems marred by miscalculation, in which would-be sentiment turns into sentimentality when committed to paper, pathos

into bathos, simplicity into banality, truth into triteness, and
sublimity into bombast. When Gerard Manley Hopkins begins a sonnet

Nothing is so beautiful as spring—

it is with the intention of conveying a sense of wonder and
enthusiasm. The rush, the exuberance, the not-to-be-denied
form of the statement are meant to sweep all before them.
But alas, it does not work. The tone is too shrill; the reader
is being hectored, and most readers sense this even if they
do not know what to call it. The language, meant to be
fresh and limpid, is shabby and second-hand. A poet who
relies on words like "beautiful" and "spring" to carry his intention is like a man drawing checks on a bank account into
which he has never deposited any money. Rather than gaining by it, in the end he loses. The best criticism of Hopkins'
first line is the rest of the same sonnet, where he sets to
work creating out of his own imaginative resources the desired attitudes toward his subject—in a sense, creating the
subject itself. At the same time that the rest of the sonnet
partly redeems the failure of the first line, it throws that
line into greater relief.

Another famous example of miscalculation is the closing of Tennyson's "Enoch Arden." This poem, once much
admired but now hardly read at all, tells the pathetic story
of a mariner who, after many years of absence, having been
shipwrecked, marooned, and given up for dead, returns
home to find that his wife has remarried and is now living
happily with a friend of their childhood days. Unwilling to
destroy their happiness, he never reveals himself to them,
and the secret of his identity comes out only after his death.
Tennyson does not describe the final revelation or its effects
on the wife, but we are given to understand that she is told
promptly, and her reaction to Enoch's quiet self-sacrifice, as
well as the depth of the love still remaining in her, are
meant to be conveyed indirectly by the last three lines of
the poem:

> So past the strong heroic soul away.
> And when they buried him the little port
> Had seldom seen a costlier funeral.

Tennyson's aim is clear. What emerges, however, is something that teeters on the verge of the ridiculous. The comfortable bourgeois connotations of "costlier" entirely cancel out any effect of pathos, and invite the reader to start comparing funerals in his imagination on the basis of their costliness, with an implied direct relation between the virtue of the deceased and the ostentation of his funeral. This is mortician's morality. Of course Tennyson did not really intend to put a pounds-and-shillings value on love, but that is the way he made it seem. Besides introducing the unwanted notion of value, these lines have a strong aura of satisfaction, as though a costly funeral were not only a fitting conclusion to the heroic sacrifice that Enoch Arden had made but were even somehow a kind of compensation for it. What Tennyson aimed at was the Doric simplicity of Wordsworth's

> And never lifted up a single stone

which testifies to the desolation of spirit felt by the old shepherd, Michael, at the absence of his beloved son, by means of his behavior at the sheep-fold which the two of them were to have built together but which the old man now has to continue alone. The sheep-fold is an appropriate symbolic focus for the emotion (the son had laid the first stone of it himself), and the restraint of Wordsworth's language emphasizes the dignity of the old shepherd's bearing. But all Tennyson succeeds in doing is to remind us of the organized hypocrisy of modern funeral customs.

In dealing with mistakes of this sort, one is irresistibly drawn to speculate about why they happened. There is something peculiarly autobiographical about them, almost as though the author's real personality had suddenly peeked through the disguise that he normally assumed while writing: here for a moment is the man, not the poet. The mistake seems far more authentic, more significant, than the fictional creation. Tennyson's mistake is most convincingly explained by the theory that Tennyson's own values gave a high place to vulgar ostentation, even though he might have denied this if he had been directly accused of it. Unfortunately for him, his success in disguising his real values through most of his work merely makes the slip, when it occurs, more telling. He is like the minister tricked by some imp of the perverse into praying, "Lead us into temptation and deliver us not from evil," who would stoutly maintain, on accusation, that his difficulty was simply a grammatical one, a matter of a wandering "not," though to some members of his congregation this excuse would never sound wholly convincing—and they would be right, according to the Freudian view of this typical error.

Poetry is fair game for psychoanalysis. Like dreams, slips of the tongue, and other symptoms of unconscious mental activity, poems can be read in terms of a "manifest" form and a "latent" content. But they cannot be read that way *as poems*. The psychoanalyst's interest in the poem as a symptom of the poet's state of mind will lead him, and anyone else following his methods, farther and farther away from the poem and into the depths of biography to the point where the work of art which started the investigation is lost from view. The reader of the poem as a poem is also interested in the "why" of things that he sees; his "why," however, refers to the artistic design only. His standard is always the fundamental unity of the poem as a work of art; any element in the poem which lies outside that unity, which has to be accounted for in terms of extra-artistic causes (whether biographical or some other kind), must be regarded as a defect. He assumes that the poem was a conscious and deliberate production. The author as a real person does not figure in his estimate of the poem. The only mind that the reader takes into account is what might be called the "authorial" mind, which is nothing more than a kind of hypothetical source for the results that he sees before him.

To insist upon the unity of artistic design in this very

rigid way is not, in fact, to isolate the poem either from its author or from the total area of real life, which includes among other things the cultural milieu and the history of the language. It is simply to assign these other influences a proper role and to delay their introduction until such time as they will not confuse the process of understanding the poem.

In all the preceding discussion it has been assumed that the only problem is one of finding or not finding an adequate justification for what the author wrote. The existence of a literary text, as an absolute and unvarying fact, has not been doubted. But the textual problem is hardly ever that simple. "What the author wrote" is sometimes a moot question, and what happened to a poem in its various publications may require the services of a technical bibliographer to straighten out. The author's changes of text may suggest some indecision on his part, and (very rarely) he may leave two different and complete versions of the same work, as Keats did with "La Belle Dame Sans Merci." The ordinary or non-professional reader of poetry seldom has any way of knowing that these problems even exist. There is no need for him to become involved with them, however, since the standard anthologies and inexpensive separate editions of poets that are currently available, with few exceptions, print accurate texts and reflect conservative editorial practices. He sees in them the same versions of poems that most other persons have read; his own interpretations will thus have an accepted basis of reference. Only at a much later stage in the study of a poem, which this chapter does not cover, would it normally be worth while for him (if ever) to investigate the text as such.

At the beginning of the chapter, after the introduction of William Carlos Williams' "This Is Just to Say," it was acknowledged that some persons might have difficulty accepting that composition as a poem because of its simplicity and naturalness. Prior to the question of whether "This Is Just to Say" is a poem, though, is the question of whether it is even a composition. Perhaps its naturalness is genuinely come by. If the reader makes a deliberate effort to view it without any preconceptions, forgetting what he already knows about poetry and asking himself only what it is that he sees on the page, what does he see? He sees a message from a husband to his wife, a private communication that shows no signs of having been meant for any eyes except hers but that somehow found its way into print and hence was made public. The message is not addressed to the reader, whose role is that of an eavesdropper, and it would surely never have been written if the author, i.e., the husband, had suspected its ultimate destination. The naïve view, thus summarized, has merits that will become more apparent later on. But inevitably it comes to grief on the hard fact that William Carlos Williams, a poet, wrote this—as we know very well—and published it in a book under his own name, along with other compositions in language with which it has more than accidental relationships. Furthermore, we know that a real husband writing an impromptu message under the ostensible circumstances would not be likely to do it with such a perfect control of language. The poem is a dramatic device, an imitation of a real action. Its naturalness is an illusion.

"Poetry is a kind of fooling that you've got to get the hang of," said Robert Frost. Poetry is never natural; it never just happens. There is always someone managing things with intent to deceive. Yet if the reader is completely deceived, something valuable goes out of the game. What magician would want to play to audiences that thought he really did saw ladies in half, and what audience would want to pay to watch him do it? The additional feature that makes poetry more than simple deception, and hence makes the analogy with the magician's performance not wholly accurate, is that the reader's most complete satisfaction depends on his perceiving how the trick is done, as well as knowing that it is a trick. Getting the hang of it means just that. The reader is not on the spectator's side of the footlights only, but is himself also and simultaneously on stage.

There is no danger that in following this role the reader will learn how to explain it all away, or even how to duplicate the poet's effects himself. If the poetry in question is good, there will always be an irreducible remnant of mystery about it. The significance of this remnant in the total design will be heightened, rather than lessened, by the fullness of the reader's comprehension of the design up to that point.

A better analogy than the magician's performance would be the football game. Surely not one of the thousands of spectators who squeeze into a typical collegiate stadium on a typical Saturday afternoon in October does so under the impression that the twenty-two men he sees running back and forth on the field below him just happened to meet there and, finding an inflated pigskin lying by, decided on the spur of the moment to pound each other into the turf for its possession; nor that they periodically stop to line up and glare at each other for no particular reason and by no prearrangement—to say nothing of the other concerted activities going on within the stadium. It is a contest played according to rules. But a spectator who knew only this fact would be a long way from understanding the football game, and his enjoyment of it, if he had no loyalties at stake, would be limited to the color and noise and excitement of the struggle. At the opposite extreme is the sports writer or the scout from another team. He knows what the rules are. Furthermore, he constantly sees things happening that the ordinary spectator overlooks. His experience is qualitatively, as well as quantitatively, richer, because he also sees things happening that the rules do not account for: the improvisations, the errors, the lucky breaks, the continuous flow of events that moves through and around the regular operation of the rules. He knows approximately how much of the game cannot be predicted, and he likes it for its unpredictability. Although he has ideas of his own about how any given game should be directed and played, he would be the first to insist on the crucial difference between having ideas about the game and being able to translate them effectively into action. If he can be said to lose anything through having fewer illusions than the average spectator, he loses only a superficial glamor, which is of very little value compared to the intimate view of the sport that he enjoys from having, in Frost's phrase, gotten the hang of it.

The particular kind of fooling involved in "This Is Just to Say" requires the reader to understand that the poem, which is a work of deliberate artifice, was designed to look natural. Some of the devices by which this design is carried out were mentioned during the preliminary analysis at the beginning of this chapter. Especially noteworthy, of course, is the absence of rime and meter, which would have tended to make the poem seem too studied or calculated—not that rime and meter are necessarily damaging to the illusion of naturalness in every case (think of Browning's "Soliloquy of the Spanish Cloister," for example), but the illusion in this case is that of a man who would not write so formally. We cannot be allowed to imagine the husband finishing his composition with the thought, "Now there's a fine poem! It even rimes." The poem, like the deed, must seem impulsive.

The artificiality of Williams' poem (the real one) and the naturalness of the husband's poem (the ostensible one) coincide perfectly, for they are related as cause to effect. The credit for this achievement goes to Williams, and the reader's having gotten the hang of it immeasurably increases his appreciation of what he sees here. Yet he must not become so taken with the "what" and the "how" of the poem as to forget the "why." If the poem was designed to look natural, what other reason can there have been except to make the reader think that it all really happened? He knows that it did not happen—that has been the burden of much of the preceding discussion—but unless he is capable of adopting the naïve point of view at least temporarily he will be failing his part of the implicit bargain with the writer. Football games are not played in order to provide scouts and sports writers with plays to be diagrammed and analyzed; these persons, as well as the ordinary spectators, applaud a brilliant run or a decisive block, are excited by the drama of two good teams meeting, and never neglect to add up the score before leaving the stadium, because they know what football games are played for. The reader who makes a similar commitment to Williams' poem will participate in the situation to the fullest extent possible, giving full rein to both his imagination and his analytical intelligence. When he does so, the poem will reveal an amazing amount of sheer information (there is no better phrase) about the character of the two persons in this episode and the nature of their married life—in spite of the fact that only one of them, the husband, is on record here.

He has come home late, or stayed up late; she is already in bed asleep. Obviously their lives are arranged so that this can happen. He is on his own, a solitary glutton prowling in the quiet kitchen which she had left all in order for the preparation of breakfast. He knows that he is invading a province that she runs by exclusive right, but he is hungry. The icebox holds a promise of relief. He opens it. We need not try to imagine the entire contents revealed to his view, for there at the front of a shelf where they can easily be taken out in the morning to start the meal is the focus of his immediate attention, a bowl of dusky plums. He picks out a plum and bites into it, holding his hand palm upward to catch the juice, as he leans on the open icebox door and peers inside for any other delicacies. But the plum is too good; he must have more. And so with undiminished zest, though perhaps with mounting uneasiness at the extent of his transgression, he finishes them all. He throws the pits into the garbage pail, rinses off his hands, and wipes them on a dish towel. He lingers, bemused, still tasting the sweetness of the last bite. It now occurs to him that there can have been only one reason for the plums being in the icebox in that accessible position, ready to eat, and suddenly he faces a problem. His wife will miss the plums the moment she opens the icebox, and there will be no doubt as to the culprit. This is not the best way to start the day. It is too late now to ask her permission to eat the plums, nor would it help matters to wake her up and apologize to her for the deed. Perhaps he had better leave a note. . . .

To the enjoyment of the plums is added the enjoyment of finding a clever solution to his difficulty. He climbs the stairs to bed, smiling.

What sort of person must the wife be, if this note is a solution to the difficulty? We know that she is provident, or the plums would not have been there to begin with. She is not, however, a fanatical menu-maker, or the note would never appease her for their loss. Of course it is more than just a matter of having her breakfast menu interfered with: she was going to eat half of the plums herself, and now they are gone. In their place—quite literally—is a note that tells her what she has surmised already and that compounds the offense by ending with the epicurean reminiscence of the last three lines. Is he rubbing it in? If we give him credit for knowing his wife better than we do, which seems proper, the last three lines must be the strongest part of his appeal and not the weakest.

But first, let us review. The beginning of the poem, "This is just to say," is self-depreciatory, a verbal clearing of the throat. The first stanza announces the deed, not bluntly (compare, "I ate those plums"), but with a super-fluous circumstantiality (*she* knows where the plums were) that indicates a delicate conscience on the part of the culprit; since he is now confessing, he cannot be satisfied unless he observes due form and completeness. (This is not the same explanation that was offered at the beginning of this chapter, but we are no longer looking at the poem from the outside.) The second stanza is in the same vein and has the same tone. Again, the "probably" is unnecessary, for there is no real doubt as to why the plums were being saved, but it would be tactless for him to claim absolute knowledge of her motives by saying "certainly." To our ears the word "probably" has a rather sad and resigned sound, much as if he were saying "Well, I always lose at this sort of gamble, and I suppose this time is no different from any of the others." Then follows the direct plea, "Forgive me." Although neither a grammatical connective nor a mark of punctuation indicates the relationship of this with the last three lines, the latter are clearly meant to give the reason why, the ground for forgiveness. They allow two different interpretations, which can be paraphrased thus: (1) "Forgive me for eating the plums, because they were so good that I could not resist them"; (2) "Forgive me for eating the plums; how I enjoyed them!" The first version is a standard excuse, resting upon the double ground of the husband's weakness and the qualities of the plums. (Note, by the way, the exact rightness of "delicious" as against any of the possible alternatives such as "tasty," "luscious," "toothsome," or "appetizing.") The second version hardly looks like an excuse at all. It is dramatic, an exclamation, almost involuntary; there is a relish in the words, just as there had been in the plums themselves. What ties it together is not the implicit logic of the first version but an assumption about the attitudes and probable reactions of the wife. We ourselves could forgive him, if we wished, on the ground offered by the first version, but only his wife could forgive him on the ground offered by the second. Just for that reason the second version is the more attractive. Since this is a dramatic poem (overheard, not heard), the excuse should not take account of what might be immediately credible to a reader or might fit in with his preconceptions and moral standards; instead, it should take account of what is probable within the circumscribed dimensions of the dramatic situation and advantageous to the end which the husband desires. Though somewhat more difficult for the reader to grasp at once than its alternative, the second version of the excuse holds much richer rewards for him by way of insight into the personalities of the man and wife and the relationship between them.

And now why is it that the husband hopes to be excused? *Because his wife will take pleasure in his pleasure.* The phrase "so sweet/ and so cold" is only in the most general sense descriptive; nearly bare of connotations, it serves mainly an expressive function. Coming at the conclusion of the poem, it is an invitation to her to participate vicariously in his experience, an invitation that he knows she cannot help accepting. And how delicate a tribute it is from him to her, to presume on her altruism! No moral weakness more resembles a moral strength than the readiness to yield when one's better nature is thus flattered. The reader of the poem is privileged to feel the sympathetic undercurrents which lend strength to this marriage and which have kept it from succumbing to the effects of time and familiarity. The poem is an exercise in the higher politeness. By comparison, our own social arrangements, at least of the verbal kind, are makeshift; our own estimates of the temper of those with whom we deal are clumsy indeed.

"This Is Just to Say" is an exemplary poem. A great deal of its value lies in the standard of behavior in marriage which it holds up before us. It does not ask that all husbands rob iceboxes and then write little apologetic poems to their wives—if anything, the conspicuous success of the poem rather discourages anyone from trying to enter such a competition—but it does, in a more general way, recommend the use of tact and imagination in this extremely important human relationship. By dealing with a marriage instead of a love affair, and by being located in a house instead of a bower of bliss, the poem stands quite outside the tradition of romance, which has typically considered marriage to be either the death of love or the final solution to all its problems. Now we see that marriage is not necessarily one or the other: it all depends. A little poem left in the icebox will not correct an unhappy marriage, and yet the happiness of the marriage depicted here must have been created by many such acts of considerateness and sympathy—in a word, by art. Still more generally, the poem recommends this approach to all human relationships. Its significance is not limited to one set of circumstances. The reader does not have to be married to appreciate it, any more than he has to be a king with three daughters to appreciate *Lear*. In light of all this, can we now say that the ultimate purpose of Williams' poem is to make the reader a better person, insofar as the exercise of these qualities will do so? The Platonist would unhesitatingly answer, "Yes." But the Platonist, according to the logic of his position, cannot really care about works of art as such. For him they are always instrumental to some end. In his terms there is no difference between a great poem such as Blake's "The Tyger" and a television commercial of the kind illustrated in the first chapter except to the extent that drinking beer is a lower type of human activity than marveling at the paradoxes of creation. We may agree with his evaluation of these two activities, but we cannot accept his reasoning, especially the reasoning that would lead us to discard the poem once its goal had been achieved. It is only necessary to point out that listening to the commercial and drinking beer are separate activities, while reading Blake's poem *is* marveling at the pardoxes of creation. The poem is its own goal. And the goal of "This Is Just to Say," a more modest poem than Blake's but nonetheless a genuine poem, is to make it impossible for the reader, henceforth, to get along without the exact words that Williams wrote. The more humanely the reader behaves, if the poem does have this effect on him, the less likely is he to forget the poem. Nor does he want to. His chief regret is that the experience of reading cannot be indefinitely repeated, and his greatest pleasure is in finding an excuse to go back to the poem and to participate once again in its miraculously unexhausted art.

The main point of this chapter is that poems do not just happen—not even simple poems. There is no such thing as words spontaneously coalescing into patterns and making themselves visible on a page. Behind each poem is a presiding intelligence, the author, who put everything into the poem that we see, and put it there for a reason. In order to understand the poem we have to understand the reason, which means, in effect, that we temporarily place ourselves on the author's side and try to see things as he saw them, making ourselves accomplices in his design. The question that must be asked, and asked incessantly, is "Why?" A good poem will always reward such effort in its characteristic fashion. As the reader's experience with poetry grows, he will find that his ability to meet the ever-changing demands upon him grows also. He will find, in addition, that the uniqueness of each poem is no obstacle to its having much in common with other poems of various kinds, and that the language these poems speak begins more and more to fall on his ear with a reassuring familiarity.

To penetrate sympathetically into the life of a poem: this is the reader's central aim. There is no road map for going about it, no recipe that will guarantee success, no way of learning it without practice. In these and other respects

the reading of poetry is an art, just as is the writing of poetry. It is a subordinate art, to be sure, controlled always by
its sense of primary obligation to the designs of the poet. Its
modest triumphs are no less real for that. In the collabora-
tive act between reader and writer the values that were
otherwise only potential come into full being, and the mere
physical pattern of the words awakens into the reality of a
poem.

4.

Irony

All poems ever written have one thing in common: they were designed to be poems. In other words, every composition properly called a poem exhibits the effects of an artistic purpose working to make language an end in itself. But this general sense of design is not the only one; there is another, at the opposite extreme, according to which every individual poem has a design both distinctive and unique. No two poems are exactly alike. Indeed, the only way in which one poem could be written so as to duplicate the design of another poem would be to make it coincide with the other at every point, word for word. And then there would no longer be two poems.

These opposite senses of design are obviously important, but their usefulness is limited because they provide no middle ground upon which poems can be related to one another. To say merely that poems are simultaneously all alike and all different is not enough. Every reader knows through personal experience that there are resemblances between poems, beyond the fact that they are all poems to begin with, and any introduction to poetry must therefore make an effort to account for these resemblances in some systematic way. For this purpose we can borrow from biology the concept of the species, which denotes a form intermediate between the genus and the individual organism. The poetic species, then, would lie between the genus poetry and the individual poem. It is because of this position that the concept is useful here, and not because the poetic species corresponds literally to the biological one.

There is no lack of material to which the concept of

species can be applied, since it has long been traditional to classify poetry under such headings as genre (lyric, dramatic, narrative, epic), form (ode, ballad, sonnet, limerick, rondeau), versification (terza rima, heroic couplet, blank verse, hexameter, ottava rima, Spenserian stanza), purpose (satirical, elegiac, mock-heroic, didactic), period (medieval, renaissance, metaphysical, romantic), and subject or occasion (religious poems, poems of feeling and emotion, poems of the imagination, poems on the supernatural, birthday poems, poems on death, love poems, philosophical poems, poems on children, poems on cats and dogs, and so on and on). Because there are so many categories, the traditional system of classifying poetry is more likely to bewilder the reader than to help him. They all appear to be more or less on an equal footing, but some of them have to do with verifiable objective characteristics, while others have to do with characteristics that depend on subjective judgment and are always open to dispute. Above all, they encourage the tendency to feel that in labeling a poem one has accomplished something significant, and that with this act the reader has discharged his obligation to the poet. There would be no great harm in calling Wordsworth's "Tintern Abbey," in the familiar handbook fashion, "a blank verse lyric of the romantic period on the subject of man's relationship to nature," adding perhaps that it is an occasional poem and written in the first person, if this were not, as it so often is, a way of concluding discussion of the poem by putting it safely to rest in a pigeonhole. In such cases the urge to classify is satisfied at the expense of any real understanding of the poem. What the reader needs is a way of bypassing the traditional categories in favor of a system that will get him into more helpful contact with the fundamental processes of composition. A further requirement is that the categories, or species of design, should be few enough so that he can become intimately acquainted with their operation and general enough so that they will apply to broad areas of his reading. After this need is met, he can return to the older system and use it whenever it is relevant, since it has not been permanently discarded. First, however, he has to shake

off the burden of tradition in order to approach the subject
with a mind receptive to fresh possibilities.

William Carlos Williams' "This Is Just to Say," which
was examined at such length in Chapter 3, provides a good
starting point for the search. The outstanding feature of
this poem is the absolute simplicity of its design. There is no
verbal ornamentation, no deviousness of approach, nothing
uncharacteristic of a plain statement in everyday language
(except that the plainness of the poem is unusually well
controlled). The fact that these qualities have to be described negatively does not make Williams' design any less a
positive achievement. But instead of calling this design
"simple," a term that is adequate only as long as one keeps
to the particular context which defines it, let us call the design "single," a term less limited in its application. Williams'
poem has a single design because it all exists on one level—
of meaning, of narrative structure, of point of view. As
Chapter 3 demonstrated, the poem has many subtleties, even
profundities, but none of these is in any sense a complication of what the reader sees on the page before him. The
poem develops straightforwardly; it is rather like an unac-
companied melody, without counterpoint or harmonic un-
derpinning, in which the listener never hears more than one
note at a time. The alternatives to a single design are designs
which involve some kind of multiplicity of means. The
poet, as the musician, can have a number of things all going
on at the same time. There is no theoretical limit to the
density of texture that he can achieve. For the sake of reducing these possibilities to manageable dimensions, this
chapter and the three chapters following it will concentrate
upon species of design characterized by *doubleness*. Of the
single design, perhaps everything necessary has already been
said. Singleness is as well illustrated by Williams' poem as it
would be by any other poem using that species of design,
and singleness per se is a concept so transparent, so lacking
in anything for a critic to grasp it by, that the best way to
appreciate it is to look back upon it from the vantage point
of a knowledge of the more complicated designs with which
it can be contrasted.

The species of design characterized by doubleness include irony, ambiguity, puns, allusion, onomatopoeia, allegory, metaphor, and symbolism—all common and familiar literary techniques, and all ways of complicating structure so that a writer can have two things going on at the same time. From the list, which is not necessarily a complete one, four species have been selected for treatment in this group of chapters, partly on the ground that they tend to pose certain difficulties in interpretation and partly on the ground that they seem, more than the others, close to the heart of the creative process.

Whether close or not, none of them is inherently *poetic*. Poetry is created by the use of language as an end in itself and not by the exploitation of devices. All of these species can be found in prose compositions, and many of them in everyday language as well. They are not necessarily better employed in poetry than in prose, or vice versa. In fact, no a priori judgments of value can be made at all about species of design, because everything depends on the particular act of composition, that is, on whether a given design functions harmoniously and effectively in terms of what the author wants to accomplish in those unique circumstances. The study of design helps evaluation only because it first helps understanding.

Two further and related points are worth making here. First, the various species of double designs are mostly compatible with one another and often occur in combination. Second, they can be used incidentally and locally in a poem, or they can be used in a general way as a basis for its whole structure. This latter point is especially worth bearing in mind as one reads this group of chapters. We should not be surprised to find an ironic phrase, an isolated pun, a single allegorical figure, a metaphor all by itself—or even to find these four, and others, in the same poem, mixed with passages of a single design. Of course, we tend to look at the large-scale uses of design as conforming somehow to an ideal or representing a state of optimum development; they appear to show us what all designs should be and could be, if allowed their proper scope. But this view is mistaken. If the study of poetry teaches anything at all, it teaches that what is good in one poem is not necessarily good in another. "Purity" of design, however this term might be understood, is a criterion only for those poems where the poet evidently adopted it himself and tried to regulate his performance accordingly. Even if the failure of a poem seems to result from an aborted or inadequate use of this or that species of design, we cannot legitimately say that the poem would have been better had the poet used his design more fully, for we do not and cannot know how he would have carried it off in those circumstances. There is always room for the suspicion that he might have made the poem still worse.

The species of double design known as "irony" is perhaps the hardest of all to include within the bounds of a satisfactory definition, because it has many different manifestations and many different uses. In order to encompass them all, a definition has to be worded so generally that it conveys little or no sense of the specific possibilities of the design. Some of these possibilities have achieved a quasi-independent rank, and might well be called "sub-species" of irony. Examples are the irony of fate (reversals of expectation, downfalls), cosmic irony (the God-like point of view, as in the novels of Hardy), dramatic irony (characters acting in ignorance of something that the audience knows), Socratic irony (self-depreciation and exaggerated deference used as a weapon in argument), and verbal irony (the irony of language itself, where words mean the opposite of what they seem to mean—which is much like Socratic irony, except that the personal element is missing). Each of these is worth treating separately and at some length. But this chapter is an attempt to say a first word about irony, not the last. Within the space available here the minimum conditions for irony can be isolated, explained, and to some extent illustrated. Discovering how and to what purpose they are fulfilled in literature is mainly up to the reader himself—it would be in any case—and his pleasure in doing so will be greater if the subject has not been trampled over too heavily by someone else before he begins.

Irony is a literary design which (1) requires, and (2)

creates the conditions for, the simultaneous perception of contrasting points of view. The stipulation "requires and creates the conditions for" is necessary because the cause and the effect are both called "irony." That is, it is not irony without the effect that irony produces ("the simultaneous perception of contrasting points of view"), while at the same time this effect is made possible by a cause or means that is a structural feature of the work in question.

So much for formal definition. Another way of approaching irony would be simply to list its characteristics, in no special order and without any pretense of ranking them according to their importance. This less formal approach has the advantage of being able to uncover more facets of the subject for inspection, and it should also tend to make the definition itself more intelligible. Such a list follows.

1. An essential characteristic of irony is that it has to do with point of view or attitude: the way one looks at something. Irony calls for the participation of the reader as a person. He is not a neutral decoder of information, an animated electronic computer translating data fed into it; his own beliefs and feelings, his "position" relative to some matter, constitute one of the ingredients of the process. (As a diagram will show later on, there are three of these ingredients, only two of which are, so to speak, "in" the literary work.) On this ground irony can be differentiated from other double designs. It is true that the reader as a person is involved more or less constantly in any kind of reading—he can never attain neutrality—but in no other case is his position marked out schematically with reference to the reading material, and in no other case is his occupying that position so important if he wishes to understand what the author is getting at.

2. The whole point of having two elements in irony is that they set each other off, or react against each other. If they simply reinforced each other, that is, if there were no contrast between them, the irony would disappear.

3. The reader's perception of the two elements in this contrast has to be simultaneous. This does not mean that he

cannot stop to consider each element separately, or perform any other act of analysis that he wishes. He can, as it were, first shut one eye and then the other. But to see the irony whole he must open both eyes again. In this way he gets something like a bifocal or stereoscopic view, except that the images are not fused into one.

4. There is no grammar of irony, no system of overt signs by which its presence is made known.

5. As a result, irony can always be misunderstood, or "taken seriously," as the phrase goes. This fate is more likely to befall good irony than bad. The most effective irony tends to be that in which the separation of the two contrasting elements is actually very wide but appears to be very small or even non-existent. The author writes as though to a restricted circle of initiates, depending wholly on their ability to read between the lines. Part of the game for him is dissimulating his real purpose. When the reader catches on to this purpose, the immediacy of the whole design is heightened. In a sense, this kind of irony implies the existence of outsiders on whom the point will be lost, and if they happen also to be the target under attack, so much the better. An author for whom the danger of being misunderstood outweighs other considerations must blunt the edge of his irony and make it obvious, perhaps even to the extent of using sarcasm.

6. Although irony has many different manifestations and uses, as already noted, generally speaking its purpose is always *critical*. This term needs careful qualification. To be critical is not necessarily to be hostile; sometimes irony is sympathetic, benignant, approving. It must, however, pursue what it takes to be the truth. Irony is in the service of reality. If there are incongruities between what appears to be and what really is, irony searches them out and exposes them—in its characteristic way. Even sympathetic irony has a deflating or minimizing effect.

7. The surface temperature of irony is cool. It can convey strong emotions—as, for example, in Swift's *A Modest Proposal*—but only indirectly. Irony involves a certain emotional distancing, in part because its structure for-

bids direct expression, whether of feelings or anything else, and in part because its critical purpose, as noted above, makes it primarily an instrument of the reason.

8. There is no one good term for the opposite of irony. "Literal" is best reserved for use as the opposite of "metaphorical." "Non-ironic" is clumsy, but at least it is not ambiguous, as something like "straight" or "serious" would be. This predicament arises because non-ironic uses of language are automatized (in the sense defined in Chapter 2); being the norm from which irony deviates, they have not been conspicuous enough to attract a name.

9. More than any other design, irony suffers by being explained. (See No. 5, above.) The damage is never permanent, but a reader who already perceives a certain irony cannot help being annoyed when someone else interrupts his view in order to tell him what he is looking at. The explicit statement of the author's meaning violates one of the basic conditions for irony, and since any such statement has to be a paraphrase, it inevitably seems weak in comparison with the original.

Most of these characteristics can be illustrated as well by one example of irony as by another, and there is certainly no lack of material on which to draw. But since this is an introductory study, the first example, at least, should be something of modest scope, preferably centered in one word. Alexander Pope's "The Rape of the Lock" offers such a word in the passage which begins the narrative of Canto I, immediately following the invocation and statement of theme:

> Sol through white curtains shot a tim'rous ray,
> And op'd those eyes that must eclipse the day;
> Now lap-dogs give themselves the rousing shake,
> And sleepless lovers, just at twelve, awake. . . .

The larger irony here is quite plain. It is created by the deliberate juxtaposition of things which not only should not be juxtaposed but which, when they are, begin to react against each other. The "elevated" style and subject matter of the first couplet contrast with the "low" style and subject matter of the second, and the result, as usual, is to pull the one down to the level of the other. There is a similar contrast within the second couplet itself. We take the lovers less seriously because they are put in the same context with lap-dogs; the implication is that the two have something really in common. In our enjoyment of the larger irony, however, we are likely to read right past a smaller one contained in the word "sleepless." It is something like a mine planted in the path: it will go off if stepped on, but it can also be missed entirely. We may imagine that Pope, who is watching from ambush, hardly cares whether it is missed or not, since there is fun in either case. "Sleepless lovers"— what does that mean? If words can be trusted, it means lovers who have not slept all night. But then something is wrong with "awake." Either it has lost its normal meaning or there is a flat contradiction built into the line. People who are not asleep cannot awake. Since the context as a whole deals with waking, we have to conclude that, whatever else may be wrong here, "awake" is perfectly normal and means just what it says. Therefore we turn back to "sleepless." Everyone knows the romantic tradition according to which the lover suffers from various physical distresses brought on by his passion, including distracted attention, involuntary sighing, palpitations of the heart, loss of appetite, and sleeplessness, all of which taken together become a kind of tribute to the merits of the young lady and all of which, we may be sure, the lover would earnestly defend as being genuine. (They are also a tribute to the fineness of the lover's nature and an implied rebuke to the rest of us for our comparative insensitivity.) Pope's "sleepless lovers" are quite traditional. But there is also a tradition of skepticism about these claims to extraordinary passion. Nothing would please the skeptic more than to find out that the lover who allegedly tosses and turns all night on his bed does no such thing, but in fact drops off to sleep immediately and sleeps quite soundly until noon. Pope seems to belong on the side of the skeptics, for he has put the lovers into a context which belittles them, but why in that event did he not write something like "And snoring lovers, just at twelve, awake"? This is the heart of the matter. The answer is that Pope knew what would get the maximum effect, which would be to take the lovers at their face value, at the height of their pretensions, and then to suggest—by a piece of incontrovertible evidence—that these pretensions are false. The lovers not only sleep soundly, but they sleep until noon. The term "just" is a kind of ironic compliment to them on their promptness and reinforces the implication that this behavior is habitual rather than occasional. If Pope had written "snoring lovers," the descent would not have been nearly as far. And the descent is abrupt, too—somewhat in the style of the movie cartoon, in which a character is pursued over the edge of a cliff but does not begin to fall until he happens to look down and see that nothing is holding him up—for Pope has allowed his quarry to take at least one full step over the edge before reminding him where he is. Or, if the first analogy is preferred, the mine has a delayed-action fuse and blows up only after the person who stepped on it has begun to congratulate himself on having escaped the danger.

What role in all this does the reader play? Insofar as he can be led to take "sleepless lovers" seriously, he is vulnerable to the shock of discovery in the same way that the lovers are. But there is more to it than that, for many readers are never taken in by the deception, and in any case the shock of discovery (or whatever it might be called) happens all over again every time the line is read. The reader may adopt the lovers' point of view, innocently or deliberately, but in some important sense he is outside the action, detached. He is, as it were, waiting with Pope in the shrubbery. He has *two* points of view, not one, and he holds them simultaneously.

The unitary or non-ironic point of view offers two possibilities: (1) we can look at the "sleepless" lover as he looks at himself, or (2) we can look at him as he really is (e.g., "snoring"). If we do both at once, the result is irony. In order to make this possible, Pope had to adjust the wording of the passage in some way, or the reader would have had no clue to direct him. The result is diagrammed below:

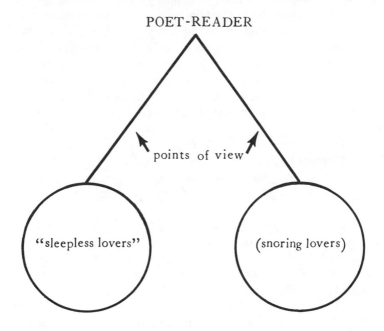

It is important to remember that the clue is not a sign; it does not say, "Warning! Irony ahead." Although it both permits and encourages irony, it does not force that interpretation. In a sense, the reader is given the materials for the double point of view, but whether he puts them together or not is up to him. If he is inattentive or if his suspicions are abnormally hard to excite, he may miss the point, and there is no way for the author to make absolutely sure that he will get the point, because the measures required to accomplish this are so strong that they will abolish the irony. A design cannot be both double and single at the same time.

Pope's irony has a cutting edge, though it is good-natured enough. For an example of sympathetic, even benevolent, irony we can turn to Edwin Arlington Robinson's well-known poem, "Mr. Flood's Party," where, in the next to last stanza, Robinson deftly inserts—as Pope did—just the one word necessary for tipping the balance. Eben

Flood is a man living out his old age in poverty, isolation, and hopelessness. As the poem opens he is returning to his solitary dwelling from the trip he has made to the town below for the purpose of filling his jug with whiskey. His "party" is an imaginary one, stimulated by draughts from the jug and attended by long-dead (or at least non-existent) friends, with whom he proposes toasts and holds conversations, taking all of the roles himself. The party terminates in a drunken rendition of "Auld Lang Syne":

> For soon amid the silver loneliness
> Of night he lifted up his voice and sang,
> Secure, with only two moons listening,
> Until the whole harmonious landscape rang—

In spite of the pathos of Mr. Flood's circumstances, he neither pities himself nor allows anyone else to pity him. Having nothing left but his self-respect, he guards that very jealously. This means that normally he must shun contact with the public; tonight he must do so at all costs, for, as he very well knows, he is making a spectacle of himself—or would be, if there were anyone around to see him. But by the time he has emptied the jug and is ready to sing, he is too drunk to care. At this point the author steps in and on Mr. Flood's behalf certifies the absence of danger, not to reassure Mr. Flood but to reassure the reader, with the line, "Secure, with only two moons listening," which could be paraphrased as "He doesn't have to worry about being overheard, because the only audience is the two moons that he sees in the sky."

There is a certain ironic contrast of tone or style between this line and its immediate context ("silver loneliness," "harmonious landscape"), but the chief irony resides in the line itself and is generated by the word "only." The two points of view involved in the irony are the author-reader's and Mr. Flood's, or, as they might be called, the objective and the subjective. All of the portion quoted above represents an objective point of view except the third line, where the author draws the reader along with him into the circle of Mr. Flood's consciousness. It is Mr. Flood's worry about being overheard that the author takes upon himself to sponsor here, and it is in Mr. Flood's blurred vision that the two moons exist. The two points of view are naturally different, but there is no inherent reason why they should clash; they would exist peaceably side by side without interacting were it not for the word "only," which smuggles into the subjective point of view an attitude characteristic of the objective, and in attempting to do the impossible— combine them into one—brings into being an unmistakable sense of their incongruity. And besides being a foreign body, an intrusion, this word has a specific tone which is dissonant with that of the rest of its context. "Only" comes from the realm of sobriety; it is critical, comparative, judicious. It could never by any chance have occurred to Mr. Flood himself, who is totally absorbed in the content of his experience now and is too drunk to judge, anyway. No doubt Mr. Flood looks at the two moons as if they were a normal phenomenon. *And so, apparently, does the author.* This is the real source of the irony. "Only two moons?" we can imagine him saying. "That's hardly worth mentioning. Now if there were sixteen. . . ." By pretending that there is no significant difference between the two points of view, the author succeeds in emphasizing this difference; by regarding the phenomenon of the two moons very soberly, he emphasizes Mr. Flood's drunkenness. Or, to put it another way, in the act of acquitting him he convicts him. If the reader were so incautious as to take "only" at its face value, he would be trapped in an absurdity. The right way to interpret this word is to turn it upside down. Robinson is playing with the reader in this passage, somewhat as Pope played with the reader in the phrase "sleepless lovers," and as usual the reader cannot appreciate this without joining in the fun himself.

But a question remains. Why does the author want to inject a note of playfulness here, interfering with the actual pathos of the situation and reflecting unfavorably on his main character? In part, it is because he wants to encourage the reader to be sympathetic toward Mr. Flood. The attitude of sympathy requires the maintenance of a certain distance between the viewer and the object, paradoxical as this may seem. Otherwise there is complete identification, loss of perspective—in a word, empathy. The rest of the poem manages to keep this distance without much effort, but here in the next to last stanza, at the emotional climax, the danger of losing it is imminent enough for the author to step in and cool things down with another touch of irony. Equally important is the fact that by doing so the author remains faithful to the spirit of the old man, who is no mean ironist himself. As long as he is relatively sober, Mr. Flood seems acutely aware of the incongruity between his real situation and those that he imagines while on the road home, and it is perhaps not too much to believe that he takes a kind of special satisfaction in deliberately exaggerating the ceremoniousness of the conversations with non-existent friends, standing a little aside from himself at these moments and viewing his own performance with the eye of a sympathetic critic.

Emphasis by understatement (as in "only") is a frequent ironic method. It is usually put in the mouth of a speaker who stands, or professes to stand, for moderation, common sense, and impartiality. He may in fact do so, but it is always in a somewhat devious fashion that requires the reader to look very carefully for the true tenor of his remarks. The game of irony, after all, cannot be played straightforwardly; there must always be a contrast between what is and what seems to be. If the contrast involves the attitudes and values of the author himself, then these attitudes and values are represented by something that looks like their opposite; when the author ostensibly speaks in his own person, we may be sure that in some very particular respect he is masking himself. There is no foolproof technique for interpreting these cases. About all that can be said in general is that the appearance in an otherwise ironic context of some especially plausible speaker or some especially attractive point of view is a sign that the irony is intensifying rather than lessening. We should be more alert than ever when the author seems to invite us to relax.

The preceding examples have been of localized irony, restricted in each case to only a few lines of a poem and generated by a single word. At the other end of the scale, irony can be used as a device for unifying and giving purpose to entire poems. Shelley's sonnet "Ozymandias" shows how this is done:

> I met a traveller from an antique land
> Who said: Two vast and trunkless legs of stone
> Stand in the desert . . . Near them, on the sand,
> Half sunk, a shattered visage lies, whose frown,
> And wrinkled lip, and sneer of cold command,
> Tell that its sculptor well those passions read
> Which yet survive, stamped on these lifeless things,
> The hand that mocked them and the heart that fed:
> And on the pedestal these words appear:
> "My name is Ozymandias, king of kings:
> Look on my works, ye Mighty, and despair!"
> Nothing beside remains. Round the decay
> Of that colossal wreck, boundless and bare
> The lone and level sands stretch far away.

The whole poem is directed toward a principal irony, which lies in the contrast between the king's boast about his "works" and what the observer actually sees. This is what might properly be called an irony of fate, since it has to do with the reversal of an expectation through the course of circumstances (here, the passage of time). The king's boast was originally not ironic at all. He cannot be excused as merely the victim of circumstances, however. He alone placed himself on the height from which he fell. Had he not been so very sure that his works would survive him, to the awe of future generations, their failure to do so would have been unfortunate or even to some degree tragic, but certainly not ironic. And still another condition is required for the consummation of the irony: that the boastful words remain themselves intact, to register on the vision of the observer simultaneously with the desolation which surrounds them. Since we are reading about the scene rather than observing it ourselves, the points of view have to be created by words. They are brought into direct conflict in the poem by the author's device of following the boastful quotation with the words which do it the most damage: "Nothing beside remains." Yet we should note that the poem leaves the reader to draw his own inferences exactly as the original scene would have done; Shelley never says in so many words that time has betrayed the king's expectation by destroying his works. He never even says that the works do not exist: he merely points out what else *does* exist, which is nothing but sand. The ironic understatement acts as a kind of emphasis.

The king's expectation has been completely reversed; his boastful words have been rendered meaningless. Just underneath the surface of this principal irony, which is created by the disparity between "works" and "nothing," is another irony created by an ambiguity in the meaning of "despair." By "despair" the king meant "give up hope of ever being able to equal my works." But to the observer "despair" can also mean something quite opposite, something like "give up hope of leaving behind you any material achievement, because in time it will all come to as little as this." There really *is* cause for despair, there is a powerful sermon in the non-existence of these stones, but it is one which never entered the king's mind when he composed the inscription. His words have been rendered meaningful in a way that he neither intended nor foresaw.

This is not the end of the irony in "Ozymandias." It is also ironic that the only surviving thing should be the sculptor's work rather than the king's, and that in spite of this the king's name should be preserved while the sculptor's is forever unknown. These further ironies are all closely related to the principal one, and instead of dissipating the force of the poem they concentrate it and intensify it. Even the narrative framework of the poem, slight though it is, contributes something. By means of the unidentified traveler, whose information about the scene is relayed to us indirectly through the poet (the "I"), Shelley achieves a lessening of our sense of direct involvement and thus a detachment or "distancing" (see No. 7, p. 95) appropriate to the irony which follows.

Both the poetic idiom used in "Ozymandias" and the sentiments which it embodies are characteristically Shelleyan, yet the total effect of the poem is quite impersonal. The poem has no distinctive tone; its focus is strictly on the subject matter, and the author himself plays no role in the irony. Although irony calls for detachment, this degree of detachment is unusual; in most cases an author manages by one means or another to make his personality felt. Since the nuances of ironic tone are multitudinous, it would be out of the question to try to cover them all here. The three poems which are to be considered in the remainder of this chapter simply illustrate three different tones out of many. In each poem the author plays a role, but in each it is a different role. What they have in common—besides being ironic—is that they all deal with some kind of contrast between youth and maturity, which in each poem is the basis of the irony. It is helpful to work with poems having thematic similarities like these because the similarities form a background against which the individual differences stand out more vividly than they otherwise would; we are better able to appreciate the distinctive achievement of each poem by having some notion, however restricted, of the range of possibilities surrounding it.

The first of these poems, taking them in chronological order, bears the date 1700 and is by Matthew Prior:

TO A CHILD OF QUALITY OF FIVE YEARS OLD, THE AUTHOR SUPPOSED FORTY

Lords, knights, and squires, the numerous band
   That wear the fair Miss Mary's fetters,
Were summoned by her high command
   To show their passion by their letters.

My pen amongst the rest I took,
   Lest those bright eyes that cannot read
Should dart their kindling fires, and look
   The power they have to be obeyed.

Nor quality nor reputation
   Forbid me yet my flame to tell;
Dear five years old befriends my passion,
   And I may write till she can spell.

For while she makes her silk-worms beds
   With all the tender things I swear,
Whilst all the house my passion reads
   In papers round her baby's hair,

She may receive and own my flame,
   For though the strictest prudes should know it,
She'll pass for a most virtuous dame,
   And I for an unhappy poet.

Then too, alas, when she shall tear
   The lines some younger rival sends,
She'll give me leave to write, I fear,
   And we shall still continue friends.

For as our different ages move,
   'Tis so ordained, would Fate but mend it,
That I shall be past making love
   When she begins to comprehend it.

In spite of its title, this witty and graceful poem is not "to" the child at all; what Prior actually wrote to Miss Mary, if he wrote anything, was some quite conventional protestation of love from which irony would necessarily have been excluded. He asks us to pretend that this is what happened. The situation, of course, is incongruous: a man of forty writing love letters to a child of five. What makes the situation ironic is the author's treatment of the incongruity. As a good ironist, he dissimulates his purpose, using the inflated language of courtly love as though it really applied here ("Lords, knights, and squires," "fetters," "high command"), and when with line six he fatally punctures the bubble he had helped to create, he gives no sign of noticing what happened. In the first three stanzas the irony is directed mainly against the conventions of love, which are made to look ridiculous by being placed, with an apparent seriousness that does not really deceive anybody, in a context where they are manifestly irrelevant. But during this third stanza the poem begins to move in another direction. The author no longer pretends to take the language of love seriously; instead, he addresses himself to the reason why this affair cannot be anything but innocent—the great difference in their ages. This theme is developed through stanzas four and five. Another poet might have ended the poem with stanza five; Prior, however, wants to follow out the logic of this difference in age by looking toward the future. He will still be allowed to write love letters to her, with no more danger of compromising her then than now, because the difference in their ages will again render his action innocent. By the time the love letters have any meaning for her, they will have ceased having any meaning for him. The villain is time, which without altering the relative positions of either person can turn a bit of idle gallantry into a confession of impotence.

Grim as this conclusion may be, it is phrased epigrammatically, and the tone of the whole poem is anything but grim. It would be better characterized as "rueful." Inviting us to compare the two situations, present and future, with their similarities and their differences, Prior does so from a point of view which he can share with the reader. He is the object of the irony, but he is above it, too.

The same kind of detachment, but with a different tone and import, is found in Thomas Hardy's "The Missed Train":

> How I was caught
> Hieing home, after days of allure,
> And forced to an inn—small, obscure—
> At the junction, gloom-fraught.
>
> How civil my face
> To get them to chamber me there—

A roof I had scorned, scarce aware
  That it stood at the place.

  And how all the night
I had dreams of the unwitting cause
Of my lodgment. How lonely I was
  How consoled by her sprite!

  Thus onetime to me . . .
Dim wastes of dead years bar away
Then from now. But such happenings to-day
  Fall to lovers, may be!

  Years, years as shoaled seas,
Truly, stretch now between! Less and less
Shrink the visions then vast in me.—Yes,
  Then in me: Now in these.

In Hardy's poem the effects of time which Prior only foresaw are now realized; the contrast is between the present and the past rather than between the present and the future. It is not a physical decline only which Hardy records, but at least equally a spiritual one, a shrinking of "visions"; the irony is divided (or perhaps multiplied), since one half of it concerns himself as he now is in comparison to himself as he then was, and the other half concerns himself in comparison to "these"—young lovers who are repeating the course which he followed, consoling themselves with visions of the future and happily unaware of the disappointment which it holds in store for them. The irony is enhanced by understatement: Hardy merely places the young lovers in the position that he once occupied and invites us to draw the inevitable conclusion, that they will in time become as he is now. A related but less clearly defined irony has to do with the misadventure which the poem records. At the time it happened, Hardy's being forced to spend the night at the inn seemed only a stroke of bad luck, fortunately redeemed and hence of no permanent significance. Now, in the perspective of the "dead years" separating it from the present, and by the act of recollection which lifts it out of the past, it becomes something like a warning sign, pointing toward the inexorable causality within which the apparent accidents of human life are bound. And not only is the meaning of the experience universalized, but so also is the intensely self-regarding emotion that once accompanied it. Beyond this point the interpretation probably should not venture, for there is no evidence that Hardy intended his poem to be allegorical. He wants us to look at, not away from, the experience at the inn. His refusal to dissipate its reality accounts for much of the strength of the poem.

The tone here is difficult to characterize. It is not rueful, though the poem records an irony in which the author acknowledges himself trapped. He makes no effort to muster a smile, as Prior did, with an epigram. It is a melancholy view that he sees, but he communicates no sense of personal grievance against fate. Instead, he places his own feelings against so large a background that they become almost irrelevant; what we notice most of all is the bleak honesty of his conception, embodied in the parallelism of the last line, and the stoic reserve which he maintains in the face of this sadly won knowledge about human life.

"The Missed Train" is a very personal poem, nevertheless, because it bears throughout the marks of Hardy's style. No one but Hardy could have written "Hieing home, after days of allure," a line that a reader sensitive to English idiom cannot view without a shudder. One doesn't "hie" home by railway train, and the word "allure," with its would-be elegance and its too-convenient rime, is more appropriate to a popular song than to a serious poem. Granted that this is the clumsiest and least idiomatic line in the poem, it is by no means unrepresentative of Hardy's taste in language. We cannot believe that these lapses were accidental, because there is too much evidence of conscious artistry at work, but Hardy must have been remarkably indifferent to the dissonance they set up. The same thing is true of his arbitrary stanza patterns, his gnarled syntax, and other stylistic idiosyncrasies. Rather surprisingly, the style does not seem to damage the poems. If it often does not have an immediate or specific function, the style contributes greatly to the design of the poems in general by uniting the substance of Hardy's uncomfortable message with the sense of a rugged authenticity in the man behind it. Here is someone who *makes* words serve his ends, however ill-adapted they may be by nature. This Olympian disdain for the smooth, the fashionable, the convenient is one of Hardy's great strengths. There is no a priori reason why it should work as well as it does—why an artistic liability should be turned to such positively successful use—but it does work: it works for Hardy. Perhaps it works for Hardy only because he is indifferent to whether it works or not, this being an essential part of the man's total honesty as an artist.

The last poem of the three also bears the marks of an unmistakable artistic personality. It is John Crowe Ransom's "Janet Waking":

Beautifully Janet slept
Till it was deeply morning. She woke then
And thought about her dainty-feathered hen,
To see how it had kept.

One kiss she gave her mother.
Only a small one gave she to her daddy
Who would have kissed each curl of his shining baby;
No kiss at all for her brother.

"Old Chucky, old Chucky!" she cried,
Running across the world upon the grass
To Chucky's house, and listening. But alas,
Her Chucky had died.

It was a transmogrifying bee
Came droning down on Chucky's old bald head
And sat and put the poison. It scarcely bled,
But how exceedingly

And purply did the knot
Swell with the venom and communicate

Its rigor! Now the poor comb stood up straight
But Chucky did not.

So there was Janet
Kneeling on the wet grass, crying her brown hen
(Translated far beyond the daughters of men)
To rise and walk upon it.

And weeping fast as she had breath
Janet implored us, "Wake her from her sleep!"
And would not be instructed in how deep
Was the forgetful kingdom of death.

The point of view is immediately established as that of
an outside observer, an adult, who looks at the child with
fondness and sympathy from the superior position which
his age inevitably confers. There is good reason to suspect
that he is, in fact, Janet's father. He is included in the final
scene ("Janet implored us") as though his right to be there
could be taken for granted, and the reference in stanza two
to what Janet's daddy "would have" done shows an insight
into her parent's mind that the parent himself is best qualified to have. Moreover, he is treated with a certain irony in
stanza two, which has a purpose only if we can assume that
the author wants to enjoy a quiet joke at his own expense;
no other member of Janet's family is thus singled out.

The tone of his language undergoes several changes. In
the first stanza it is admiring, as befits the subject. A possible
divergence in point of view is suggested very delicately by
the use of a somewhat heightened style: "beautifully,"
"deeply" (there are reasons why these seemingly interchangeable adverbs cannot be interchanged), and of course
"dainty-feathered." The last term—courtly, archaic, almost
arch—is certainly not one that would have been used by
Janet herself. The tone of the second stanza is set by the
rueful but amused account of Janet's whirlwind passage
through the gathering of her family, perhaps at breakfast,
on the way to see Chucky. The observer's point of view is
sharply differentiated from Janet's for the first time in his

statement: ". . . But alas,/ Her Chucky had died." "Her" Chucky is one thing; the actual hen that the adult world sees is another. In an earlier version of this stanza Ransom had written "Running on little pink feet upon the grass." Besides the awkwardness of "on . . . upon," the original line is marred by the heavy-handed condescension of "little pink feet." This sentimental phrase, which Ransom wisely altered, causes the points of view to diverge much too widely here. Moreover, its tone is out of harmony with the tone adopted elsewhere in the poem, and though her feet were doubtless little and pink, this is about the least relevant fact that one could imagine for the context. "Running across the world" is a fine intuitive look into Janet's own attitude toward her life, phrased, of course, in the observer's words.

It is in stanzas four and five (unified by the run-over sentence) that the irony becomes most prominent. Before we start congratulating the poet on the effective way in which he met the problem of describing the hen's death, we ought to pause and remember that he created the problem for himself in the first place, since the manner of the hen's death might have been silently omitted. The reader would never have known the difference. (But then it would have been another poem.) One reason why Ransom wanted to describe the hen's death may have been that this episode is his best opportunity for neutralizing in advance the potential for sentimentality in the concluding scene. The reader might fail to keep his adult perspective and sense of values in the face of a small child sobbing over the death of her pet, and it would have been difficult, perhaps impossible, to include enough irony in the scene itself to prevent this effect without at the same time destroying the seriousness of the conclusion. Furthermore, the manner of the hen's death is part of Ransom's subject. Consider what a difference it would have made if the hen had died of old age, or disease, or perhaps had been carried off by a natural predator. The oddity, the pure happenstance, the grotesqueness of the hen's fate are intensely real and belong to the world which Janet will have to understand some day, even if she cannot understand it now. It is a world which offers no finality except death, and in which death can come through weird and inappropriate accidents.

The language in this section is mock-heroic. The bee is preceded by a thunderous five-syllabled adjective, "transmogrifying," and it comes "droning down" like a bombing plane "on Chucky's old bald head." The latter phrase institutes the other half of the ironic contrast, and it is reinforced by "sat and put the poison," which makes the deadly blow (as it would be called in the language of epic battle) sound more than a little like the laying of an egg. In the next sentence the language is again ironically inflated, only to come abruptly down to earth with ". . . Now the poor comb stood up straight/ But Chucky did not."

Janet's "waking" in the ordinary sense took place when she got up that morning. The grotesque accident caused her to wake in another sense by revealing to her that life contains tragedies, or at least irreversible events. But did Janet really wake to the significance of what happened? The final, and main, point of the poem is that she did not. Not understanding death, she thought that her hen was only asleep. She knew that there was something very wrong with this condition, but she *would* not wake to its significance, even though her preceptors tried to explain it to her. In the heedless and self-centered world where she had lived so far in paradisal innocence, the word "death" had doubtless intruded now and then, but the reality of death never. By sheer force of will she tries to exclude it now. Why should things ever be different than they are? Why should something loved cease to exist? It is a fact that this happens, but even when fully apprehended a fact is not a reason, not an explanation. And here the omnipotent parents are betraying her by refusing to do something that she wants with all her heart to have done, and offering instead of action only some empty words. We notice that Ransom writes "would not" rather than "could not." It is a nice question whether or not the former can be taken to imply the latter. In any case, it is evident that Ransom wanted to emphasize the willfulness of Janet's behavior. In this response to the fact of death Janet very much resembles the heroine of Wordsworth's "We

Are Seven," who "would have her will," insisting that the brother and sister who lay buried in the churchyard are to be counted in the family along with those still living, and she also resembles Margaret, in Gerard Manley Hopkins' "Spring and Fall," who "will weep and know why"— though Wordsworth's little girl is quite cheerful, seeming to feel that death makes no essential difference, and Hopkins' Margaret, whose melancholy is decorous, weeps (rather improbably, some readers feel) not over the death of a relative or a pet animal but over the falling of leaves in autumn.

As the poem comes to an end, the divergence between Janet's view of death and the adult view stands fully revealed. Both Janet and her parents are trying without success to wake someone from a "sleep." This word is ambiguous, just as "wake" is. Together they bring to a focus and make explicit the principal irony. The two points of view on death would still exist without these words, but without them the reader would not be encouraged to see the two points of view simultaneously, which he must do if the irony is to be realized. The structure of this principal irony is diagrammed on p. 115. One of its components, the adult view of death, is not normally a "view." That is to say, most of the time adults simply take death for granted. They may not be reconciled to death or profess to understand it, but they do not feel called upon to choose sides among possible interpretations. Since the question of death is seldom present in their consciousness in that form, they are not aware of taking a stance in regard to it. The reader of "Janet Waking" belongs in this group, of course. But the pull of a much different point of view forces him to look at his own *as* a point of view (according to the law of contrast, which was introduced in Chapter 2). This process of distancing or objectification is furthered by the very noticeable role the author takes in shaping the poem. The reader tends to assume a position alongside the author; this vantage allows him to see his own point of view as one of the two components active in the poem, more or less as if he were a spectator at a drama.

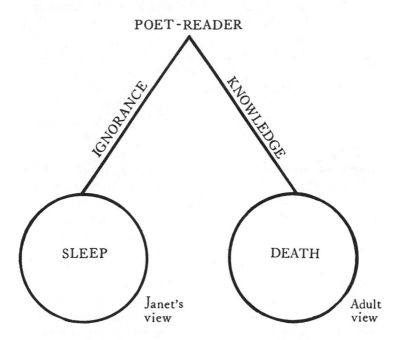

POET-READER

IGNORANCE

KNOWLEDGE

SLEEP

DEATH

Janet's
view

Adult
view

Although there are two small clues, noted earlier, by which one may identify the probable narrator of the poem as Janet's father, they are very small and very well hidden; he is a nearly invisible character. But that is not true of John Crowe Ransom. The author of "Janet Waking" is felt as a distinct presence in every line of the poem; he has chosen to accentuate and exploit his own personality, rather than submerge it as Shelley did. He has accomplished this solely by the force of his style, without ever using the personal pronoun "I" or allowing himself to figure as a participant in the action. The questions *Who is he?* or *What is he like?* are answered by pointing to features of the poem—for example, to the controlled irregularities of its form. The line lengths are varied a good deal within an approximate general pattern, the rimes are sometimes askew ("daddy—baby," "Janet—upon it"), and the ends of four of the sentences do not correspond with the ends of lines. As we have seen, the fourth and fifth stanzas are bound into a unit, although all the rest are independent of one another.

It is in the diction, however, that Ransom's personality is most evident. On the one hand there is the almost Biblical resonance of lines such as "Translated far beyond the daughters of men," and especially the two concluding lines of the poem; on the other hand the calculated oddity of "dainty-feathered hen," "transmogrifying bee," ". . . exceedingly/ And purply . . . ," and their like. The difference between Ransom and Thomas Hardy, who also raised idiosyncrasy to a kind of artistic principle, is not so much that Ransom writes more gracefully (though he does) as that he writes deliberately, with an eye to the effect of his idiosyncrasies on the reader. The phrase "transmogrifying bee," for example, is an act of stylistic bravura, meant to be seen as such. It functions perfectly in its context, and yet it has an extra charge of purposiveness that its context does not demand. In Hardy and Ransom the artistic process is visible, making a texture that runs parallel to, but is not submerged within, the meaning of the poem. Accordingly it becomes a separate component of the aesthetic experience. In Ransom's case the texture would include the irregularities of form noted in the preceding paragraph as well as these incongruities of diction.

Ransom's poem is a tightrope exercise: serious writing that defies gravity. If it had failed, we would not waste a moment asking why. Since it succeeded, we have a number of questions about its success, particularly about the way in which it manages to evade the rules on harmony and consistency of design that have been a principal topic of this book so far. How can language be incongruous and appropriate at the same time? How can a poem violate rules it has made for itself, without nullifying them as rules? How can it ask the reader to give a portion of his attention to the style as such and still maintain the integrity of poetic language as an end in itself? The answer is that the poem does not evade any rules on harmony or consistency of design: it transcends them. "Janet Waking" has a superordinate design that requires these inconsistencies and dissonances. This design is ironic; its components are (1) the poem as a created thing, and (2) the process of poetic creation. As the preceding paragraph has already suggested, we are normally made aware of the poetic process only through the instances where it has not become thoroughly assimilated into the product—where there is some kind of roughness (like the chisel marks on a marble statue) remaining on the finished poem, some noticeable gap in the appropriateness usually demanded of poetic language, some excess either of material or of artistic energy. The absolute rightness of poetic language, when it is right, tends to blind us to the possibilities for wrongness; in the face of the poet's success, we cannot imagine the creative effort having turned out in any other way. (The technique of substitution recommended in Chapter 2 is a way of learning to appreciate this rightness by temporarily disturbing it.) The poet, of course, knows differently. But how is he to communicate his own sense of the miraculous chance by which something was made out of nothing? How is he to assert his own role in the process? The moment a poem of his enters the public domain, it begins a life of its own over which he has no control; in effect, it renders him superfluous. Most poets react to this situation by turning once more to the act of composition, to the next—as yet unwritten—poem, which is always much more interesting to them than the poem they have finished. In this case Ransom has taken an alternative course, which is to incorporate a measure of visible process into the product, reminding the reader that the poem was *made* and by a writer with the power to have done otherwise than he did, if he had wished to. He tells us that the poem is not something that always had to be, nestled snugly in a cultural milieu and bringing to focus a long series of historical antecedents; it exists because Ransom willed it into being, and for no other reason. This wayward or willful element is not a sign of the relaxation of control, though it may seem so from the outside; it is a demonstration of absolute mastery. Ransom is like the equestrian who is so much in command of his steed that he can release the reins and let the animal apparently guide itself. He has developed that quality of nonchalance or studied negligence which became an ideal of gentlemanly behavior in the Italian Renaissance and which the Elizabethan English admired and copied, along with its Italian name: *sprezzatura*. He can take chances; he can play with his work.

"Janet Waking" presents the ironic situation which develops from a child's first encounter with death. This is the substance or content of the poem. The poem itself is included within a larger irony constituted by our awareness of the author's presiding intelligence as a force separate from his poem, playing freely above it and giving hints of a purposiveness that is not wholly engaged by this one artistic design.

The word "play" when applied to this kind of activity is quite literal. Play is essentially the expression of surplus energy, physical or other, under conditions of freedom from the normal constraints of life and with no object other than itself. As we know, the pre-eminent playing animal is man, and one of the most significant formal embodiments of this ability to play is his art. Poetry is the use of language for its own sake; a poem is a kind of game insofar as the rules according to which it is played, though they are of the utmost strictness, are self-determined. *Insofar as*. Because a poet is bound, and his poem determined, in many fundamental ways by the culture in which he lives; not the least of these is the English language which this culture presents him with, ready-made. He cannot say, as the inventor of a game: "I will take a ball of a certain size, or a stick of wood; perhaps an arbitrary distance measured out on the ground, a board ruled into squares, some stones marked with dots—or anything else I please." His poem exists for more reasons than simply his will that it should be. But a good poem creates the illusion of total freedom within the limits of what is necessary to account for its existence; it appears to be self-determined because it contains implicitly all the causes for all its effects. This much was established in the opening pages of Chapter 3. What we are faced with now, in the type of ironic poem represented by "Janet Waking," is the design of an author to disengage a certain amount of his creative energy from the immediate ends proposed by his composition and to assert this freed energy as itself a legitimate artistic goal, also existing for its own sake. Thus he tells us that the poem is not autonomous but that the poetic process is. This too is an illusion—the poet, after all, did not create the art of poetry—but it is an illusion on a higher plane. The design of "Janet Waking," which was double to begin with, is doubled again by this aura of energy playing around it, through which its elements are refracted as they come to us, subtly qualified by signs of their relation to a purpose not immanent in the poem.

And now the inevitable question: Is "higher" also "better"? Some critics and students of poetry would answer "Yes" without hesitation, and others who might be put on their guard by the directness of the question would still come out on the affirmative side after rephrasing the issue in their own terms (i.e., "higher" might be changed into "more complex"). In this way some rather extravagant claims have been made for the value of irony in general, and no doubt they would apply with still greater force to the type of doubly ironic poem represented here. The problem is that there is no ground on which such claims can be judged. Species of design are incommensurable. Would anyone want to argue that "Janet Waking" is a better poem than "This Is Just to Say?" Better as to what? A reader can prefer doubly ironic poems over other kinds if he wants to, but it is a personal preference and will have to be defended as such. His chief obligation is to understand and appreciate them as they are.

Founded as it is upon contrasting points of view, irony tends toward the condition of drama. Because with rare exceptions the author plays a role in the design, either as himself or behind some more or less transparent disguise, there is usually the potentiality for a dramatis personae. The clash of points of view generates dramatic impetus. The reader's active participation in what is going on, his function as an audience, resembles the condition that obtains in the theater. For this reason the design of irony commands an interest that other species of design do not, even though it cannot be said to have an intrinsically higher value. In particular the assertion of creative energy as an autonomous activity, as defined above, seems to have captured the imaginations of authors in our time, and we are now often treated to the spectacle of poetry as process and poetry as product clashing upon the stage. The major focus of attention is upon the author's battle with his medium and his vocation—even the subject matter of the poem, as it were, becomes the author *agonistes*, establishing by skill of arms the possibility of new and further poetry in an age when all possibilities had seemed to be exhausted. This post-romantic development may not be the final sophistication of irony, but it is one which has certainly revitalized the design and has put readers still more on their mettle. It will be worth watching.

5.

Allegory

The design of allegory has at least one distinction that the other species treated here cannot claim, since allegory is not used in ordinary speech, as the others are, and is even rather rare in writing outside of works intended specifically as literature. As a result it has a somewhat bookish flavor; one cannot imagine allegory being used other than deliberately, with an eye to effect. This quality is enhanced by its formal symmetry and by the fact that it is capable of great explicitness if an author wishes his intention to be visible to the reader. Up to a point all this makes allegory rather more accessible than the other designs, but allegory has its own problems, too, which this chapter will attempt to illustrate, along with as many as possible of its modes and applications. Its past, rich and significant though that is, will have to be omitted as a topic of more interest to literary historians than to non-specialized readers.

Allegory is a design of narrative, a way of telling a story. It is not restricted to poetry alone, and in fact the allegories with which most readers are familiar are likely to be prose works of one kind or another, such as Aesop's fables, the New Testament parables, or *The Pilgrim's Progress*. In allegory the narrative is conducted on two levels: (1) the *ostensible*, which is the meaning of the participants, events, and situations taken at their face value, and (2) the *actual*, which is a parallel meaning corresponding point for point with the ostensible but not intermingling with it, requiring the reader to take things at something other than their face value. This kind of doubleness in basic structure allegory shares with the logical device known as "analogy,"

and indeed the clearest insight into how allegory operates
can be obtained by imagining what an author would do if
he began with a simple analogy and proceeded systematically to articulate it. For example, consider the very old and
very common analogy between life and a play, which
Shakespeare expressed by saying, "All the world's a stage,/
And all the men and women merely players." The diagram
on page 123 indicates how this might be worked out. Note
that for every element on the ostensible level, there is a corresponding element on the actual level above it. Although not
all of the elements are temporal events, the whole complex
tends to move forward horizontally in time, which is the
normal direction of narrative.

Here is how the analogy appears in a short poem by Sir
Walter Ralegh, who gives it a characteristically mordant
touch:

WHAT IS OUR LIFE?

What is our life? The play of passion.
Our mirth? The music of division:
Our mothers' wombs the tiring-houses be,
Where we are dressed for life's short comedy.
The earth the stage, Heaven the spectator is,
Who sits and views whosoe'er doth act amiss.
The graves which hide us from the scorching sun
Are like drawn curtains when the play is done.
Thus playing post we to our latest rest,
And then we die in earnest, not in jest.

Ralegh's poem is a good one to start with because it exhibits the bare bones of allegory, which are often well concealed. It should not, however, be regarded as an archetype
or model, the norm from which all others vary. This is only
one of the many possible allegorical structures, some of
which do not appear to derive from an underlying analogy,
and most of which, in any case, are less explicit and four-
square in their development. The next example represents at

FIG. 4

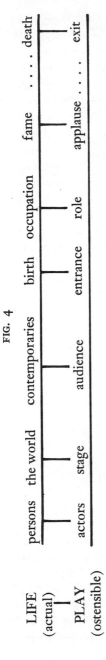

| LIFE (actual) | persons | the world | contemporaries | birth | occupation | fame ..... death |
| PLAY (ostensible) | actors | stage | audience | entrance | role | applause ..... exit |

Note: The two levels can be, and often are, called the "literal" and the "allegorical." These terms are not used to designate the two levels in the present chapter because they are potentially confusing. It is true that the existence of an "allegorical" (i.e., actual) level of meaning is what makes a given work an allegory, but since both the noun and the adjective are commonly applied to the total work, they should not also be used for one of its parts. As for "literal," it too often connotes "real," and which level of the total allegory is real depends upon the direction it is viewed from. The ostensible level is real in the sense that it is made up of what the reader sees on the page before him. It really exists; everything else is supplied, imagined. But the actual level is real in the sense that it is what the poet means to be saying—what he is *really* writing about; the rest is just appearance, a veil for the reader's eye to pierce. By changing terms, perhaps some of this confusion can be avoided.

least one step away from Ralegh's poem in the direction of greater subtlety. It is Matthew Arnold's "To Marguerite":

Yes! in the sea of life enisled,
With echoing straits between us thrown,
Dotting the shoreless watery wild,
We mortal millions live *alone*.
The islands feel the enclasping flow,
And then their endless bounds they know.

But when the moon their hollows lights,
And they are swept by balms of spring,
And in their glens, on starry nights,
The nightingales divinely sing;
And lovely notes, from shore to shore,
Across the sounds and channels pour—

Oh! then a longing like despair
Is to their farthest caverns sent;
For surely once, they feel, we were
Parts of a single continent!
Now round us spreads the watery plain—
Oh might our marges meet again!

Who order'd, that their longing's fire
Should be, as soon as kindled, cool'd?
Who renders vain their deep desire?—
A God, a God their severance ruled!
And bade betwixt their shores to be
The unplumb'd, salt, estranging sea.

The analogy here is between individual human beings and islands in the sea—not a particularly novel one, since it is implied in the very word "isolation." The qualities Arnold contributes to the analogy are a perfect appropriateness and resonance of language and a great energy of movement that simply overwhelms the reader's natural resistance to cliché. The only interpretative difficulty in the poem concerns the images in stanza two and in the very last line. The moon-light, the spring breeze, and the nightingales' song all function in the allegory—that is clear—and yet they themselves do not have to be taken at other than face value, since a heightened awareness of human isolation often comes most strongly to people in the springtime and following such stimuli as these. On the other hand, these three elements, together, may stand for the periodic awakening of love in human hearts, an event that often serves only to dramatize the impossibility of any absolute union between two human beings. The result for the poem is much the same in either case. The "estranging sea" is a different problem. It cannot be taken at face value, any more than "islands" can; in the allegory it stands in a general way for the omnipotent circumstances enforcing human isolation. These circumstances are themselves vague and hard to imagine in concrete terms. They are less important to the poem, however, than are the qualities suggested by the three adjectives attached to the noun "sea." Whatever they may be, the forces that isolate people are of undetermined extent (and probably unknowable—to "plumb" is to "fathom" and to "fathom" is, in one sense, to "know"); they are sterile, or sterilizing, and bitter to experience; and they do not merely keep people apart but also "estrange" them in the sense of making them strangers to one another.

The diagram on page 123 shows that an allegory contains a number of discrete elements or components which, it now appears, have a certain interest in themselves. The nightingales' song, the moonlight, the spring breeze, and the estranging sea in Arnold's poem could all be arranged in sequence on one level, as in the diagram, and each connected by a short vertical line with a corresponding element on the level above; the higher element would be the "meaning" of the lower one. Each pair of connected elements can be called a "symbol."

But there are symbols and symbols. The poetic symbol, as it will be defined in a later chapter, has little to do with allegory and is best kept separated from that topic. The reason why Arnold's "estranging sea" seemed different from the other elements in the poem is that it approaches the condition of the true poetic symbol, i.e., it has a meaning, but this meaning is nothing specific or definite that could easily be written on the upper line of a diagram. The meaning of "estranging sea" is more like the sum of its qualities, of all the things it suggests or connotes. If the poet had stopped to dwell on this symbol, he would not only have given it still greater significance (without necessarily making it more definite) but he would also have begun to weaken the force of his allegory. A symbol is static; an allegory moves—it must move. An allegory is not indifferent to the need for apt and suggestive symbols, but its main object is to present a complex of narrative relationships. The symbols in an allegory therefore tend to be clear-cut, almost schematic.

Inasmuch as the allegorical symbol has this nature, it is not surprising that writers have often gone to the logical extreme and given the ostensible element its actual meaning as a name. The implicit reasoning would be: X (the ostensible element) stands for so-and-so—then why not *call* it "so-and-so"? Probably no writers ever reasoned it out quite this way. It is more likely by far that they began, not with the ostensible element, but with the actual meaning, which they then crowned with a capital letter and moved down to the level below. This process is called "personification." (The capital letter itself is incidental to the process and is not always used.) For example, here is a familiar passage from Gray's "Elegy":

> Let not Ambition mock their useful toil,
>   Their homely joys, and destiny obscure;
> Nor Grandeur hear with a disdainful smile,
>   The short and simple annals of the poor.
>
> . . . .
>
> Nor you, ye Proud, impute to These the fault,
>   If Memory o'er their Tomb no Trophies raise,
> Where through the long-drawn aisle and fretted vault
>   The pealing anthem swells the note of praise.

Can storied urn or animated bust
    Back to its mansion call the fleeting breath?
Can Honour's voice provoke the silent dust,
    Or Flattery sooth the dull cold ear of Death?

In a sense, two distinct levels are not involved here, since "Ambition," to take the first personification at hand, is only a quick and ready way of extracting from ambitious *persons*, generally considered, the one quality that they possess in common. The persons are really impossible to visualize, and there is no reason for supposing that Gray wanted us to try to visualize them. Still, "Ambition" takes a predicate; it does a man's work. There is nothing inherent in the device to prevent Gray, if he so desired, from elaborating "Ambition" into a very solid and life-like figure and giving it more to do. This is the mode of allegory used in *The Pilgrim's Progress* and in much of medieval literature. There is a great difference in effect upon the reader between the two extreme types of allegorical personification—the one in which the ostensible and actual dimensions are virtually identical, and the other in which only the occasional recurrence of a certain name reminds us that an abstract "meaning" hovers over the character whom we see—but they are still basically the same device; it is best not to divide them here and attempt to treat them separately.

Modern readers tend to be unsympathetic to the device as Gray uses it, feeling that no great credit can be given to an author for the simple act of personifying an abstract noun. In Gray's defense, it should be said that his practice was consistent with the aesthetic beliefs of his age, and furthermore that these stately and sonorous abstractions harmonize very well with the design of the poem. They all apply in some fashion or another to the "great world," the society from which the obscure persons whom the elegy commemorates were excluded by birth. Gray's language when he is writing directly about humbler persons tends to be much more concrete—a feature particularly noticeable in the three stanzas preceding those quoted above. As a matter of practice, readers should judge each case of personification on its own merits, rather than apply a blanket condemnation to the device regardless of where it is found or how it is used.

What allegorical personification is capable of when it is well handled, and something of the depths it can sink to when it is not, can both be illustrated by passages from Keats. The first is the opening of his "Ode on a Grecian Urn":

> Thou still unravish'd bride of quietness,
>   Thou foster-child of silence and slow time. . . .

The second is from his "Ode to a Nightingale":

> Where Beauty cannot keep her lustrous eyes,
>   Or new Love pine at them beyond tomorrow.

The first line of the "Ode on a Grecian Urn," flawless as poetry, is puzzling as allegory because "quietness" seems merely to duplicate "silence" in the following line, though how this quality can be husband and foster-father both is not clear. And if the marriage with quietness were consummated, would the result be less quiet or more? It seems nonsensical to propose that the result of consummating a marriage with quietness would be noise, but if the result were greater quietness, what is gained, for the urn, by the lack of consummation? Why is it better off the way it is? No doubt these questions are pedantic. Nevertheless, they have to be asked, and it is the poet's use of allegory that calls them forth, not the critic's pedantry.

The puzzle in Keats's lines yields to careful analysis, once the reader senses the very special nature of this marriage and its unstated analogue in human life. *Any* bride of quietness would be "still unravish'd" (note, by the way, how much better a word "still" is than "yet"), because quietness is incapable of consummating a marriage. That is why the marriage was made. To marry quietness, in this context, means to enter into a perpetual virginity by embracing the absolute and final aesthetic conditions of sculp-

tural art. It is as much like becoming a nun as becoming a
bride. (The word "bride" itself—instead of "wife"—
indicates a marriage that has perpetually just taken place;
the domestic and connubial implications of marriage are
excluded here.) The work of art renounces the world of
motion and time. The price that has to be paid for this
haven from change is incompleteness, as the figures on the
urn demonstrate. Is such gain worth such a loss? According
to what Keats says further on about the failure of human
passion, the answer would seem to be "Yes." Unfortunately,
this is not a choice that human beings can make for themselves. What they can do is participate in the temporary
consummation which occurs when the imagination of the
spectator, from the world of time, meets the urn, from the
world of art, and supplies it with the missing dimension.
(All consummations are by their nature temporary, but this
one at least can be repeated and is stable in its character.)
This interchange between the urn and the spectator is itself
in time, and hence cannot really affect the urn, which remains exactly as it was ("still unravish'd"). The act affects
only the spectator, or, if he happens to write a poem about
his experience, other persons as well—but they are affected
through the medium of a poem, a work of art of an entirely
different kind.

The allegory in the lines from the "Ode on a Grecian
Urn" is pregnant with meaning. The more carefully it is
analyzed the more meaning it reveals; at the same time its
integral connections with the rest of the poem become
more and more striking. As the preceding paragraph demonstrates, it cannot really be understood without invoking
the whole of its context. The allegory in the lines from the
"Ode to a Nightingale" is quite a different matter. The personification of beauty and love is not only easy but also
rather carelessly executed. Keats wants to make lustrous
eyes a possession of "Beauty," although in fact beauty is a
quality of lustrous eyes. "Pine" is a deliquescent word, of
the sort that Keats was unfortunately still capable of using
at times in his mature work, and it introduces all of the connotations of bad romantic love, which is passive, self-

indulgent, sorrowful, remote—and unreal, for nothing would be more irksome or fatal to love in reality than an endless time spent pining at (or into) the eyes of one's lover. (It is interesting that the last objection does not come up in one's reading of the "Ode on a Grecian Urn.") The general sense of these lines is that both beauty and love are temporary, and that this is a cause for regret. The difficulty comes when the reader tries to read them as the allegory seems to require him to do, assigning specific functions to the elements and relating them to one another. "New Love," we are told, cannot pine at Beauty's eyes beyond tomorrow. Is this because "new Love" is no longer new or because the eyes have lost their luster and charm? The reader is tempted to answer, "Both." But this is hardly a fruitful, or even a possible, ambiguity. If love fails because of the passage of time, then it cannot matter whether its object, beauty, fails or not. The two occurrences are independent, and Keats should never have presented them as though they were related. On the other hand, if love fails because beauty fails, implying that new love requires an object always new, the failure of beauty is also irrelevant, since the real fault lies in the inconstancy of the human heart and its penchant for fastening on external appearances.

If these lines from one stanza of the "Ode to a Nightingale" are defective, the stanza in which they appear is not less so; it is inadequate to its subject (the sorrows of human life) and inadequate to the rest of the poem. Hence the defects are not solely caused by the allegory. The conclusion to be drawn from this example is that allegory cannot be used to cover up such weaknesses in the poet's design as a lapse into sentimentality or a failure to think the subject through; the added dimension of meaning, instead of hiding confusion of feeling and thought, is likely to add its own confusions to the total. In a good allegory the basic analogy should be apt, the relationships between the two levels should be consistently worked out, and (especially) the allegorical pattern imposed on the subject should expand rather than limit its potential meaning. All three of these requirements were more than met by the allegorical passage from the "Ode on a Grecian Urn."

The one benefit that overt personification always confers upon allegory is that of making its interpretation easier. It may be helpful, in that case, to look at a few allegories where personification is not used and to consider what the reader must do in order to understand the allegory, i.e., in order to get beyond the ostensible level in his reading. The following sonnet by W. H. Auden, from a sequence entitled "In Time of War," presents typical difficulties:

> And the age ended, and the last deliverer died
> In bed, grown idle and unhappy; they were safe:
> The sudden shadow of the giant's enormous calf
> Would fall no more at dusk across the lawn outside.
>
> They slept in peace: in marshes here and there no doubt
> A sterile dragon lingered to a natural death,
> But in a year the spoor had vanished from the heath;
> The kobold's knocking in the mountain petered out.
>
> Only the sculptors and the poets were half sad,
> And the pert retinue from the magician's house
> Grumbled and went elsewhere. The vanquished powers were
>   glad
>
> To be invisible and free: without remorse
> Struck down the sons who strayed into their course,
> And ravished the daughters, and drove the fathers mad.

Not many readers would be willing to guess off-hand what the subject of this poem is, though the poem is clearly about something. It has a cast of characters, a setting or settings, and it narrates a series of events that seem to be causally related. Since the poem is presented here out of its normal context and with no commentary or background information, it will have to be interpreted by means of inferences based on clues in the text itself. This process is no different from the one followed when one interprets non-allegorical poems that are similarly isolated, except, of course, that in this case the goal is a double instead of a single level of meaning. The value of isolating a poem in this way is that the process of inference becomes easier to follow when strictly confined to a narrow range of evidence. It is not necessarily the best way to interpret a poem; on the other hand, the proper interpretation of outside evidence— biographical, bibliographical, historical, and so forth—is itself an art which requires special training. The reader is usually safer sticking with the text. Outside evidence can be used as incidental support for an interpretation based on the text, occasionally even to verify an interpretation, but never to *produce* an interpretation—assuming, as always, that the poem has the artistic integrity that we have a right to demand of it.

The reader might very well begin with the point of greatest obscurity: the word "kobold." A trip to the dictionary reveals that "kobold" comes from Germanic folklore and that it may refer either to a mischievous domestic spirit or to a gnome who haunts underground places. The latter sense is obviously preferred here. The kobold belongs in the same category with the giant and the dragon, not only because they are all imaginary beings from the realm of folklore but also because, as a second look at the text reveals, they all suffered a comparable fate: the giant disappeared, the dragon died, and the kobold fell silent. (It seems reasonable to infer that the poet is talking about more than one being of each kind; the definite article is used here with the same purpose as in a sentence like "The dog is a domestic animal.") Since the end of the age coincided with the end of these three beings, it was probably the age in which they flourished: the age of giants, dragons, and kobolds. We now need an inclusive term for this age, one that the poem seems to want us to supply. The age of imaginary beings? The age of legend? The age of superstition? It is a little hard to say, because the poem refers to these events as though they had actually taken place, whereas what we might call the age of superstition is the age when they were merely believed in; we are quite confident that they never took place. Perhaps by design, the first eight lines of the poem do nothing to resolve this ambiguity.

The poem takes a turn of some sort with the beginning of the ninth line; the word "only" signals an exception to the condition described earlier, and sculptors, poets, and "the pert retinue from the magician's house" are associated in some reaction to the end of the imaginary beings which differentiates them from the "they" in lines one through eight. Some persons were "safe," and some others, safe or not, were far from being pleased by the outcome. Again a term is needed under which these persons may be grouped. Sculptors and poets are artists, but are magicians? Magicians are practitioners of make-believe. But then so are sculptors and poets, in a sense—and magicians are a kind of artist, when it comes to that. Their common stock in trade is fiction, which comes from and appeals to the human imagination. They are all engaged in kinds of fooling. It is understandable that they would be disappointed by the end of such an age, in which giants and dragons preyed on the countryside and kobolds stormed underground. The poets and sculptors were deprived of subjects, and the magicians' magic, without the support of a common belief in the supernatural, became nothing but sleight-of-hand. "They" wanted safety, normality, peace, and "they" were the great majority. How appropriate that the age should end, not with a mighty confrontation of forces, an Armageddon, but diminuendo, with senility and natural death occurring in scattered places over the countryside and mostly out of sight! "They" had won.

Except that the poem is not over. " . . . The vanquished powers were glad/ To be invisible and free. . . ." One kind of problem had merely been exchanged for another, and apparently the new one was far worse. "Vanquished" must be ironic, for the "powers" operate completely at will now. The word "vanquished" ties these powers in some manner to the giants, dragons, and kobolds; it was the defeat of the latter that ended the age. But how are the two groups related? Could it be that the defeat of the imaginary beings was a condition for the liberation of the "powers"? The powers are said to be invisible and they have no names; the imaginary beings, however, were at least all known if not all visible—they were specific, clearly differentiated, and had the characteristics of persons. They might be considered personifications of otherwise abstract forces—and why not of the "powers"? According to this hypothesis, then, the age did not end but merely changed its outward character: with the disappearance of the objective manifestations of these malign powers—their poetic versions, as it were—the powers were at last free to operate as they wished, and the safety of the people turned out to be an illusion.

This interpretation is internally consistent and seems to make sense of the poem as far as it goes, but it is nearly all on the ostensible level, which explains why most readers would still feel that there is as yet no *point* to all this. It is remote and unreal; how could we be expected to care? We could be expected to care if Auden were describing some actual, historical event in which our ancestors had been involved, that is, if "they" means the human race, or that part of it which contributed to Western civilization. Our ancestors believed in supernatural powers hostile to mankind, and their imaginations gave concrete substance to these powers in the forms of giants, dragons, ghosts, witches, elves, and other such beings whom we dismiss now as the products of superstition. These beings existed as long as they were believed in; when modern scientific rationalism (itself a curious mixture of skepticism and credulity) came into possession of men's minds, after a process that continued over several centuries, superstition died a natural death. Along with it died the pantheon of minor deities who had been of such great use to artists. The public at large, characteristically, cared nothing about this incidental result. They were all much too busy congratulating themselves on their emergence from darkness. But the world itself does not change, however much our ways of looking at it may do so, and the reality which man's imagination had once dealt with by giving it visible form in the creatures of superstition persisted unharmed, invisible now, and the more dangerous for being invisible because there was no longer any way of coming to grips with it—in fact, most persons did not even believe that it existed. This reality, which Auden symbolizes ironically with "the vanquished powers," is not overtly defined in the poem, but there is little question that it is the reality of evil *—hence the murder, rape, and madness which flourish in consequence of man's entering the modern age. The pathos of his situation (if "pathos" is not too feeble a word) is that he can no longer explain what is happening to him with the old, satisfying fictions of art; he is self-constrained to pretend that evil is merely an aberration that can be taken care of in due time by the moral equivalent of sewage disposal or slum clearance. If evil can somehow be made illegal, all we need to do is enforce the laws. As this continues not to happen, modern man faces the most unmanning of all states: despair. His fate, in literal terms, is perhaps no more grim now than it ever was, but there is no longer animus in it. Fate is impersonal. There is satisfaction of a kind in being defeated in battle against a known and visible enemy, but none at all in being struck down from behind by an invisible, abstract force.

If the "powers" are indeed those of evil, then (in nontheological terms) no deliverance from them is possible. The deliverers mentioned in line one had no more corporeal existence than the giants, dragons, and kobolds; they too were creatures of the imagination—saints, folk heroes, and the like—and it is clear that their function was not that of abolishing evil but of permitting man to come to terms with it. Their victories and sacrifices were ritual, part of a great continuing drama. And though they were of the age, they did not work for the age: they worked for individual persons. The battle was fought out again and again in the arena of the individual human mind through a direct confrontation of personified forces. Man cannot escape from the conditions of human life, but he can transcend them by the exercise of the imagination.

Auden's poem can be read as allegorical because, and only because, there really has been a turn in human history away from the forms and rituals of the moral imagination

---

* Instead of "evil" the psychoanalyst might prefer his own term, the "id."

and toward the hygienic myths of scientism. Otherwise the poem would remain merely a kind of fairy story that would hardly repay the small effort needed to take it at face value. One could object that Auden's view of history is oversimplified; a professional historian, while conceding that something loosely resembling what Auden describes did take place, would go on to insist that human attitudes toward evil have never been consistent and uniform in any age and that the overthrow of superstition by science (which is not itself a monolithic structure) is a long way from being complete even now. True. But Auden is dramatizing the facts, and since he has not pretended to write an exact history it is unfair to criticize him as though he had. To a certain extent his schematizations and simplifications are dictated by the allegorical method. But we must not forget that through them he has gained great force and vividness, nor that the historian would be exceedingly hard pressed to record his own version of the events in fourteen lines of prose without distorting them to a similar degree. History, in any case, is not a bare chronicle but a *story*, a product of the imagination seeking to provide an intelligible form for the meaningless raw material of events.

Auden's poem was introduced partly as a way of testing whether it is possible to arrive at a satisfactory interpretation of an allegory in the absence of outside evidence, if the allegory itself does not provide specific clues to its meaning. The conditions were as fair as they can be: the reader's mind was assumed not to be empty of all information (here he needs to know something about the intellectual and cultural history of the past few centuries), for he could not understand any poem if he were totally ignorant. The point is that he need not know anything *specially* for this poem. There are, of course, some allegories of which this cannot be said, but precisely because each of them offers a unique interpretative problem there is nothing to be gained by studying them as a class. They demonstrate only that the design of allegory will help a poet be obscure who does not do what is necessary to make himself clear.*

* If space permitted, Auden's "And the Age Ended" might be compared here with Wordsworth's sonnet, "The World Is Too Much

On its surface the next example of allegory is a much more straightforward poem than Auden's. Unlike his, it makes good sense when taken at face value, and for this reason many readers probably fail to notice the allegory. It is A. E. Housman's "Fancy's Knell":

When lads were home from labour
   At Abdon under Clee,
A man would call his neighbour
   And both would send for me.
And where the light in lances
   Across the mead was laid,
There to the dances
   I fetched my flute and played.

Ours were idle pleasures,
   Yet oh, content we were,
The youth to wind the measures,
   The old to heed the air;
And I to lift with playing
   From tree and tower and steep
The light delaying,
   And flute the sun to sleep.

The youth toward his fancy
   Would turn his brow of tan,
And Tom would pair with Nancy
   And Dick step off with Fan;
The girl would lift her glances
   To his, and both be mute:
Well went the dances
   At evening to the flute.

Wenlock Edge was umbered,
   And bright was Abdon Burf,
And warm between them slumbered

With Us." The two poems complement each other in many respects. Wordsworth's is not allegorical, but its major theme is the destruction of man's rapport with the world of nature—a rapport that at one time in the past was close enough to allow the personification of natural forces.

The smooth green miles of turf;
Until from grass and clover
    The upshot beam would fade,
And England over
    Advanced the lofty shade.

The lofty shade advances,
    I fetch my flute and play:
Come, lads, and learn the dances
    And praise the tune to-day.
To-morrow, more's the pity,
    Away we both must hie,
To air the ditty,
    And to earth I.

Superficially, this poem is another graceful variation on the familiar *carpe diem* theme: country pleasures do not last forever, "more's the pity," so catch them while you can. But two things happen in the last stanza that cast doubt on this interpretation. The first is a dramatic shift from past to present tense (e.g., "advanced" to "advances"). Suddenly we are no longer in a timeless pastoral world where all events can be described in terms of customary action ("would call," "would send," "would turn"), where the participants are more like players cast in roles that never change than human beings with histories of their own, and where the unfailing cycle of night and day within which these individual lives are ordered subtracts no quantum from the future with each of its twenty-four hours and adds none to the past. We are now in the real world. "To-day" and "to-morrow" are divided by more than a mark on the dial; the "lofty shade" of the penultimate stanza, which was only the shade of night, is now the shade of approaching death. With this sudden broadening of significance, the poem has taken a turn toward allegory. The second thing is a shift in emphasis from the country pleasures to the artist who provides them. The phrase "we both" excludes the audience. Housman is saying that while there will always be an audience of some kind needing entertainment, there will not always be this particular artist with his distinctive repertory. (Tom, Nancy, Dick, and Fan are individually named, but they are no less generic than "the youth" and "the girl" and will surely repeat themselves in succeeding generations.) The unexpected emphasis on the artist gives the poem a personal tone that it would otherwise not have had. And since the last stanza has thrust us into the real world of death and change, what is more natural than to suppose that the "I" is not the conventional dramatic fiction, but is Housman himself? Following this hypothesis, only a few more translations are necessary to make perfect sense of the whole work. The "tune" is poetry, the rustic folk are Housman's audience, and "Fancy's Knell" is his poetic valedictory. Two further bits of knowledge, which some readers may already possess, support this interpretation: in pastoral poetry (long a favorite genre of allegorists) the poet is traditionally represented as a player on some instrument—most often the shepherd's pipes or flute; and this poem is the last one in the volume that Housman entitled *Last Poems*.

The immediate topic of the allegory in "Fancy's Knell" is a very personal one: Housman's conception of himself as poet, in relation both to his art and to his audience. But this is imbedded in the context of something that might fairly be called a philosophy of life. The pastoral world is meant to be the allegorical counterpart of the real world, and what Housman says about himself and his audience, he implies, is true of poets and audiences in general. A rough paraphrase of the philosophy would go something like this: "Life is transitory, and labor is its main ingredient. However, there are moments of respite, and these ought to be spent in innocent pleasure while we still have the power to enjoy them. The function of the poet is to aid this pleasure—not for the few but for the people in general, of whom he is one, differentiated mainly by his special talent, the exercise of which requires him to stay apart from the rest. His reward is the approbation of this audience. When their time is up, both the artist and his work disappear."

Unhappily, some of this philosophy is denied by the

very poem which presents it. The existence of this poem, in its present state, testifies to Housman's belief that the function of the poet is to create enduring works of art for the minority who can appreciate them, not ephemeral amusements for the public at large. If poetry is only a diversion for idle hours, why did he write this poem, which is demonstrably so much more? The ditty does not go "to air"; if it is any good it stays on paper, and Housman knew this better than most men. Perhaps this conflict of values might be avoided by blurring the focus of the poem, so to speak, and refusing to look beyond the most general features of what it presents, concentrating on the flavor or tone or sentiment at the expense of the philosophy. But it is hard to see how the results of the tactic would justify its use, for a poem as vague as that would scarcely be worth reading at all. Anyhow, this poem is not in the least vague or ambiguous; a more detailed analysis than the one above would reveal many more instances of precise calculation on Housman's part. The problem has nothing to do with Housman's craftsmanship, which is faultless, but with something far deeper and more pervading: a kind of artistic schizophrenia. Housman is willing to take his art seriously, it would seem, but he is unwilling to *say* so. Since he is also unwilling to keep silent, he writes a poem by which he hopes to indicate covertly something of the high value he places on himself and his function, while overtly minimizing these things. It may be that he mistrusts his twentieth-century audience; it may be that he is genuinely reticent— we do not know. But what he produces is grossly oversimplified, stagy, false in fact and—what is worse—false in spirit. As allegory, the poem thoroughly misrepresents the poet's situation in twentieth-century England, yet where and when was the England that could have permitted us to accept all this at face value?

Housman's other poems are not open to the same objection. Although there is more than a little incongruity in one's mental picture of the mustachioed and reclusive Professor of Latin at Cambridge, the fiercest classical scholar of his day, disguised as an apple-cheeked Shropshire lad, with

very few exceptions the poems themselves do not require
one to make this identification. They are impersonal; the
characters are dramatic fictions, even when the "I" is used.
And for all its being a never-never land, with the artificially
clarified atmosphere of the pastoral, Shropshire is a very
grim place. There is no attempt on Housman's part to miti-
gate or conceal the realities of life—in fact, his main themes
are death, defeat, and estrangement. When he thinks of
himself as a man, and universalizes his predicament, Housman is on safe ground. He falters only when he thinks of
himself as a poet.*

The objection to "Fancy's Knell"—let it be clear—is
not that Housman used the method of allegory or that he
disguised himself as a rustic musician, but that he constructed a poem with basic inherent contradictions of fact,
value, and attitude: between the real status of the poet in
modern England and the wished-for status, between poetry
as enduring art and poetry as temporary entertainment, between actual pride and pretended humility. And yet, in a
surprising way, the contradictions do not destroy the poem.
They remain unresolved, for if Housman did not resolve
them the reader certainly cannot do it for him. But after a
while they begin to take on an aesthetic interest of their
own. They form a design which includes the poem that
Housman thought he was writing, and they enable the
reader to view the poem from an ironic perspective apparently unintended by its author. A somewhat similar criticism was made of Tennyson's "Enoch Arden" in Chapter 3,
except that in Tennyson's case the poem did not survive
nearly as well. Both poems are defective in design, Housman's perhaps the more so because the defect is spread
through the whole poem and not localized in the final line.
What saves Housman's poem is that his dilemma is genuine:
if he is attempting to conceal a problem, at least it is a real

* The exception is No. LXII in *A Shropshire Lad*, " 'Terence,
This is Stupid Stuff,' " which is wholly successful. But the poem
following it, "I Hoed and Trenched and Weeded," which occupies
the same position and serves the same function in that volume as
"Fancy's Knell" does in *Last Poems*, and is likewise allegorical, reeks
of sentimentality and self-pity.

problem. Tennyson, on the other hand, created a problem that need not have existed, and he created it simply by a lapse of taste or sensitivity. There is no such lapse in Housman's poem. And the unintentional standard of value advanced by the concluding line of "Enoch Arden" is not one that we would accept even if Tennyson had meant it deliberately, whereas there are no moral reasons, at least, why we should reject the idyllic and unreal picture of the poet's role in society that Housman gives us.

Housman's picture of the nature and function of the poet is untrue, but what is more important is that Housman wished it to be true—wished it to the extent of writing this poem. He was powerfully attracted by the vision of an organic society, related to the land, in which the poet would have a respected and necessary function. In this picture all of the complexities of modern life are ironed out smooth; everything is direct and simple. Even the hedonism and the pessimism balance exactly. Thus it is remarkable that Housman should have used the complex design of allegory in order to convey all this to us. The design of the poem is more than just the allegory itself: it is the *choice* of allegory as design, the author's commitment to the method. This choice is the most eloquent admission possible of the distance between the world which Housman imagined and the one in which he really lived. We may be sure that Housman's rustic musician would never have sung "Fancy's Knell."

Within the space of a few paragraphs the treatment of Housman's poem has moved from the realm of explication to that of evaluation and judgment. This is a normal process, one that ought not to be interrupted if a reader wishes to do anything like full justice to a poem. Allegory in particular requires this kind of treatment, because allegory is habitually concerned with problems of value, moral issues, and even outright doctrine, and to leave these concerns unrecognized would be a disservice to the poet who chose to express them.

A poet uses allegory because he wants to teach, but allegory is not the only way of teaching. There is always the alternative of presenting a doctrine straightforwardly and without disguise. Allegory must have qualities that make it especially attractive for teaching or poets would not use it. And indeed it does. For one thing, allegory can sugar-coat an otherwise unpalatable truth by surrounding it with the vividness, energy, and human interest of narrative, so that the reader is often won over to the author's point of view before he realizes what is happening to him. At the same time, by leaving much or all of its actual meaning for the reader to infer, allegory permits ambiguities and equivocations for the author who does not want to commit himself too definitely. (The method of symbolism is still better adapted to this end.) We must also recognize that allegory is already halfway along the road to didacticism because of its very structure, which embodies the principle of the extrinsic goal, with the ostensible level of meaning functioning as the vehicle for the actual level of meaning. It would be hard to write an allegory that did not make a point of some kind on which judgment might be passed.

These qualities help explain why an author who wants to teach writes an allegory, but they do not quite touch upon the reasons why an author who wants to write an allegory decides to write a poem, rather than something in prose. It must be that the didactic urge is not the only cause operating here. The most likely, or at least the most obvious, explanation is that he wants to add the qualities of poetry to those of allegory. While true enough in its way, this explanation hardly represents the real complexities of the situation. To begin with, the writer has probably dedicated himself to poetry long before the issue of composing this particular allegory arose; whatever he writes, it will be some kind of poem because that is his characteristic mode. Moreover, it is surely the case that many allegorical poems began simply as poems; the author's original conception had allegorical potentialities, and as he saw them adumbrated in the language of his earlier sketches he allowed them to develop themselves and take over the direction of the poetic design. Hence there was never any point in the sequence at which a decision between poetry and prose had to be made, and the allegory developed naturally, almost spontaneously, out of the exigencies of the creative process. The result of this process unites the qualities of poetry with those of allegory ("adds" is too static, too arithmetical a term). The truth of the allegorical meanings, besides being made concrete in the forms of allegory, is transfigured by the language of poetry. We shall never return in our minds to the idea of human isolation without remembering Arnold's "unplumb'd, salt, estranging sea," nor encounter persons who believe that science will save the world without thinking of Auden's ironic "they were safe" and its aftermath of horror, nor shall we reflect upon our own roles in society and the necessarily brief span in which we can exercise such talent as we have without hearing the echo of another spirit who was moved by the same concerns to write:

> The lofty shade advances,
>   I fetch my flute and play:
> Come, lads, and learn the dances
>   And praise the tune to-day.
> To-morrow, more's the pity,
>   Away we both must hie,
> To air the ditty,
>   And to earth I.

If this is *tristesse* rather than tragedy, and if it does not stand up under criticism as well as it should, still the craftsmanship in language cannot be lightly dismissed, and we do not soon forget the tone, so apt and finely modulated, nor the Roman dignity Housman manages as he confronts his vision of the nothing beyond this life.

Because the great achievements of allegory, like Spenser's *Faerie Queene* and Dante's *Divine Comedy*, belong to earlier epochs, students of literature tend to assume that allegory is not much practiced now. This assumption is reinforced by the common knowledge that poets in our own time have put themselves on record as being against the use of poetry for didactic, moralistic, or propagandistic purposes. It would be wise, however, to give more attention to what poets do than to what they say they do. The urge to teach is as strong now as it ever has been. If anything has changed, it is the poet's willingness to admit, perhaps even to himself, that he does so. In accordance with this change of attitude, allegory appears nowadays in more varied disguises than ever before, and the relationships between its actual and ostensible levels of meaning are likely to be more complex and more difficult to schematize than in allegory of earlier periods. One sometimes finds a certain diffidence or even playfulness in the poet's approach to his task, as though he had a message to deliver but would rather slip it under the door than ring the bell and hand it over in person. The work of Robert Frost is particularly illuminating in this respect, since so much of it is a kind of running debate that he conducted, half with himself and half with the public, on the issue of whether it is possible to write meaningful allegory at all. (See, for example, "For Once, Then, Something" and "Directive.") One also finds that modern poets have developed their own analogies and symbols, so that even if they write about familiar subjects they produce works which cannot be easily referred to some allegorical tradition. But this discussion has perhaps already gone farther than it should in attempting to generalize about the status of allegory today. The topic is a very complicated one and deserves treatment in more detail than is possible here. It will be more helpful to close the chapter with a brief examination of a specific poem; this one is from the decade of the fifties in our century. It is by Adrienne Rich and is entitled "The Celebration in the Plaza":

The sentimentalist sends his mauve balloon
Meandering into air. The crowd applauds.
The mayor eats ices with a cardboard spoon.

See how that colour charms the sunset air;
A touch of lavender is what was needed.—
Then, pop! no floating lavender anywhere.

Hurrah, the pyrotechnic engineer
Comes with his sparkling tricks, consults the sky,
Waits for the perfect instant to appear.

Bouquets of gold splash into bloom and pour
Their hissing pollen downward on the dusk.
Nothing like this was ever seen before.

The viceroy of fireworks goes his way,
Leaving us with a sky so dull and bare
The crowd thins out: what conjures them to stay?

The road is cold with dew, and by and by
We see the constellations overhead.
But is that all? some little children cry.

All we have left, their pedagogues reply.

Here is a bit of genre painting that we instantly recognize: has not this, or something like it, appeared on calen-
dars and magazine covers ever since we could remember?
The place is the standard interchangeable timeless Smalltown, U.S.A. of the television and movie screens, which
exists not in a geographic area but in a state of the mind. Its
chief industry, someone has said, is the exportation of
freckle-faced boys. The event is a municipal celebration in
the town square, probably for the Fourth of July, complete
with speeches, souvenirs, refreshments, fireworks, and a
chance to see a platform full of dignitaries (we know that in
daily life they are the banker, the grocer, and the hardware
salesman) who consent to join the fun just like everyone
else, though at some risk to their top hats and their temporary eminence. The crowd is happy, appreciative of the
desultory entertainment. They will stay as long as anything
is going on. Everything seems to work to perfection on this
charmed evening—but of course it cannot last forever, and
so finally, when the resources for entertainment are used
up, the celebration concludes and the crowd slowly leaves,
straggling homeward in quiet under the stars. The children

are still looking up at the sky for another pyrotechnic display; all they find, however, are the constellations.

Miss Rich's poem is immediate and dramatic; it places the reader in the middle of the events, along with the author. But the author's participation (and hence the reader's) is a qualified one. Her point of view is ironic. The irony is most obviously created by the contrast between certain explicit moral judgments ("sentimentalist," "pedagogues") which could come only from an outsider and certain passages where she adopts the attitude of the other spectators ("Nothing like this was ever seen before"). Even without the ending of the poem to tip the balance, we would incline to be suspicious, for the expression on the author's face—so to speak—is just a little too bland, and the naïveté with which she reports the incident is so artless that it has to be artful. All well and good: that is exactly what she wants. The most significant irony in the poem, however, is created in the last four lines, where the constellations replace the fireworks. The children, and their elders, too, would gladly exchange the former for the latter. Stars are tiny, colorless, apparently immobile, a poor substitute for the gorgeous display that man can make with his pyrotechnic art. And they are boring: every night the show is the same. It is sad, not ironic, that fireworks are preferred to stars. The irony is in the phrases, "But is that all?" and "All we have left," because they have implications that neither the children nor the pedagogues are aware of. The stars really *are* "all"; they are the whole visible universe. The language used to minimize the stars has the unintended effect of calling attention to their transcendent status—and to the blindness of the viewers.

No specific verbal clue tells us that the poem is allegorical. Rather, the general setting does so: the Smalltown, U.S.A., which can be paralleled, in respect to its function, with the never-never lands of Auden's "And the Age Ended" and Housman's "Fancy's Knell." (In other respects these imaginary locales are quite different, of course.) We very quickly sense that this stereotyped portrait of the small town, though enlivened with gay and colorful touches, is not in itself adequate to account for the existence of the poem. The author must have had something more in mind, or she would not have bothered to write the poem at all. Our suspicions are encouraged by finding that the author's point of view is ironic, which indicates that she herself recognizes the stereotype and is using it deliberately. To what end? Thus we begin to look beyond the ostensible surface for other and more final meanings.

We must be careful not to attribute the same kind of significance to every detail in the poem. The sentimentalist and his meandering mauve balloon are one thing; the mayor and his cardboard spoon are another. It is true that the mayor can be said to "stand for" petty officialdom, and the spoon for his condescension when he behaves like ordinary folk in taking refreshments, but these are hardly allegorical meanings, since they would still mean the same things in any other context. They are picturesque touches to the painting; they have no further dimension beyond the ostensible. The mauve balloon, on the other hand, is a different case. It is more than simply a spot of color floating across the view, and the context of this particular poem is required in order for us to understand how much more than that it is. Mauve is a civilized, some would say a decadent, color; we do not associate it with nature. (A few readers will think of the so-called "mauve decade" of the late nineteenth century, a time of luxury and artificiality.) Furthermore, the balloon is released by a "sentimentalist"—someone who enjoys the experience of emotion as a thing in itself, i.e., unnaturally—and it meanders into the air, just as passive and aimless as the crowd of people below it. Everything these people see is judged for its effect, nothing for its intrinsic value. Thus in the second stanza the sunset is viewed as an arrangement of colors, needing perhaps a touch of this or a touch of that to bring out its full impact; nature is like a shop window, or a room to be decorated. When the artificial blooms of the fireworks erupt into the sky, it is the high point of the celebration. There is some unconscious irony in the exclamation, "Nothing like this was ever seen before," for the pattern of the fireworks is in-

deed unique, momentary, unrepeatable. It was never part of
nature's design (in either sense of the term). What nature
has to show, instead, is the majestic order of the constellations. The stars are not personified in this poem, as they are
in Blake's "The Tyger" or in George Meredith's sonnet,
"Lucifer in Starlight," where they become "The army of
unalterable law," nor do they proclaim to the ear of reason,
as in Addison's hymn, "The hand that made us is divine."
Yet they have a symbolic function, one that by now is
probably so evident that it hardly needs stating. They stand
for the permanent as against the temporary, the important
as against the trivial, and of course the natural as against the
artificial. The town is the whole civilized world in micro-
cosm, its citizens the human race. The "pedagogues" are the
grownups, the elders, whose responsibility it should be to
communicate knowledge and, especially, values to the children, who cannot be expected to work things out for themselves unaided. Alas, all that the elders do is to echo the
question of the children in their answer. The title of "peda-
gogue" has not only the unflattering connotations that normally attach to it, but also an ironic one here, since these
teachers teach nothing.

"The Celebration in the Plaza" makes its point deftly,
demonstrating that an allegory need not be mechanical or
heavy-handed. The seriousness of its purpose is not incompatible with a certain playfulness of texture. One feels that
the author, in spite of her ironic point of view, is sympathetic with these people. Had she wished to strike out sav-
agely at the blindness of the human race, she would not
have used the picturesque and somewhat folksy celebration
as a basis for the poem. And this fact reminds us that the
ostensible meanings in allegory are not meant to be used and
then discarded, as though once we had got past them to the
actual meanings we had found, in the latter, everything that
the author wanted to say. A good part of what the author
wanted to say is the *way* it is said. This is no less true of
allegory than of any other poetic design. When all possible
credit is given to the author here for the wisdom and the
pertinence of her moral lesson, we must still acknowledge

that the lesson would fail to gain more than a routine assent from the reader were it not presented through language which is charged with the unmistakable qualities of poetry. The celebration in the plaza ended, as we know, but thanks to Miss Rich the celebration in the poem will always be going on.

6·

Metaphor

The study of metaphor has a long and honorable history which goes all the way back to Aristotle, but during much of this time metaphor was considered to be only one of a number of devices—what we know as the "figures of speech"—used to heighten the effectiveness of language. Since the beginning of the Romantic movement, however, metaphor has tended more and more to take the center of the stage at the expense of the other figures. This change in the value assigned to metaphor parallels (and is in part caused by) a larger change in attitudes toward the nature of poetry during these last two hundred years. Because we now think of poetry as being the result of a creative act in which form and content, or language and thought, are fused into an integral whole, we cannot admit the legitimacy of any devices in the language of poetry if they are merely added for the sake of enhancing or ornamenting it. No common figure of speech better avoids this proscription than metaphor, beside which the rest seem external and mechanically applied. And because the process of metaphor has strong analogies with the creative act, it has come to be regarded as typically poetic—at least in theories which place their emphasis, following the Romantic precedent, on the poet's mind or imagination. Metaphor becomes the poetic figure par excellence, and poetry itself, in one view, nothing but metaphor writ large.

It is quite true that we can no longer believe with Pope that expression is the dress of thought. The poet does not first conceive of something that he wants to say and then, separately, clothe his ideas in appropriate language: this is the method of prose rather than of poetry. But we are not obliged on this account to place so exalted a value on metaphor. Poetry is not made out of devices, metaphorical or otherwise. One can easily find many passages of authentic poetry that are non-metaphorical and many passages of authentic prose that are rich in metaphors. Thus if the two modes of writing are to be kept separate, metaphor cannot be regarded as intrinsically poetic; it cannot be a defining characteristic of poetry. The special importance of metaphor in poetry arises from a rather different cause, which is the fact that metaphor alone, among the various species of design, is a *linguistic* design.

To say that metaphor is a linguistic design implies, first, that metaphor is never found outside of language. This is not true of irony. For example, there are ironic events or circumstances which we can experience directly, without the medium of language. Nor is it true of allegory, for there are such things as allegorical paintings and motion pictures which do not depend upon language for the communication of their meanings. The next chapter will point out how symbolism is also independent of language. But there is no such thing as a non-linguistic metaphor. The second and more significant implication is that metaphor occurs, when it occurs, because language makes it possible. The causes of metaphor are rooted in the very nature of language itself. Since poetry itself is made out of language, the student of poetry needs to know what these causes are.

Happily, the word "metaphor" gives a clue to its own definition. It is nothing more than the Greek version of "transfer," a familiar word derived from Latin. Thus:

meta—phor
trans—fer

Both words add up to exactly the same thing—a carrying over or across (cf. "ferry"), a change of location. In a metaphor a word or group of words is transferred from one place to another. But rather than "place," it is better to use the universally accepted technical term, "context," defined as the surroundings or environment in which a given word exists. A context has two different aspects, the verbal and the non-verbal. Contexts always have non-verbal aspects, if only because all uses of language are events which take place within the physical world we inhabit and to which, in some fashion or other, they can be related. Language, fundamentally, is a response to this world. Nevertheless, non-verbal contexts will be largely ignored in this chapter, and for three reasons. (1) The influence of non-verbal contexts on language is quite variable and often merely fortuitous, and so it cannot be taken into account in any systematic way. Sometimes it matters a great deal, and sometimes it matters not at all. (2) The virtue of language, as this was explained in Chapter 1, is that it frees us from the tyranny of the environment. Language is a way of dealing with the world in the abstract. If we could only talk about things when they were right in front of us, we would hardly be better off than the philosophers in Swift's account of the Academy of Lagado, who tried to dispense with words altogether by discoursing in *things*, bundles of which they had to carry upon their backs in order to have at hand the materials for a conversation. (3) The proper and natural environment for words is other words. Words join with other words to form organized utterances, according to grammatical laws, and they all have more in common with one another than any of them has with any non-verbal thing.

A verbal context has no fixed or predeterminable size, and its boundaries cannot be decided except in a somewhat arbitrary manner. The phrase in which the word occurs, the sentence, the paragraph, the chapter, the book, the collected works of an author—all are verbal contexts, radiating like concentric circles outward from the central word. (There would be an analogous set of contexts for a spoken word.) But as they move farther from this word the degree of their relationship to it rapidly diminishes. For this reason discussions of verbal context usually refer to a rather small area, the immediate context of the word. In order to free a discussion from unnecessary complication, one would want to choose the smallest possible immediate context, perhaps beginning with the grammatical unit to which the word is directly related, the phrase or clause, and only moving beyond that to the sentence or paragraph if the smaller context did not provide the answers one was looking for. This is only common sense.

However small the immediate verbal contexts of a particular word may be when taken individually, their number is very large. Taken together, they form a kind of composite environment which is typical of that word. It is upon these that the best dictionaries draw in making their definitions, placing them in separate categories accordingly as they demonstrate different uses of the word. In even the best dictionaries the significance of this procedure is obscured by the need to provide brief verbal translations or equivalents of the meanings of words. Most persons assume that these definitions are themselves the meanings, but the meaning of a word is in the way the word is used, not in what can be said about it in other words. (If this were not so, then one would have to conclude that most language is meaningless, since the ordinary person is quite incapable of giving satisfactory definitions of more than a few of the words he uses—and uses correctly—in his daily life.) As children, we learn the meanings of words both by associating them directly with objects and by hearing them repeatedly used in certain distinctive verbal contexts. We may be assisted by parents, teachers, or dictionaries telling us what they "mean," but as anyone who has dealt with children realizes, the true test of whether a child understands a word is his ability to use it himself or to respond properly to it in a variety of typical contexts. Actually we do not so much learn words one by one as we learn them in groups, already related and grammatically organized, and this is a further reason for stressing the importance of contexts in language. The oftener a word is encountered along with other words in a certain context, the stronger will be the bond tying it to them. The result is that for each word there is built up a range of permissible uses, permissible combinations with other words, and this constitutes a rule or norm for that word. It is not a rule of law, natural or manmade, but a rule of custom, of propriety, and of course it is not consciously apprehended as such; rather, it is unconscious, an intuition or feeling that the speaker himself need not be aware of.

The rule or norm which governs the use of a word is in fact a number of different rules operating simultaneously, having to do with such various things as grammar, rhetoric, style, social taboos, and substance or content. Only this last, however, is relevant to the study of metaphor. It is the rule of substantive propriety. As the term "substantive" indicates, except in certain expressive and ritual uses language has a subject: our universal and surely well-founded assumption is that when we use language to say something we say *something*. The content of an utterance is determined by, and determines, the particular words used. If someone intends to talk about typewriters, for example, he does not use words like "horsepower," "acceleration," "braking," "gear ratio," and "wind resistance," because these words are proper to the subject of automobiles. As we learned the words proper to typewriters and to automobiles we learned them in different verbal contexts, and at the same time we learned (unconsciously) that these words should not be interchanged if we want to communicate intelligibly with other people. The more familiar we are with the respective verbal contexts, the more strongly entrenched does this propriety become and, as a consequence, the less likely we are to be aware that it is operating. It is without doubt the strongest of the proprieties governing the use of language because it concerns the fundamental need of language to be about something.

In executing its substantive function, its "aboutness," language operates according to the principle of nominality. That is, the abstract signs by which language refers to its subject have no necessary connection with that subject, being purely arbitrary; they did not have to be the way they are, and they can always be changed if enough speakers of the language collaborate in making substitutions. Yet most speakers of a language are quite unaware that they possess the theoretical freedom implied in this principle, and insofar as they have any opinion on the matter at all they tend to believe that language is not nominal—that there is a real and necessary connection between things and the names of things. There are no quotation marks around the words they use; they do not deal in as-it-were's and so-to-speak's. They believe that things have their names in the same way that things have their attributes of shape, size, weight, and color. A spade is called a spade because it *is* a spade. The nature of language conforms to the nature of the world.

This notion that language has a real and necessary connection with things underlies the popular concept of literality. Literal language, people suppose, is what they use when they give things their proper names, the names which they "have." It is therefore a kind of standard against which deviations can be gauged. The principal deviation is metaphor, a fact that is attested to by the common use of the terms "literal" and "metaphorical" as correlative opposites. It will now be necessary to point out (1) that the concept of literality is untenable in this form, and (2) that some form of the concept, along with the distinction between literal and metaphorical that it implies, is both valid and worth preserving.

As a deviation from literality, metaphor is often defined as a process of interchanging the names of things or of attributing to things qualities which they do not really possess. For example, one may take the opening lines of Hamlet's famous soliloquy:

> To be, or not to be—that is the question.
> Whether 'tis nobler in the mind to suffer
> The slings and arrows of outrageous fortune,
> Or to take arms against a sea of troubles
> And by opposing end them. . . .

The third line would be called a metaphor because fortune does not really use "slings and arrows" in attacking its victims, or alternatively because fortune itself is an abstraction that does not really exist in a concrete and personal form. Furthermore, troubles do not really come in "seas"—they are not made of water and they do not break on the shore

—and even if they did, one could not "take arms" against them. In a rough and ready sort of way, these results are quite acceptable. The difficulty arises when the definition is given critical attention or applied rigorously; then its inadequacy for the serious study of metaphor becomes apparent. In the first place, it obscures the nominal character of language. Why cannot a man call the sum of his troubles a "sea"? For that matter, why cannot he call the sea a "sum"? There is nothing inherent in these combinations of consonants and vowels, merely as such, that makes them unfit for other uses, and the objects do not own the names as exclusive property, like trademarks. In the second place, this definition introduces an alien term, "really," which it silently substitutes for "literally," even though the two are in no sense equivalent. Thus the whole question is prejudiced, for the way things really are is the province of science or metaphysics, not of ordinary language. Does the great bulk of language used in everyday communication habitually and consistently correspond with the way things really are? Are the findings of science and metaphysics embodied in this language? We may study science or metaphysics, but do we *talk* them? Even if literal language always says things that are so and metaphorical language says things that are not so, we are left with no means of indentifying the sub-class of metaphors within the larger class of not-so things. It is false to say "The sun circles the earth," and it is also false to say "The sun is the eye of heaven," but everyone knows that the second statement is a metaphor while the first one is not. In order to explain the difference between them we need something that this definition of metaphor cannot supply.

The crucial point in all this is the relationship between language and the external world, or the non-verbal environment of language. There can be no doubt that language is fundamentally a response to this world. But it responds to the world mediately, through the activity of the human mind, rather than directly. The proof of this is that language can refer equally well to real things—concrete external objects such as individual tables and chairs—and to unreal ones—abstractions and fictions such as "justice" and

"Santa Claus." In modern semantics the tendency has been to accept the first kind of reference as a standard for meaningfulness and to look with suspicion on the second kind as being inherently deceptive and perhaps even illegitimate. A better way of looking at the situation would be from the opposite side, taking as standard the kind of reference which is made to things that do not have a concrete objective existence. These things exist only in the mind; but so also do tables and chairs, as far as language is concerned. The world which language refers to, the world which it is about, is an interior world of perceptions, feelings, ideas, dreams, beliefs, attitudes—a world in which the line between real and imaginary things is by no means sharply or consistently drawn, and at times is not drawn at all. This is not a pathological state: it is perfectly normal. The functions of language must therefore be judged in terms appropriate to and consistent with human psychology. It may not have escaped notice, by the way, that the term "really," as it was used in the paragraph above, is potentially equivocal. If someone who explained the metaphors from Hamlet's speech in that fashion were challenged to show what scientific proof he had that troubles do not come in seas, as alleged, he might, on discovering that it was just as hard to prove that they do not as it would be to prove that they do, then fall back upon some translation of "really" into the equivalent of "as we suppose" or "according to universal belief" or "in our manner of thinking"—which immediately negates the intent of "really" by putting the whole matter on the basis of human psychology, where it should have been all along.

Literality must be defined so as to include the great bulk of language used in everyday communication. This is axiomatic. If we now ask ourselves what characteristics this language has, we can only point to its complete ordinariness, to what seems rather than anything else to be a lack of characteristics. It is colorless, neutral. But perhaps literality is just this: being colorless and neutral. Metaphor would then be anything that stood out against the background of ordinary language. Unfortunately, a number of different things, profanity for one, also stand out against this background, and so the definition does not sufficiently discriminate metaphor from the rest. What is needed is a concept of the *kind* of ordinariness involved in literal language, so that the kinds of deviation from it can be indentified. The popular concept of literality held that such language is proper to the subjects it refers to because it has a real and necessary connection with them. Substitute for this untenable notion the concept of substantive propriety which has already been explained and at one stroke the problem is solved. Literal language is language which regularly observes this propriety, i.e., words are used to refer to subjects according to linguistic precedent, based on their previous and repeated use together in typical verbal contexts. Metaphor departs from substantive propriety by introducing into a given context a word which is proper to another and different kind of context. This is often done, of course, but it is not done so often as to become itself a normal procedure, and thus the distinction—the vital distinction—between the literal and the metaphorical is maintained.

In regularly observing substantive propriety, literal language is automatized. We do not notice this propriety as long as it is observed, but when a word from another context intrudes and violates it the violation at once draws our attention. The violation takes on immediacy. If this were all that happened, however, metaphor would be nothing more than using the "wrong" word instead of the "right" word for a given context. The essential further step is that the metaphor, the "wrong" word, is somehow assimilated and temporarily made the "right" word. Our instinct to make sense out of the language we encounter comes into operation, and the rule or norm which governs the context and determines which words are proper for its subject is modified just enough to allow the violation to pass muster. It is accommodated. Although a new norm, a norm *ad hoc*, is created in the process of accommodating the intruding word, this word does not entirely cease to be "wrong" for the context. To be accommodated is not to be naturalized. The foreignness of the word remains perceptible, and our understanding of the situation includes our assumption that the word will, as it were, return home after its present duty is done. Our understanding of the situation also includes an appreciation of the author's or speaker's intention. This is certainly the case when a metaphor is bizarre or far-fetched, because such a metaphor puts us on our guard and makes us suspect that its creator might have been using words irresponsibly. Before we accept the metaphor as legitimate we want to see what the author was up to. That is, we want to see that there was a genuine substantive propriety in the first place and not just a random collocation of language; to put it another way, we want to see that when the intruding word entered the context and changed its direction there was indeed a direction to be changed. We also want to see the effort we make in accommodating the violation justified by some gain in the vividness, force, or meaning of the altered context.

Metaphor may therefore be defined as an *accommodated violation of substantive propriety*. This is a formal, objective definition, and it does not convey much sense of how a metaphor actually seems to the person who experiences it. To a certain extent that is a weakness in the definition, since metaphor exists only as it is experienced. If a given word does not strike anyone as metaphorical, then it simply is not metaphorical, whatever its form may be. So-called "fossil" metaphor is a good case in point. A fossil metaphor is a word which presumably once existed as a metaphor but which through constant use has become naturalized and is now taken to be literal. Its substantive propriety is automatized. For example, the word "shambles" once meant "slaughterhouse," and the dictionary still lists this meaning, but though the word is in common use today it now means something much less specific: a "mess" or an "area of destruction." It occurs in such contexts as "Their play deteriorated, and the second half of the game was a complete shambles." One can see, by taking into account its original meaning, how the word could be metaphorical in the modern context, but no one understands it that way. The reason is that no one remembers "shambles" as "slaughterhouse." The latter word has completely supplanted it in contexts having to do with the killing and preparing of animals for food. Hence there are two processes at work, one of them being the constant use of the word as a metaphor and the other being the disappearance of the word from the contexts in which it had been literal. An example of a metaphor which has not yet been fossilized would be the word "harness" in contexts having to do with atomic power: "harnessing the atom," as we say. "Harness" will remain a metaphor as long as it lives in its original and proper contexts, and it will not become literal in the contexts of atomic power until we no longer have cause to use it in talking about straps, bits, and collars. Words are also maintained as metaphors by the continued existence of literal alternatives to them. Thus it is literal to speak of the leg of a chair but metaphorical to speak of the eye of a hurricane, because there is no other word to use for the former, whereas for the latter we can use "center" as well. Finally, there is a large category of words which have latent or at most very feeble metaphorical uses, the classification of which depends almost entirely on whether some accidental circumstance gives them immediacy and allows their latent character to emerge. In such a context as "I was overwhelmed by his arguments," one feels very little sense of metaphor; but change this to "I was overwhelmed by the keenness of his arguments," and "overwhelmed" begins to stir uneasily in the reader's consciousness. Because "keenness" is indisputably metaphorical and lends its immediacy to the whole context, we are reminded of the metaphorical possibilities of "overwhelmed," and the incompatibility between the two, far from convincing us that we should not understand "overwhelmed" as meaning "to submerge or cover completely," makes it difficult for us to think about it in any other way.* The moral of this for a writer is that he can introduce a great many potential metaphors that his readers

---

* Here are some further examples, from the thousands possible, of fossil metaphors in ordinary speech which could on occasion become more actively metaphorical: a *stilted* style; to *touch off* an argument; a *pitfall* in one's path; to *make headway* against opposition.

will never notice, as long as he makes sure to avoid clashes among them. He must curb his imagination and sift out all weak spots in his writing with a sharp eye.

For an illustration of how metaphor works, we can turn again to Hamlet's "sea of troubles." There is a slight preliminary difficulty here which is not typical of all contexts: before proceeding with the analysis we first have to determine what Hamlet is talking about. In other words, what is the substantive norm? This norm must be found, because if it is not, there will be nothing against which to measure any violation. We quickly discover that the norm or subject is Hamlet's troubles. What settles the question beyond doubt is the larger verbal context of the speech and the still larger one of the play itself up to that point, both of which establish "troubles" as the governing term. In that case, "sea" is the intruder. (It could be the other way around if Hamlet were at that moment on shipboard battling a storm.) By what new norm, then, can "sea" be accommodated to "troubles"? It is the fact that Hamlet's troubles, as he views them, are overwhelming (note the latent metaphor here), that they are so numerous as to have lost for the moment any individual characteristics and have merged into one homogeneous mass, and that they are comparable in their impersonality to a force of nature. So vivid are the connotations which "sea" brings with it from its proper contexts that they dominate the metaphor, but they cannot actually become the subject of it. The accommodation of "sea" is not made possible by reference to the real world, the non-verbal context, although the sea does have the three characteristics listed above. Rather, it is made possible by reference to the connotations of the *word* "sea," which may or may not correspond to the way things really are. Whatever the sea may really be like, in a scientific or metaphysical sense, it is what we think about the sea, as it is embodied in our language, that underlies this metaphor.

In order to analyze the process of metaphor, one has to slow it down artificially. The above example may create the impression that a reader or listener who encounters a metaphor has to stop in his tracks and work through a series of analytical problems before he can understand it. In fact the process occurs very rapidly, almost instantaneously. There is no reason to suppose any perceptible gap between the question, "What's this doing here?" and the answer, "Oh, I see now." (Nor does anyone normally ask this question as such.) And too, it must be admitted that most of the metaphors we encounter, whether in speech or in reading, are familiar to us from previous encounters or belong to some easily recognizable family of metaphors. Many of them are clichés. Nevertheless, a metaphor must make a difference, for if it does not, if it becomes itself automatized, then practically speaking it no longer exists.

The process of metaphor can be represented visually in terms of its components by the diagram on p. 164. Each circle stands for a substantive area: one for the primary or governing context, the context which determines the subject, and the other for the context from which the metaphorical word is drawn. Inside each circle (but in no particular order) are placed the connotations which linguistic custom or usage has established as appropriate to that context, and in the area where the two circles overlap are placed the connotations which they hold in common. The metaphor represented in this diagram comes from the last line of Wordsworth's sonnet, "Composed Upon Westminster Bridge":

> Earth has not anything to show more fair:
> Dull would he be of soul who could pass by
> A sight so touching in its majesty:
> This City now doth, like a garment, wear
> The beauty of the morning; silent, bare,
> Ships, towers, domes, theatres, and temples lie
> Open unto the fields and to the sky;
> All bright and glittering in the smokeless air.
> Never did sun more beautifully steep
> In his first splendour, valley, rock, or hill;
> Ne'er saw I, never felt, a calm so deep!

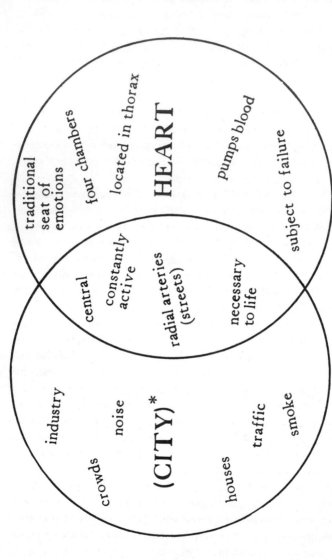

HEART

traditional seat of emotions

four chambers

located in thorax

pumps blood

subject to failure

central

constantly active

radial arteries (streets)

necessary to life

(CITY)*

industry

crowds

noise

houses

traffic

smoke

* It is understood that "this city" is a capital, as the connotations show.

The river glideth at his own sweet will:
Dear God! the very houses seem asleep;
And all that mighty heart is lying still!

Although the circles stand for whole substantive areas, in the interest of simplicity they have been limited so as to include only the major connotations adhering to the two words, "city" and "heart," the former of which is placed within parentheses because it does not occur as such in the last line of the poem. On the left-hand side one should imagine this line, which is the immediate context, beyond that the sonnet itself, and beyond the sonnet all the contexts having to do with cities. On the right-hand side one should imagine all the contexts having to do with animal anatomy and physiology. It is important to understand the diagram in this fashion, because metaphor is the interaction of entire contexts, not of separate words only. Another possible source of confusion is the fact that the only visible manifestation of metaphor in a context is likely to be the intruding word, in this case "heart." Hence we commonly speak of a word like "heart" as if it were itself the metaphor. Not so: "heart" is the *cause* of the metaphor, or what sets the process in motion, but the metaphor proper is the *result* of the process, i.e., all that happened because "heart" was introduced into this context. One is also tempted to go astray by considering metaphor as a case of substitution of words or a replacement of one word (the literal one) by another word (the metaphorical one). That certainly seems to be true of the example from Wordsworth. If so, however, one should add that substitution or replacement does not imply equivalence: the comparatively small area of overlap between the circles demonstrates how little the two words have in common. Furthermore, there are many instances in which the supposed original word cannot be reconstructed. Something literal might have been used, but it is impossible to guess what it might have been. Thus in the ninth line of the sonnet occurs the word "steep," which is metaphorical (and was commented upon back in Chapter 2). What does "steep" replace? Not "sweep," surely. "Bathe"? "Drench"?

"Cover"? "Immerse"? "Soak"? "Embrace"? "Gild"? Not only is there no clue to what Wordsworth might have said if he had wished to be literal, but most of the words suggested for this role tend themselves to be metaphorical. Perhaps there is no other way to say this than by a metaphor.

In diagramming this latter metaphor from Wordsworth's sonnet, one would put "steep" in the center of the right-hand circle, and in the center of the left-hand circle one would put something like "action of the sun," an expression much too vague to be considered as in any sense the literal equivalent of "steep," but an expression the connotations of which overlap to a certain—and significant—extent with those of "steep."

The reasons for Wordsworth's using "heart" in the last line of his sonnet are implicitly contained within the overlapping area of the two circles. These four connotations, with the delicate overtones of meaning that accompany them, function integrally with the rest of the poem to bring into being a major paradox: that when the city (London) is least animated, it seems most alive. The architecture of man is usually inferior to the architecture of nature (note that in the sonnet nature is presented without its color and movement, and only in large, formal outline: "valley, rock, or hill"). But astonishingly, when the veil of smoke is lifted from the city, and the bustle of everyday activity ceases, the city rivals the very finest scenes of nature in its beauty, taking on the quality of inward life which nature characteristically revealed to Wordsworth's imagination. The pulsing metropolis, with its arteries of commerce reaching out to the farthest regions of the country, without which the country would certainly die, is suddenly revealed as what it has been all along—the heart of England—but only because the by-products or concomitants of its own vitality have been temporarily removed.

If we see from this demonstration how important the overlapping areas in a metaphor are, we should also see how important are the areas of difference. The position of "crowds," "noise," and "smoke" outside the area of overlap is not just a matter of fact but also makes possible a meaningful contrast. It is, among other reasons, *because* the city lacks crowds, noise, and smoke at this moment that Wordsworth can see it as alive in the manner of a heart. To be sure, some of the connotations which exist alongside these are merely irrelevant, but these are not. If there were no difference between the contexts involved in a metaphor, and the two circles coincided, there would be no metaphor. Our perception of the differences is required along with our perception of the identities. Or to look at the matter once again from the strictly psychological point of view, there must be a certain tension between the governing context and the intruding word; if the word is wholly assimilated and does not appear to violate substantive propriety, then it becomes literal.

The definition of metaphor that most handbooks of rhetoric would probably apply to this instance explains it as an implied comparison between "city" and "heart." (If the comparison were stated—"The city is like a heart"—it would be called a simile instead of a metaphor.*) There are two general objections to this view. First, to say that the author is comparing the city with a heart belies his real intention. Had he really wanted to compare the two, he would surely have written something rather different, perhaps like Shakespeare's "Shall I Compare Thee to a Summer's Day?" which goes on to do just that. If two things are compared, one is not ordinarily transformed into the other, as happens in Wordsworth's sonnet. Second, the definition of metaphor as comparison fails to provide any basis for discriminating metaphors from literal comparisons. To "compare" London with a heart is quite different from comparing London with Paris, as anyone can tell, but the difference has nothing to do with the act of comparison per se. An-

---

* The distinction between metaphor and simile, which rhetoric handbooks make so much of, is based entirely on whether the words "as" or "like" are used. The significance of this distinction is often exaggerated, but it remains true that the verbal separation which simile imposes on the two elements of a metaphor tends to limit their interaction by introducing a sense of deliberate appraisal and judicious balancing into what would otherwise be the very different process of violation and accommodation.

other and almost equally popular definition of metaphor is open to similar objections: this is the definition of metaphor as an analogy of proportion. Thus the implied form of Wordsworth's metaphor would be, "The city is to the country as the heart is to the body," and an earlier metaphor in the sonnet would be paraphrased as "The beauty of the morning is to the city as a garment is to the body." This is fair enough and is even of some help in getting us to understand these two metaphors, if not, perhaps, in getting us to understand why they are metaphorical. But what is one to do with the metaphor created by "steep" in line nine? One *could* say that the sun is to the landscape as hot water is to tea leaves, but a responsible reader would be very loath to do so, for the excellent reason that Wordsworth had no such analogy in mind. In a sense, he undoubtedly was thinking of the action which hot water has upon objects immersed in it, but no specific object can be suggested to furnish the fourth term of the analogy in place of "tea leaves," because no specific object is involved. At most the analogy has only three terms. Hamlet's "sea of troubles" is similar; it yields, if squeezed hard enough, "My troubles are to me as the sea is to me." Canceling out the terms common to both sides of the equation leaves "sea" and "troubles," and brings us right back to the starting point. Furthermore, the relationship between terms, which is the essence of this kind of analogy, is not always the important aspect of a metaphor. Wordsworth's "heart" metaphor was not intended primarily to convey the relationship between the city of London and the country of England but, as we have already seen, the life implicit in this great human artifact when beheld under certain special conditions. A final example could be the well-known opening lines of T. S. Eliot's "The Love Song of J. Alfred Prufrock":

> Let us go then, you and I,
> When the evening is spread out against the sky
> Like a patient etherised upon a table. . . .

The evening is to the sky as a patient is to a table? Hardly. The relationships of evening to sky and patient to table are comparatively insignificant, and indeed it would be hard to explain how "evening" and "sky" are two separate terms. What counts here is the image of Prufrock's helplessness. Something vital is lacking within him, or is mysteriously inhibited by a kind of moral disease, and yet of all things he fears the operation which would expose it in order to cure him. *He* is the patient. With unconscious irony this morbid egoist projects his feelings into the scene before him, transforming it into the theater of a cosmic surgical inquisition. To explain Eliot's metaphor as an analogy is, in the most generous view, irrelevant, and an explanation or a definition which produces this kind of irrelevance is not to be trusted.

In the passage from "Prufrock" two very different kinds of context are brought together: those having to do with sunsets and those having to do with sickness. Words appropriate to the one do not belong in the other. The sunset context dominates: it is the subject of the passage and provides the norm against which intrusions are judged, but it does this neither because of any inherent strength of its own, any inherent rigidity or invulnerability, nor because of any corresponding weakness in the intruding context. The sunset context dominates simply because it dominates —the poet has chosen to begin his poem by locating it in time, and "when" introduces a complicated adverbial clause that modifies "let us go" and is already well on its way before the intrusion occurs. A reader who makes sense out of the passage makes *this* sense; recognizing the dominance is part of understanding the passage. As the two contexts meet, they collide with great force. Though we later see that "spread out" is an integral part of the sickness context, it has an innocent and almost literal look when first encountered in the sunset context, so that the real shock comes only with the line, "Like a patient etherised upon a table." The virtual separation of the two contexts intensifies the shock. With this, the poet has handed to the reader what amounts to an ultimatum that he accommodate a violation of substantive propriety. But it is an invitation as well as an ultimatum. By exercising his imagination as he is invited to do, the reader can see a partial common ground for the two contexts. The word "etherised" is particularly active in this process. The evening is flabby, inert, comatose. It is naked —stripped of its superficial glamor, its romantic associations. It is about to expire into night, but not, apparently, before some gratuitous injury is inflicted upon it. The atmosphere is clinical. It is also characteristic of a modern industrial city, with its chimney pots, smokestacks, and burning dumps exhaling their gases into the air. Whatever life the evening once had has been anesthetised by modern civilization. The personification of "evening," as the paragraph above suggested, is a detail with special psychological significance. But it also helps somewhat in the accommodating process because the trick of personification, as we know from our reading, is a standard poetic device and has a kind of propriety of its own. Thus we do not question the legitimacy of personifying evening and are already half prepared to accept the consequences of doing so. For our coöperation we receive a peculiar reward, since Eliot's image, though drawing its life and force from the romantic tradition of personifying nature, turns that tradition against itself, subverts it with irony, and leaves it at a kind of impasse from which it has yet to be rescued. The life of nature is invoked only as a means of asserting its essential automatism, its deadness. How opposite this is from the personification in Wordsworth's sonnet! Whether we agree or disagree with Eliot's point of view, we are by now so thoroughly implicated in it, through the strategy of metaphor, that we find ourselves seeing things through Eliot's eyes, and the imaginative truth of the situation becomes the only truth we know or need to know.

We must recognize that Eliot's metaphor is a local feature of the poem in which it occurs. After line three, it is all over. Eliot then goes on by other means (including other metaphors) to develop the tone and psychological content which his opening metaphor has helped to establish. Similarly, the metaphor in the last line of Wordsworth's sonnet is confined to that line, though unlike Eliot's it is climactic rather than introductory, bringing to a focus in itself the central meaning of the whole sonnet. These examples of what may be called "local" metaphor are quite representative of metaphors in general, which usually function as subordinate parts of a total poetic design. Yet there are cases in which a single metaphor pervades a whole poem. It is not so much that the whole poem becomes a metaphor, strictly speaking, as that the metaphor serves as an organizing principle around which the whole poem is built and to which its various parts are related. This structural use of metaphor is much less common than the local use, but it has a certain interest because it affords us a chance to see how much potentiality for development certain metaphors have when skillfully handled, and because it is a kind of way station along the road to allegory.

A good example of structural metaphor is found in Robert Frost's sonnet, "A Soldier":

> He is that fallen lance that lies as hurled,
> That lies unlifted now, come dew, come rust,
> But still lies pointed as it plowed the dust.
> If we who sight along it round the world,
> See nothing worthy to have been its mark,
> It is because like men we look too near,
> Forgetting that as fitted to the sphere,
> Our missiles always make too short an arc.
> They fall, they rip the grass, they intersect
> The curve of earth, and striking, break their own;
> They make us cringe for metal-point on stone.
> But this we know, the obstacle that checked
> And tripped the body, shot the spirit on
> Further than target ever showed or shone.

The entire poem develops out of the metaphor announced in the first line. The two contexts (human beings on the one hand and instruments of war on the other) have their common ground in the notion of aim: humans can be aimed at a target or goal just as lances can. They can also fall short, strike the earth, and end their flight (die). Not only can they, they must, since human life is finite and earth-bound, and no matter how far the flight may be, it is inevitably interrupted by the harsh fact of human mortality. These subordinate metaphors are all implicit within the basic one. What gives the sonnet its special value and keeps it from being merely ingenious is the final sentence, where Frost draws one further and unexpected implication from his metaphor. Freed by death, the soldier's spirit continues its flight beyond mortal eyes. His goal cannot be discovered by sighting along his earthly trajectory, the career of his body, because the true aim of the man was toward immortality.

The ingredients of allegory are all present in this sonnet. It is kept from becoming an out-and-out allegory by a certain reserve in the handling of them, a certain lack of commitment to the implications of the basic metaphor. The circumstance which the poem explores is not inherently static, but the poem is satisfied to present it instead of drawing it out in narrative fashion, with the incidents separated by intervals of time.

A poem that treats death by means of unmistakable allegory is Emily Dickinson's "Because I Could Not Stop for Death," and it might well be considered here for the purpose of making the difference between structural metaphor and allegory more evident:

> Because I could not stop for Death—
> He kindly stopped for me—
> The Carriage held but just Ourselves—
> And Immortality.
>
> We slowly drove—He knew no haste
> And I had put away
> My labor and my leisure too,
> For His Civility—
>
> We passed the School, where Children strove
> At Recess—in the Ring—
> We passed the Fields of Gazing Grain—
> We passed the Setting Sun—
>
> Or rather—He passed Us—
> The Dews drew quivering and chill—

For only Gossamer, my Gown—
My Tippett—only Tulle—

We paused before a House that seemed
A Swelling of the Ground—
The Roof was scarcely visible—
The Cornice—in the Ground—

Since then—'tis Centuries—and yet
Feels shorter than the Day
I first surmised the Horses' Heads
Were toward Eternity—

The basic metaphor here is "Death is a journey," and the journey is narrated to us in retrospect from the grave. Objectively, the journey is the author's funeral procession. It is paralleled by a subjective or psychic journey, not from the home to the grave but from ignorance to awareness. Each detail that the author encounters is thus both literal and symbolic. The symbolism is only suggested, since the author herself does not recognize it. It is conveyed to us by the slight and inexplicable aura of strangeness enveloping the details as she records them. At the end of the journey is the literal grave (seen by her as a "House"); also at the end of the journey, however, is the awareness of death. This awareness—so terrible that she cannot describe it directly —is the real point of the poem. It is withheld from us deliberately by the author's device of recounting her experience just as it seemed to her at the time. By forcing us to relive the events with her, she makes it possible for them to have an effect on us something like the effect they had on her. But only something like, for there are quite enough clues (beginning with the word "Death") to ensure that we are never in real doubt as to what is happening. (And it might be argued that we are never in real doubt as to what *will* happen, for as soon as we see the author's naïveté we realize that it cannot last very long.) The poem is fascinating for its multiple ironies, and some careful map reading is required if one is not to get lost among them. One begins, of course, with the fact that dead persons don't write poems. Although the narrator has been called the "author" in this analysis, the real author is the living poet Emily Dickinson, who has invented a fictional counterpart of herself to tell the story in the first person. There is a split point of view between the "I" of the poem as she now is and as she once was, involving her present awareness and her former ignorance of the meaning of death; in "real life" one point of view develops and displaces the other, but in the poem, which is a work of art and subject to different conditions, they exist simultaneously, thus making the irony possible. There is also a third point of view that partly coincides with each of these, as the reader, who is inevitably outside of the experience depicted in the poem, accompanies the narrator in his imagination on this journey while at the same time he also divines the meaning of the events which she is not fated to realize until it is all over.

The cluster of symbolic details in stanza three creates the only real problem of interpretation, and here it is mainly the problem of how far to push or how much to emphasize the symbolism. The children, the grain, and the setting sun must represent youth, maturity, and death. The author passes life on her way to death—not her own life, but life in a generalized representation. The fact that the three phases of life are represented by three different orders of things helps to veil their common import. But the suspicions of the reader, at least, are immediately alerted, and he cannot help feeling that there is more than meets the eye. "Strove" seems to tell one something about human nature, though on the surface it is just a description of how children play; the oblique adjective "Gazing" personifies the grain and lends a tone of puzzling suspense (clearly the grain is gazing at *her*, and why?); the ambiguity as to how the sun and the carriage are moving in relation to each other somehow hints at a detachment from the certainties of life. The symbolism of the setting sun is too obvious to need comment.

There is more to Miss Dickinson's poem than simply its allegorical design, though that is why it was introduced into this chapter. One cannot leave the poem without taking note of one or two further points. Out of all the possible ways of representing death, she has chosen to represent it as a gentleman caller. This device (which has some precedent in literature) is particularly significant when the dead or dying person is a young woman. The author's dress in the poem is as much appropriate to a bridal as to a burial, and the permanent union with death is a kind of marriage. But it would spoil the mystery essential to the poem if any motive were given for the author's consenting to this unexpected invitation; her riding off in the carriage, all unprepared as she was, has precisely the flavor of actions in dreams, where we do things without any apparent reason and yet with the firmest possible sense of their rightness. And as in dreams things are merely *there*, without being accounted for, so is the third passenger in the carriage. Since nothing further is said about this vaguely personified Immortality, are we to suppose that he disappears from the story? Is he only an extraneous detail? Almost certainly not. The prominence of death in the story is misleading, for it is not death but immortality which is the real villain. Immortality, conventionally thought of as a great blessing, is here reduced to nothing but eternal consciousness, a consciousness existing in a void, and if there appears to be a certain anodyne in the mere emptiness of experience beyond the grave, still it is this consciousness that has made possible the author's knowledge of death. Inasmuch as "stop for" is a pun to begin with, perhaps one may read into it yet another level of meaning, and an irony as well. Death does not stop for her, after all: she has been taken out of time and into a realm where the sole fact is the reality of her death, holding true forever in an endless present tense.

The distinction between metaphor and allegory can be drawn quite clearly in theory, but it is not always clearly maintained in practice. That such is the case is no indictment of the poets whose poems have contributed to blurring the distinction, for poets are not bound to observe the categories that other persons invent to apply to their works, nor is it, either, a reason for abandoning the attempt to define and analyze the two as separate devices. Whatever their allegorical potentialities may be, very few metaphors in actual use are pushed so far as to become allegories. Furthermore, without an understanding of these devices based upon the strictest possible definition of each as it occurs in its "pure" form, the reader would be unable to appreciate fully their blending or coalescence.

The serious reader of poetry studies metaphor because poets have used metaphor; for him this is an entirely sufficient motive. But why have poets used metaphor? The answer to this question, if implicit in the analyses of metaphors given above, still needs an explicit statement. In answering it one operates under the assumption which it has been the object of this book to urge as primary for all readers and critics, namely, that whatever occurs in a poem is there for a purpose. Whether the poet was himself conscious of having such a purpose when he wrote is irrelevant, and in any case we cannot discover that he did not have it unless we first assume that he did. Assuming, therefore, that every particular metaphor can be justified in terms of what it contributes to a particular poetic design, we now have to ask what it is that metaphor in general contributes to poetry as a whole. It must be something that cannot be furnished by literal language.

The structure of metaphor as a double design suggests the first answer: metaphor is a way of amplifying meaning, without necessarily increasing the amount of verbal space required, by adding the connotations of one word to the connotations of another. As the diagram on p. 164 illustrates, these connotations overlap in a certain area, which is the immediate usefulness or *raison d'être* of the metaphor. But though metaphor is in one sense a kind of semantic bargain, a "two-for-the-price-of-one," it is also something more than that. Even a connotation which both sides of the metaphor share, such as "constantly active" in the example from Wordsworth, retains and communicates a sense of its double provenance, for we do not think of the activity of a heart in quite the same way as we think of the activity of a city, and on each side of this area of overlap lie the connotations not shared, which are by no means unimportant to the metaphor. In the example from Wordsworth their "outside-ness" was shown to be a contributing factor. In more radi-cal or far-fetched metaphors, such as those in metaphysical poetry, the incongruity of the constituent parts is fully as important as their congruity. The excitement, the risk, the tension which the poet wants to communicate cannot be achieved by terms that are too docile because too closely re-lated. The aptness of the sunset-sickness metaphor to the design of Eliot's "Prufrock" depends in part on its inaptness to the purposes of literal speech, which is our norm, or in other words on the shock we receive when two such nor-mally disparate contexts are found yoked together. And Eliot would have been the last one to wish it otherwise. Thus metaphor is not just an economical way of extending the connotative range of language, quantitatively speaking; metaphor is a way of bringing together contexts that other-wise would never have met or interacted, without at the same time destroying their individuality, and this process creates a qualitative difference that is distinctive. The resonance of a metaphor—to pick up a term introduced in Chapter 2—is notable both for its range and for the promi-nence of its dissonant overtones.

How nearly impossible it is to talk long about the structure of metaphor without considering also the topic of its psychological effects, the above sentences testify. The second general contribution of metaphor to poetry is an in-tensification or heightening of effect which springs from the immediacy that all metaphors possess, as opposed to the automatization of literal language. Again, as the resonance of metaphor is qualitatively distinctive, the intensity of metaphor is not like the intensity that other forms of lan-guage can have. We are not only aware of a word or ex-pression that stands out, but of one that stands out as a violation of substantive propriety. In the profile of intensity that every poetic composition has, the metaphors at least the best metaphors—are usually reserved for the highest points.

Finally, metaphor contributes a kind of creative novel-ty better suited to poetry than to any other use of language.

The Romantic theorists who saw in metaphor an analogue or small-scale repetition of the fundamental poetic process were not entirely wrong, for just as poetry is the art of taking language which has no intrinsic poetic character and turning it into something which has this character, so metaphor is the art of taking the ready-made materials of literal language and, by transferring them out of context, creating unique entities of meaning. These entities are more than just the sum of their constituent parts: they are really new. Since the poet, who is engaged in the conquest of new territories for his art and in the extension of human experience, moves into the unknown by means of the known, one of the most appropriate devices at his command is that in which two familiar verbal contexts are brought together in an unfamiliar way and set to producing a meaning that did not exist before. The significance of this possibility is not diminished by the fact that many metaphors are traditional and are listed in the dictionary along with literal terms. The point is that the poet need not use these if he does not want to: he can make others for himself. Only with great difficulty can he invent a new literal term, but he can invent metaphors with complete freedom and in any numbers that his poetic design requires.

The value of metaphor as a resource for poetry lies in the characteristics here described, and they are characteristics absent, or nearly so, from literal language. Nevertheless, we cannot say that metaphor is better suited to poetry than literal language, unless we are prepared to say—as surely we are not—that any passage of literal language in any poem would be better if somehow it were rewritten metaphorically. There are no a priori laws governing the language used in poetry, and both metaphors and literal expressions are judged by the same standard, i.e., according to the way they further the design of the poem in which they appear. Our appreciation of metaphor should not be hindered in the least by this condition. If anything, it should be enhanced, for we now see that metaphor in poetry is an integral component of poetic design rather than an extrinsic ornament. Such value as metaphor might be thought to have independently is minor indeed compared to the value that it actually has when functioning in the context of a poem, and surely no one would give up the latter in order to have the former. These are the alternatives between which we must choose. As readers, we need to train ourselves in the indentification and analysis of metaphors because metaphor is a special linguistic device with a structure all its own. It simply requires more attention than literal language. But our investment of effort is at bottom a tribute to the value of poetry.

7·

Symbolism

A literary topic or literary device may suffer as much from overzealous attention as from neglect. This is certainly true of symbolism, the great preoccupation and almost the *idée fixe* of our era. No academic figure is better known to us than the symbol hunter, who may be found on either side of the lectern, and such has been his influence that even comparatively unsophisticated readers tend to behave as if the interpretation of a work of literature begins and ends with the discovery of its symbols. Whether the author himself intended his work to be symbolic is not always considered a relevant question. This kind of undiscriminating approach to literature not only damages the literature on which it is used, but it also puts an obstacle in the way of understanding symbolism, which is to some extent valuable and significant because it is *not* omnipresent. Like irony, allegory, and metaphor, it depends for much of its force upon the contrast provided by the "normal" or ordinary literary contexts in which it is not employed. If everything were symbolic in literature, symbolism would cease to exist as an identifiable literary device.

The fashionable status of symbolism has its legitimate causes. For one thing, symbolism is widely used in modern literature. There was a so-called "symbolist movement" in the latter part of the nineteenth century, and during this period many authors adopted symbolism as their primary aesthetic commitment. The influence of these authors is still with us. In modern philosophy there has been a corresponding, though not directly related, movement which is based on the doctrine that man is the symbol using animal, and which treats not only language but all aspects of human culture as manifestations of this unique capacity. The effects of the movement can be seen even more clearly in such disciplines as linguistics, anthropology, cultural history, and literary criticism than in philosophy itself. Psychoanalysis has also made its contribution by teaching that the unconscious mind habitually disguises unwelcome thoughts and desires before it allows their expression, and thus that human behavior is often symbolic and must be "read," like a work of literature, for its hidden meanings. But however welcome these movements may be, they have contributed to making serious difficulties for any attempt to view the topic of literary symbolism afresh, without preconceptions and in its basic outlines.

Perhaps the best way to begin this attempt is by making a simple distinction between literary symbolism, the kind we are concerned with here, and the symbolism of language in general. It has already been argued that the characteristic function of words is to stand for or refer to things in the human environment. This act of "standing for" can be understood as symbolism.* The word "table," for example, stands for or symbolizes the flat surface supported by four legs on which I am writing. Insofar as the literary symbol is embodied in a word or words, it is exactly like the linguistic symbol. But here the resemblance ends, for the object itself which the word "table" symbolizes has no meaning, whereas the object in a literary symbol does—indeed it is precisely because the object has such meaning that it can be so used.

To say that a table is meaningless does not deny it all value. It may have any kind of value, save one. Consider what happens when the wood that is fastened together to make this useful object is fastened together in a somewhat different way and made into a cross. Identical in material

* Because the term "symbol" has a non-linguistic application, as this paragraph brings out, and because not all words refer to things (many of them have strictly logical or grammatical functions), it is preferable to call the word something else: a "linguistic sign." But this terminological problem is not of real importance here.

and at least comparable in construction—but how different in meaning! The cross, of course, is a symbol.

A process of abstraction has occurred since the original wooden Cross stood on Calvary, so that for many centuries the mere geometrical figure of two crossed lines has been an adequate substitute for the real object. These crossed lines are also a symbol, no different in effect from the wooden Cross. So too, by another kind of abstraction, is the *word* "cross." Depending on circumstances, I can use two sticks of wood, two crossed lines, or a word. (The circumstances must make it evident that I have a symbolic intention in using them, for a cross does not always or inevitably refer to the Crucifixion.) The only difference between the word and these others is that the word does not look like a cross, so that an intermediate mental operation is required before the meaning is complete. The verbal symbol is a meaningful object translated into or conveyed by language.

This definition points to the fundamental difference between symbolism and metaphor. Metaphor is a linguistic device, whereas symbolism has no necessary connection with language at all. As we meet them in literature, however, the two often appear quite similar, and sometimes they can be discriminated only after careful analysis. This is not surprising when we remember that metaphors very commonly involve "images"—references to concrete objects or perceptible actions—and that both metaphor and symbolism are species of double design. Each of them can be diagrammed by means of two overlapping circles. The difference is that in metaphor the two circles represent verbal contexts, focusing upon a word and a word, while in literary symbolism they represent a thing and an idea, expressed in language but not dependent upon it for their existence. Symbolism might be defined as a way of thinking with things. In theory, at least, the doubleness of a symbol is more distinct and radical than that of a metaphor, since it is caused by the interaction of human thought with objects of the material world and is not confined to the realm of language alone, as metaphor is. Because the poem of James Shirley's that was quoted in part in Chapter 2 contains good examples of both metaphor and symbolism, it can serve now to illustrate this point:

> The glories of our blood and state
>> Are shadows, not substantial things;
> There is no armour against fate;
>> Death lays his icy hand on kings:
>>> Scepter and crown
>>> Must tumble down,
> And in the dust be equal made
> With the poor crooked scythe and spade.
>
> Some men with swords may reap the field,
>> And plant fresh laurels where they kill;
> But their strong nerves at last must yield;
>> They tame but one another still:
>>> Early or late,
>>> They stoop to fate,
> And must give up their murmuring breath,
> When they, pale captives, creep to death.
>
> The garlands wither on your brow,
>> Then boast no more your mighty deeds;
> Upon Death's purple altar now,
>> See where the victor-victim bleeds:
>>> Your heads must come
>>> To the cold tomb;
> Only the actions of the just
> Smell sweet and blossom in their dust.

Life is a battle—this is the basic metaphor of the poem. The metaphor is introduced in line three by the word "armour," but it is not really developed until the second stanza; the first stanza speaks of the glories of heritage ("blood") and status (though "state" could also be taken in the sense of "nationality"). Interestingly, when the poet begins this development of the life-battle metaphor, he is speaking in literal terms: one of the ways to win renown in life is to kill other men with the sword. At this point another metaphor has been introduced, following the theme suggested by "scythe" and "spade" in stanza one, in respect to which battle is shifted back toward literality. A diagram of the complex metaphor would show three overlapping circles, one each for life, battle, and something we may call "farming," with a small area common to all three. The farming metaphor is appropriate because the least glorious humans are poor peasants, the victims of war are metaphorically "reaped," the laurel (symbol of victory) is a plant, and finally because the "dust" to which we all come is the soil tended by farmers. Although important, the farming metaphor is not continuously active in the design of the poem, being brought in here and there when needed. Its most striking use is at the very end, where the "actions of the just" are suddenly exempted from the judgment on human mortality.

This complex metaphorical design offers a number of symbols: "blood," "scepter," "crown," "scythe," "spade," and "laurels." (The list may not be quite complete, but these at least will be conceded by everyone.) We note that they are all standard and conventional; their meanings are obvious. We note also that some symbols are formed by the process of synecdoche, by taking a part of something and using it to stand for the whole, as the spade stands for agricultural labor and its lowly status. Death and fate, of course, are merely personified abstractions, not symbols. The local metaphors are not so easily identified, but some of the important ones in the earlier part of the poem are "shadows," "armour," "lays . . . hand," "tumble down," and "reap the field." The question now is why these are metaphors rather than symbols. Is not "shadows," for example, a symbol of the fleeting and immaterial quality of earthly fame, in the same manner as the garlands that wither on the victor's brow? The garlands, however, have been arbitrarily given their meaning by the tradition which awards them to victors; in their own right they are just plants. Shadows *are* fleeting and immaterial. Again, armor is not a symbol of protection: it *is* protection. These objects—the shadows and the armor—have no meaning as objects, and the only process of symbolization at work here is the one that is at work all the time in language as a whole, where a word stands for something in the human environment. The words are metaphors because they do not normally occur in the kind of context that we see here, to which they become appropriate only after a process of accommodation. The words "scepter and crown," on the other hand, stand for objects which themselves stand for an idea, the idea of monarchy, or for the royal persons who possess them as symbols of power.

The difference between metaphor and symbolism can also be illustrated by the imagery of politics. One of the most popular and durable political metaphors in this age is that of the "iron curtain." It was widely taken up following Winston Churchill's famous post-war speech and later received the ultimate tribute of extension by analogy, turning into such things as the "bamboo curtain" and the "paper curtain," though this process often ignored the logical basis of the original metaphor. The phrase "iron curtain" is a linguistic device for expressing a sense of Russia's intransigent isolation. The lack of physical communication between Russia and the Western world (more real then than now) was so complete that it seemed as if a curtain had been dropped between the two, and this curtain was metaphorically given the substance of iron because it was enforced by tanks and guns. Thus the metaphor is a double one. The "as if" quality of the expression—because there is no such thing in fact as an iron curtain—is not what makes it a metaphor: rather, it is the intrusion into a context having to do with physical communication of terms taken from the contexts of war and the theater, combined into the one phrase "iron curtain" and accepted in the new context by reason of certain appropriate connotations. Political cartoonists at once went to work trying to convert it into a symbol by drawing pictures of it, but they did not change its linguistic status in so doing. The awkwardness of their attempts served merely to emphasize how poorly it was adapted to symbolic use. There is no lack of true political symbols, however. We may cite Uncle Sam, the Republican elephant, John Bull (rather out of fashion now), the stars and stripes, the sombrero (used indiscriminately to characterize all residents south of the Rio Grande), and of course the hammer and sickle. None of these objects has anything we could call "meaning" until it is put into a political context. The hammer and sickle, whether separately or together, are simply instruments of labor, but because they are instruments of labor they have been chosen as the symbol of international socialism, and this is now what they commonly stand for. They may be represented equally well by words or by a picture; no connotations are gained by verbal and none are lost by pictorial expression.

Symbols do not only accompany us to the voting booth and the firing line; they are part of the texture of everyday life as a whole. They might therefore be classified according to whether they are religious, political, commercial, athletic, artistic, etc., but there would be little point in doing so now. A classification more relevant to the purpose of this chapter is one that ignores these boundaries and instead takes into account the process by which the symbol was derived, i.e., whether the symbol is natural, conventional, or personal.

NATURAL

This kind of symbol is "natural" because it is found in nature and because the objects which have symbolic meaning are thought to have it naturally and inherently, not depending on the human mind to give it to them. One of the classic statements of this position is Emerson's: "It is not words only that are emblematic; it is things which are emblematic. Every natural fact is a symbol of some spiritual fact." The notion is attractive; it suggests that man does not inhabit a blank and irrelevant universe, but one which is somehow congenial to him, reflecting his mind in its own structure and its component parts, providing incessant material analogies to the human spirit. The visible surface of nature is eloquent. As Emerson goes on to say, "Who looks upon a river in a meditative hour and is not reminded of the flux of all things? Throw a stone into the stream, and the circles that propagate themselves are the beautiful types of all influence." The mountains seem to speak of aspiration and nobility, sunrise and sunset of birth and death, the stars of permanence and order. There are sermons in stones, books in the running brooks. Attractive though it may be, the existence of a natural symbolism has to remain a matter of faith alone, since the conditions for submitting it to proof are nearly impossible to obtain. In order to prove it one would have to find a person whose mind was uncontaminated by any previous notions of natural symbolism, explain to him somehow, without prejudicing the experiment, what one was trying to do, and then confront him with an allegedly symbolic natural object to see whether he would spontaneously find meaning in it. What actually happens is that we are already conditioned to see certain meanings in objects by our cultural tradition, meanings that have been read into, not out of, these objects. If that is the case—and only a mystic of some sort could long believe that it is not —natural symbolism is basically identical with the conventional symbolism which is discussed next.

CONVENTIONAL

This kind of symbolism is always arbitrary. Something, natural or artificial, is chosen to have a certain meaning. Since the origins of many conventional symbols are very ancient, we can only hypothesize that an original act of choice must have taken place, but we can see the choice of other symbols taking place around us now. The hammer and sickle were chosen not long ago, as history runs, and even the Cross has a reasonably definite historical date. Though the basic meaning of a conventional symbol is fixed, it is still capable of being interpreted or used with a good deal of individual flair, and one should not suppose that these symbols, however frequently they appear in literature, are mere stereotypes.

PERSONAL

Nevertheless, many authors have not been content to explore traditional symbolism, but have set to work to create symbols of their own. Here the meaning must somehow be communicated at the same time as the symbol is presented —not an easy task. The rewards can be great if the attempt succeeds, but the liabilities can be great if it fails. In fairness to authors, it must be granted that their apparent failure is often due to the inadequacy of the reader when confronted with something that taxes his powers of interpretation, as also to a certain vagueness which the author may have deliberately left in his symbol for the legitimate purpose of extending its suggestiveness. In the former case, a little research will many times solve the problem. Yeats's "gyres" should not long remain puzzling. In the latter case, research and mental effort are likely to prove the biggest obstacle to understanding unless they are guided by the utmost tact. Melville's Moby-Dick, the white whale, is a personal symbol —that much is clear—but what is it a symbol of? The reader's efforts to pin Melville down are at odds with Melville's purpose to leave Moby-Dick surrounded by the mystery that the whale, both as a creature and as a symbol, deserves. The ghost of Melville peering down on his twentieth-century reader must surely wish that the reader would relax a little. After all, it was Ahab who demanded to strike through the mask.

Since by their very nature all cases of personal symbolism are somewhat different, it is dangerous to generalize about methods the reader should use in handling them. At the very least, however, he should not try to force an interpretation on them. To use a homely simile, it is something like screwing a cap on a bottle: as soon as he feels resistance the reader should back off and try again with less force, or otherwise he may damage the threads and make his subsequent attempts all the more difficult. If an easier approach yields better results, he has his answer. Many authors do not want to have their symbols carry a single clear-cut meaning. They feel, with justice, that life is usually complex and fraught with ambiguities, and they wish no less for the art that attempts to cope with life. Something is lost when the interpretation of a symbol results in the substitution of a bloodless abstraction for what had been a concrete and integral object. The concrete object itself may be more interesting, may have more immediacy and resonance. Such an object is the fly in Emily Dickinson's "I Heard a Fly Buzz When I Died":

I heard a Fly buzz—when I died—
The Stillness in the Room
Was like the Stillness in the Air—
Between the Heaves of Storm—

The Eyes around—had wrung them dry—
And Breaths were gathering firm
For that last Onset—when the King
Be witnessed—in the Room—

I willed my Keepsakes—Signed away
What portion of me be
Assignable—and then it was
There interposed a Fly—

With Blue—uncertain stumbling Buzz—
Between the light—and me—
And then the Windows failed—and then
I could not see to see—

Here again is Miss Dickinson's favorite theme, developed with multiple ironies and from a retrospective point of view, but the muted horror of "Because I Could Not Stop for Death" is absent—perhaps because the author in this case does not explore death beyond the instant of its occurrence. Some of her irony is at the expense of the mourners, who are reduced by synecdoche to "Eyes" and "Breaths," that is, to the external symptoms of grief, and whose grief moreover has a certain *willed* quality (the eyes "had wrung them dry"). Some of the irony is at her own expense, as she conforms to the traditional pattern of death-bed behavior by signing away her worldly possessions, which, being of little value, are hardly worth the formal ceremony. Still, she dutifully plays her part along with the others, awaiting the "last Onset." But the fly was not on the program. The poem ends on a note of surprise as the author's fading consciousness, narrowed to a view of the intruder, vainly confronts its meaning.

Readers who are alerted to the possibilities of symbolism frequently want to translate the fly into an abstraction such as "death" or "immortality," or into something hardly more concrete, "the soul." The fly's struggle to leave the room may be a paradigm of the soul's struggle to leave the body, and the choice of the fly instead of something more dignified may be a further instance of the author's belittling irony, but to stop with this interpretation is to shut off a whole range of other possibilities. The poem then becomes more allegorical than symbolic. Furthermore, such an interpretation tends to assimilate the event into everything else that is happening in the room, making it congruous rather than incongruous; the author's surprise, and the reader's as well, is surely because the fly (so to speak) has no business being there at all. This is not to say that the fly is wholly meaningless, but only that its meaning has to do somehow with its being a genuine and irreducible concrete object. Yet it would not be doing justice to the poem if one dismissed the problem by saying, "The fly is a fly, and that's all there is to it." Miss Dickinson herself has put us on guard by referring to the fly twice, the first time in her opening line, which as much as tells us that the fly is the most significant detail that she has to convey.

A helpful way to approach a symbol of this kind is to approximate its meaning by listing all the connotations that it suggests, without any special order of precedence. The method is deliberately unsystematic. Thus for the sake of getting at the meaning of Miss Dickinson's fly we can draw up two sets of connotations, one for the fly itself and the other for everything else in the poem (though mainly focused upon the author):

> little—big
> animal—human
> living—dying
> noisy—quiet
> active—still
> uncertain—certain
> striving—resigned
> spontaneous—planned
> trivial—important
> out of place—in place
> continuing—about to end

The incongruity which the fly brings into being extends point for point through the whole series. What the fly stands for, then, is a system of relationships polarized in the manner indicated. When we have discovered this much, it should no longer trouble us that we lack a word or a short phrase to express the meaning of the fly, since we realize how imprecise, how limiting, that would be. Listing these connotations is like making a circle by drawing a number of straight lines perpendicular to the radii coming from a single point. The result is actually a polygon, but the more elaborate it is the more it approximates to a circle. If this process never yields *the* meaning of the symbol, it still comes closer to doing so than any attempt to seize that meaning directly can, and at the same time it respects the integrity of the symbolic object.

Miss Dickinson's fly is an ordinary prosaic insect. Readers often overlook the accuracy of her observation (this is another consequence of searching too intently for symbolic meanings); her fly is doing just what all of us have seen flies do many times—it is bumping against a window, trying to get out toward the light through the barrier which it cannot see. The marvelous synaesthesia of "Blue . . . Buzz" should not cause us to miss the rightness of "uncertain stumbling." That the author's last sight on earth should be of a fly is

ironic, considering that she and the others had been prepared to witness "the King." Like Lear's button, the fly
represents both a drastic reduction in scale and a narrowing
of point of view. It, too, communicates the pathos of the
familiar. Perhaps the reality of life is not in its formal occasions, its ceremonies, its human constructs, but in the multi-
tude of small details that the external world offers to the
senses of the living, even the most trivial of which is
unimaginably beyond the grasp of the dead. Perhaps here is
the moral of the poem. What was indeed "witnessed"
(testified to, acknowledged) in the bedroom was the irrelevance of these elaborate preparations for death. Yet it is not
as though nature were solicitous for man, trying to draw
him into itself, trying by means of natural symbolism to
communicate a sense of his belonging. The fly does not
know where it is; it is acting instinctively and could not be
more indifferent to the tableau beneath it. The whole situation, in fact, is a comedy of irrelevance, with each side, the
natural and the human, acting on its own as if the other did
not exist. This strange contrast develops within the sight of
the dying woman (there is no reason to believe that the
"Eyes around" see the fly), but before she can make anything out of it the light is withdrawn from her and then, as
she says in the wonderfully metaphysical closing line, "I
could not see to see." The final irony is that death comes as
the failing of the external world while the personal consciousness, as it seems, is still eager and capable of experience—a complete reversal of expectation.

All three kinds of symbolism can be seen in another
death-bed poem, John Donne's somber and powerful
"Hymn to God My God, in My Sickness":

> Since I am coming to that holy room
>   Where, with thy choir of saints for evermore,
> I shall be made thy music, as I come
>   I tune the instrument here at the door,
>   And what I must do then, think here before.
>
> Whilst my physicians by their love are grown
>   Cosmographers, and I their map, who lie

Flat on this bed, that by them may be shown
 That this is my south-west discovery,
 Per fretum febris, by these straits to die,

I joy, that in these straits I see my west;
 For though their currents yield return to none,
What shall my west hurt me? As west and east
 In all flat maps (and I am one) are one,
 So death doth touch the resurrection.

Is the Pacific sea my home? or are
 The eastern riches? is Jerusalem?
Anyan and Magellan and Gibraltar,
 All straits, and none but straits, are ways to them,
 Whether where Japhet dwelt, or Cham, or Sem.

We think that Paradise and Calvary,
 Christ's cross and Adam's tree, stood in one place;
Look, Lord, and find both Adams met in me;
 As the first Adam's sweat surrounds my face,
 May the last Adam's blood my soul embrace.

So, in his purple wrapped receive me, Lord;
 By these his thorns give me his other crown;
And as to others' souls I preached thy word,
 Be this my text, my sermon to mine own:
 Therefore that he may raise, the Lord throws down.

  The drama in this poem is the drama of ideas, not of events. Donne's mortal sickness forms the basis for a meditation on death, and his physical circumstances are important only in setting the stage for this meditation. Flat on his back, surrounded by physicians who are characteristically more interested in the disease than in the patient and who pore over him as though he were a map on which some discovery had been noted, he ironically accepts the implications of their "love." The discovery is that his straits are those of fever; he will die *per fretum febris.* A strait is a narrow and difficult passage, and as such is a kind of natural symbol for what Donne is at present going through. The pun is intentional. It is a voyage with no return, physical or financial (the exploitation of the Indies was under way in Donne's time), but the sight of the west (a symbol for death) instead of making Donne despair fills him with joy, since he knows that longitude is only relative and that at some point the west will always touch the east, or lead to resurrection. The personal symbolism of the map has been used to produce this consolation.

After the fourth stanza, which dwells on the significance of straits in the geographical sense and makes the suggestion that one must always go through some strait to travel anywhere at all, Donne turns to the old legend that the Crucifixion took place on the same spot where the Tree of Knowledge had grown in Eden. Both the Cross and the Tree produced suffering; the blood shed by Christ and the sweat of Adam, who was condemned to toil for his living, are thus analogous, and with this Donne also reminds us that Christ is prefigured in Adam. The blood and sweat are symbols of suffering, but the blood is also a Christian symbol of redemption, and if it embraces the soul as the sweat had embraced the body, the man is saved, elevated, made fit for a royal reception in heaven. If the crown of thorns which Christ wore was a prerequisite to his being crowned as Savior, then on a human level Donne's suffering promises a similar reward. But the reward cannot be achieved without the suffering: "Therefore that he may raise, the Lord throws down." This final consolation as to the purpose of suffering also derives from the symbolism of the map, after having been enriched by further appropriate symbolic associations, all of which deal in some fashion or other with the meeting and reconciliation of extremes.

Although Donne's religious symbols are conventionally derived, they bear the unmistakable stamp of his own imagination; in this poem the distinction between personal and conventional symbolism soon becomes blurred, and we find ourselves more interested in watching Donne's strategy than in categorizing his materials. The chief point that one would want to make about Miss Dickinson's fly vis-à-vis

Donne's map is not that they are both personal symbols, but that the fly is wholly idiosyncratic while the map, odd and "conceited" as it seems at first, has an explicit meaning and a kind of logic that all readers accept without difficulty. The map has none of the vagueness about it that the fly does, in spite of the fact that the fly is a specific and concrete object and the map a very generalized one. The nature of the symbol is much affected by its use. It is thus necessary to give some attention to the ways in which symbols are used in poems, though in doing so we shall have to resort once again to categorizing, which means restricting our point of view and excluding a great many poems which do not lend themselves very well to this process. Aside from local and structural symbolism, which can be passed over here because they are exactly parallel to local and structural metaphor, the well-defined symbolic strategies fall into three main groups: the deductive, the inductive, and the imitative.

As their names suggest, the first two of these are opposed but complementary, and they are analogous to certain basic strategies in logic. The deductive strategy is the taking of an abstract idea, state of mind, or feeling and the finding of a concrete symbolic equivalent for it; the inductive is the taking of a concrete object and the finding of an abstract idea, state of mind, or feeling that it can symbolize. Neither strategy is necesarily as cut-and-dried as these definitions make it seem, but it is true that the first one tends toward the schematic pattern of allegory, the crucial difference being, as we know, whether or not the pattern involves narrative movement. Deductive symbolism in its pure form is well illustrated by Theodore Roethke's "A Light Breather":

> The spirit moves,
> Yet stays:
> Stirs as a blossom stirs,
> Still wet from its bud-sheath,
> Slowly unfolding,
> Turning in the light with its tendrils;
> Plays as a minnow plays,

Tethered to a limp weed, swinging,
Tail around, nosing in and out of the current,
Its shadows loose, a watery finger;
Moves, like the snail,
Still inward,
Taking and embracing its surroundings,
Never wishing itself away,
Unafraid of what it is,
A music in a hood,
A small thing,
Singing.

The poet has begun with an abstract generalization about the human spirit, which ". . . moves,/ Yet stays." The generalization is also a paradox that needs to be explained. He has chosen three concrete objects to symbolize the paradox of the spirit—a blossom, a minnow, and a snail. There seems to be a descending order of value in these objects, at least as we ordinarily regard them, but there is no real progression in them. Rather than being stages in some kind of development, each of them by itself fully possesses the main characteristics of the spirit. But though parallel and equivalent, they are far from identical, and each maintains its own unassimilable character. This is important, because the poet is as much interested in their differences as in their similarities; some part of the meaning of the poem is just the fact that the human spirit is mirrored, so to speak, in many aspects of the outside world. The careful and affectionate attention that Roethke gives to these three concrete objects tells us that he values their individuality. Moreover, the actions they perform do differ: one "stirs," another "plays," and the third "moves" (i.e., from place to place). The meaning adumbrated in the symbols of the blossom and the minnow is made clear in the final symbol of the snail, which as it crawls embraces its surroundings: the spirit does not reject the external world, but finds it congenial, "Never wishing itself away." It freely accepts itself ("Unafraid of what it is"), and more than that it is happy in the acceptance. The spirit inside the shell of the body is "A music

in a hood . . . Singing." Though a small thing when measured on the scale of the whole universe, the spirit is a universe in itself, and it confronts its environment with the
serene confidence of an equal. It "moves," or explores this
environment, but is not itself determined or shaped by the
forces acting upon it; rather, it "stays," keeping its integrity
and autonomy, its status as a unique living thing. The self-
sufficiency of the spirit is developed through its relationship
with the world in which it lives and on which it depends for
life. This great paradox, which has teased the imaginations
of philosophers through the ages, is—not solved, for who
would want to solve it?—memorably and finely expressed
by Roethke's poem.

In a sense perhaps not consciously intended by the
poet, the poem itself moves yet stays, and to the extent that
this is true the poem also illustrates the imitative strategy of
symbolism. Its gross structure, at any rate, is deductive.
What went on in the poet's mind when he was conceiving
his subject we do not know; his mental processes could as
well have been inductive as deductive, or (more likely) a
complicated mixture of the two. Hence these terms should
be taken to refer only to the design of the poet's thought as
it is revealed on the printed page.

A good example of the inductive strategy is Richard
Wilbur's "Years-End":

Now winter downs the dying of the year,
And night is all a settlement of snow;
From the soft street the rooms of houses show
A gathered light, a shapen atmosphere,
Like frozen-over lakes whose ice is thin
And still allows some stirring down within.

I've known the wind by water banks to shake
The late leaves down, which frozen where they fell
And held in ice as dancers in a spell
Fluttered all winter long into a lake;
Graved on the dark in gestures of descent,
They seemed their own most perfect monument.

There was perfection in the death of ferns
Which laid their fragile cheeks against the stone
A million years. Great mammoths overthrown
Composedly have made their long sojourns,
Like palaces of patience, in the gray
And changeless lands of ice. And at Pompeii

The little dog lay curled and did not rise
But slept the deeper as the ashes rose
And found the people incomplete, and froze
The random hands, the loose unready eyes
Of men expecting yet another sun
To do the shapely thing they had not done.

These sudden ends of time must give us pause.
We fray into the future, rarely wrought
Save in the tapestries of afterthought.
More time, more time. Barrages of applause
Come muffled from a buried radio.
The New-year bells are wrangling with the snow.

The poem begins with a familiar scene. There is a snowstorm on the last night of the year, and the poet is standing or walking outdoors in the falling snow. From the darkness he can look into the lighted rooms of houses. They remind him of frozen-over lakes, each one a little world separated from the hostile climate by a sheet of protective ice (window glass) that allows observation of the remnants of normal life preserved within. This image leads him to remember another familiar sight, that of autumn leaves frozen where they fell into the water. It seems as though they would continue falling if they could, that their motion was arrested prematurely by the ice that holds them. Unable to go further, they dance in place, each one in the pose it had when overtaken by the magic touch of winter. Since dancing is the *raison d'être* of autumn leaves, the characteristic and proper expression of their inward being, it is appropriate that in death they should still be dancing and that they should be preserved doing so, forming their own visible memorials or monuments. (At this point one may recall Hopkins' "Scotist" sonnet, "As Kingfishers Catch Fire," and Keats's "Ode on a Grecian Urn.") The perfection that Wilbur finds in the leaves comes from this sense of an appropriate end. But because they are now exempted from change, remaining as they were in life, the leaves are perfect in another sense as well. This is true of ferns that we discover preserved in stone, exact in every detail, and of other kinds of fossils—the wooly mammoths of the Pleistocene, for example, which have been dug out of ice, untouched by the passing of many thousands of years. This trance-like state is doubly composed: peaceful and resigned, ordered and harmonious.

The first image was only an illustration, but the later ones are now beginning to turn into symbols, though symbols whose full import remains to be seen. The instances of buried life already given now lead naturally to that archeological wonder, the Roman city of Pompeii, which was overwhelmed by the ashes of Vesuvius in A.D. 79. As we know, the ashes came so suddenly that they caught many people in the act of fleeing, struck them down where they were, and held them in the very postures of life for future generations to discover. But there was no composure here, no resignation. Everyone had expected to go on living, everyone had unfinished business. Another day, perhaps, would have brought for some of them the chance to complete the work that was to have allowed them to die in peace—or so we like to think. Their bodies have been perfectly preserved, like fossils, but their lives were anything but perfect. This chronic unreadiness for death seems to be a characteristic of humans alone; it does not appear in the other instances that Wilbur has cited. The symbol of Pompeii, then, brings a new dimension to the poem. With Pompeii the "sudden ends of time" take on human significance. They "give us pause": (1) they put a stop to our lives when they occur; (2) they make us stop and think about our lives with some alarm when we see examples of them. We live always at loose ends, "we fray into the future." Our lives show a complete and ordered pattern only when we look back upon them, but these "tapestries of afterthought" are imaginary, reconstructed after the fact, and true (so Wilbur seems to imply) as artistic creations rather than as history. To *do* a "shapely thing" is not the same as to think about doing it. But, we cry, if only there were more time! As the poem closes, the reader senses an ominous parallel between the snow in this scene and the ashes that fell, smothering Pompeii. The calendar declares that this is the year's end, but what if this moment—right now—were really an end? We would be no better off than the citizens of Pompeii; their example has taught us nothing. The sounds of celebration that come over the air, tokens of man's perennial optimism, his faith that life will perpetually renew itself and that second chances are infinite, have an ironic ring now to the listener in the snow and to us. What had been an observation of the picturesque has turned, through the contemplation of symbols, to a disturbing lesson on human folly.

Wilbur's basic strategy is inductive. The poem is developed first by means of a simile (the "frozen-over lakes"). From it the poet moves next to a comparable image, that of the "late leaves . . . frozen where they fell." The next step is a deductive one, as the idea of perfection leads him to think of fossils, which are also analogous in other ways to the leaves, not least in that each is held fast by a substance that covered it and solidified. The latent symbolism in these fossils is energized by the image of Pompeii. That image is both literal and symbolic: literal for the people of Pompeii whose lives were cut off suddenly and left unfinished, symbolic for us who think about them and see the meaning that their fate suggests for us. In retrospect from this point, all of the images in the poem are seen to be symbolic. They all show us life arrested by a cataclysm of nature, buried and preserved for the future in exact detail. But the leaves, the ferns, and the mammoths were ready for death; it froze them complete. When it freezes man, he will always be incomplete. Perhaps a man's reach should exceed his grasp, as Browning's Andrea del Sarto claimed, but what if there were no heaven to reward the unfulfilled ambition? What if his conduct were not so much the result of romantic aspiration as of heedlessness and unfounded optimism? We can now find this chilly thought, thanks to the process of induction, even in the snug and comfortable image with which the poem began.

The third symbolic strategy, the imitative, is the use of the form of the poem itself as a concrete verbal or structural equivalent of an abstract meaning. What the poem says is reinforced by what the poem sounds or looks like, or by the way it is constructed. The most familiar variety of this is onomatopoeia, in which the sounds of such words as "cluck," "hiss," "tinkle," "thump," "gurgle," and "buzz" approximately reproduce the sounds that the words refer to. There is no "meaning" to these words other than their own sound. The term is also applied to another class of words in which there is a definable meaning that includes sound as well as other components (e.g., "spatter," "rip," "crash," "sneeze," "groan," and "chuckle"). These two classes are so similar that they are usually not worth separating. In any case there is universal agreement over their right to be called imitative and the limited nature of their role in poetry.

But there is another and much vaguer kind of onomatopoeia, or sound symbolism, about which a long controversy has raged. These words do not imitate sounds at all, and yet their own sounds are felt to be somehow appropriate to their meanings. The word "sneer," for example, denotes a facial expression, but it almost seems as though one has to adopt that facial expression in order to pronounce the word. There seems to be a smooth gliding effect in the word "slippery," a soft and dull one in the word "muffled," and a hard and bright one in the word "glitter." It is very popular, also, to find symbolic effects in phonemes, the separate sounds that make up words. Thus *l* suggests something flowing or liquid, short *i* suggests smallness, long *o* and *oo* are solemn, *f* is forceful, *d* is dull and heavy, and so on.

There would be no point in entering this controversy here if the notion of sound symbolism were not so alluring to inexperienced readers, who tend to adopt and apply it

quite indiscriminately, and if the critics who sponsor the
notion were more careful in the way they phrase their
claims. Complex relationships between sound and sense do
exist in poetry—that much is certain. But the sound-
symbolists too often appear to maintain that sounds have
meanings *as sounds*, independently of words. They are fond
of quoting examples like the following lines from Tennyson's "The Passing of Arthur":

> Dry clash'd his harness in the icy caves
> And barren chasms, and all to left and right
> The bare black cliff clang'd round him, as he based
> His feet on juts of slippery crag that rang
> Sharp-smitten with the dint of armed heels—
> And on a sudden, lo, the level lake,
> And the long glories of the winter moon!

The onomatopoeia in such words as "clash'd," "clang'd,"
and "rang" (reinforced by "chasms," "black cliff," and
"crag") is unmistakable. In addition the sound-symbolist
would point to "juts," which by the configuration of its
sound creates the impression of a sharp outcropping of
rock, and he would find in the last two lines a liquid calm in
the repeated *l*'s and an openness, radiance, and wonder in
the sounds of *o* and *oo*. The problem is this: would we
know that the sound of "juts" symbolizes a sharp outcropping of rock if we did not already know what the word
denotes, or would we know that the sounds of *l*, *o*, and *oo*
symbolize what they do if we had not already received
these suggestions through the meanings of the words?
There is no dispute about the appropriateness of the sounds
to the meanings, though there is still a great deal of mystery
about how they get that way. The sound-symbolists, however, will not be satisfied with mere appropriateness or with
the conclusion that the sounds have the effect that they do
because of the meanings of the words in which they occur.
Yet it is possible to write other lines containing the
phonemes in question with an exactly opposite effect. The
liquid calm of *l* disappears in

Limping along the lumps of livid lime. . . .

and the general phonetic pattern of Tennyson's last line can be reproduced in such a way as to abolish most of its sound symbolism:

And the strong loathers of the wimpled prune.

Other such easily manufactured examples will show that sounds per se do not have the meaning that is claimed for them. As a way of reinforcing sense in poetry sound is a valuable device, but aside from cases of out-and-out onomatopoeia it has little or no independent symbolic value, and nothing is gained by exaggerating its role in a fashion that cannot withstand analysis.

The reinforcement of meaning by the manipulation of the actual shape of a poem, so that it more or less resembles its subject, is best observed in the "pattern poems" of the sixteenth and seventeenth centuries. By varying the lengths of lines, poets fashioned on the page such simple visual forms as altars, eggs, pillars, wings, and diamonds. This is not a very imaginative device (at best, as in the mouse's "tale" in *Alice in Wonderland*, it is merely witty) and it quickly becomes mechanical if overused. It could also be disapproved of on the ground that it attempts the fusion of two incompatible arts, the verbal and the graphic, but there is no real issue here because the number of extant pattern poems is not very large, and the number of those with any poetic merit is even smaller. In our era the pattern poem has been sporadically revived, in greatest quantity, it would seem, by E. E. Cummings. Yet on careful inspection the visual symbolism in Cummings' poems tends to disappear, and the reader discovers that the bizarre typography is expressive rather than imitative—which is a different function altogether.*

* In something of a class by itself is Dante's *Divine Comedy*, the form of which is elaborately symbolic of the Trinity, being in three parts of thirty-three cantos each (plus one introductory canto which brings the total to one hundred, the square of the perfect number, ten) and written in three-line stanzas. This form is not wholly visible as

A more respectable and certainly more interesting kind
of imitative symbolism is that in which the poetic (as distinguished from the visual) design supports the meaning of the
poem. Here the opportunities are enormous and the effects
capable of great subtlety. Since poetry no less than other
linguistic constructions is normally made up from sequences
of different words, one of the commonest imitative devices
in poetry is that of repetition, which runs counter to this
norm and achieves immediacy by doing so, as in this well-
known stanza from Coleridge's "The Rime of the Ancient
Mariner":

> Water, water, every where,
> And all the boards did shrink;
> Water, water, every where
> Nor any drop to drink.

The repetition not only communicates a sense of weariness,
but it actually imitates the monotonous and unchanging
character of the mariner's surroundings—the "everywhere-
ness" of the water. There is a comparable use of repetition
in the stanza preceding this one ("Day after day, day after
day,/ We stuck, nor breath nor motion") and in these later
stanzas:

> There passed a weary time. Each throat
> Was parched, and glazed each eye.
> A weary time! a weary time!
> How glazed each weary eye,
>
> . . . .
>
> Alone, alone, all, all alone,
> Alone on a wide wide sea!
>
> . . . .
>
> I closed my lids, and kept them close,
> And the balls like pulses beat;

such, nor does it enter immediately into the reader's experience of the
poem, though he can be made aware of it in an abstract way.

> For the sky and the sea, and the sea and the sky
> Lay like a load on my weary eye,
> And the dead were at my feet.

We notice also in this last example a certain effect of meter, as the "beat" of the poetry imitates the pulse of the eyeballs. Meter is used as a symbolic device in poetry even more often than repetition, but partly on that account it is too complicated a subject for treatment here and will have to be deferred until the next chapter.

The device of fragmentation or discontinuity is sometimes used by poets who want to emphasize these qualities in their subject matter, the most famous example probably being the close of Eliot's *The Waste Land*, where the chaos of modern civilization is directly symbolized by the chaotic form of the poem. The theory underlying Eliot's practice has been attacked as fallacious by an unsympathetic critic, Yvor Winters, on the ground that it violates a basic law of literary aesthetics: literature is the giving of form, or meaning, to the formless, and if literary form attempts to imitate the formless it destroys itself. There is no reason to take this argument more seriously than any of the others based upon the supposed "laws" of literature; if the device works, the critic would be better occupied examining his prejudices than in giving vent to his outrage. Formlessness is not often directly imitated in poetry, but the reason has less to do with poets' scruples concerning the device than with the fact that a poem seldom provides a canvas broad enough for its effective display. A brief excursion into formlessness may seem like a temporary loss of control; something as big as a novel is usually needed to make the enterprise convincing.

All of the symbolic devices mentioned so far, including onomatopoeia, are found in William Carlos Williams' poem, "The Dance," which attempts to imitate the intricate mingling of figures in its subject, their motion, and the noise they make:

> In Breughel's great picture, The Kermess,
> the dancers go round, they go round and

around, the squeal and the blare and the
tweedle of bagpipes, a bugle and fiddles
tipping their bellies (round as the thick-
sided glasses whose wash they impound)
their hips and their bellies off balance
to turn them. Kicking and rolling about
the Fair Grounds, swinging their butts, those
shanks must be sound to bear up under such
rollicking measures, prance as they dance
in Breughel's great picture, The Kermess.

In one respect the poem is a more successful imitation than the painting, since it can at least approximate the noise of the dance, which the painting cannot do at all. On the other hand, the painting can better communicate a sense of the perpetual motion of the dancers, who (like the figures on the Grecian urn) are always doing exactly the same thing. Being a construction in time rather than in space, the poem has to symbolize this paradoxically static motion by inviting the reader to take its last line as its first one and begin all over again.

A poem that uses a circular design with very similar effect but with a far different tone and import is George Herbert's "Sin's Round":

Sorry I am, my God, sorry I am
That my offences course it in a ring.
My thoughts are working like a busy flame,
Until their cockatrice they hatch and bring:
And when they once have pérfected their draughts,
My words take fire from my inflamèd thoughts.

My words take fire from my inflamèd thoughts,
Which spit it forth like the Sicilian Hill;
They vent their wares, and pass them with their faults,
And by their breathing ventilate the ill;
But words suffice not; where are lewd intentions,
My hands do join to finish the inventions.

My hands do join to finish the inventions,
And so my sins ascend three stories high,

As Babel grew before there were dissensions.
Yet ill deeds loiter not; for they supply
New thoughts of sinning: wherefore, to my shame,
Sorry I am, my God, sorry I am.

This solemn and measured poem is a sinner's act of contrition. Herbert offends God in three separate but related ways: in thought, in word, and in deed, and the three ways are presented in that order by three separate but related stanzas. As thought leads to word and word to deed, so stanza one leads to stanza two and then to stanza three, the specific poetic links being the repetition of the last line of a preceding stanza as the first line of the following one. Just as the process of sinning is not finished with the sinful deed, because the deed produces a sinful thought and starts the round again, so the poem ends with a line which is not a conclusion but a repetition of the line with which it began.

Although it may be turned to artistic advantage, as these examples show, imitative symbolism is not a common strategy in poetry. One can read through many pages of a standard anthology without finding instances of its use. It is not for that reason less important when it is found, but it is clearly something that poets resort to only under special circumstances. No poem is ever harmed by not containing imitative symbolism. Why this should be so is a question that takes us back once more to the nature of the language from which poems are made. Onomatopoeia again excepted, language is a means of dealing with the world in the abstract. A linguistic sign *represents* what it refers to, but need not *resemble* it. Language is not iconic: neither in its content nor in its form, in spite of what some linguists have maintained, does it habitually picture the world. This fundamental characteristic is also assumed by artful uses of language, such as poetry, the difference being that because they are artful the user can, if he wishes, deliberately add imitative symbolism to his work as a means of giving it an extra dimension. On the whole this state of affairs works to the advantage of imitative symbolism, since it always has immediacy where it occurs, and there is no danger that its

effect will be diminished by familiarity or taken for granted. Poetry also gains, asserting its unique values and its artistic autonomy better because it is not saddled with that kind
of requirement.

The other kinds of symbolism discussed in this chapter
are much more common in poetry, and the reason is not
hard to find. The poet is often concerned with expressing
intangibles—attitudes, feelings, beliefs, intuitions—which
do not lend themselves well to literal and abstract statement.
To say that "only virtue survives death" is true enough and
has momentous implications, but unfortunately when put
this way the idea is not at all impressive. Stated symbolically, as in Shirley's poem, it comes magnificently to life.
What Shirley did was to find objective equivalents for an
abstract idea, giving it the resonance and immediacy that its
intrinsic value deserves. Poets write in language, of course;
they do not draw pictures. But of all those who use language in an artful way, poets are most inclined to see the
world in terms of concrete objects. What they have to convey are ideas about love, fear, hope, doubt, courage, pity,
honor; in doing so they fill their poems with roses, swords,
mountains, sunsets, hearts, arrows, birds, ships, caves—and
one poet whom we have met even found some application
for an ordinary housefly. Because symbols concentrate
meaning so well, they are especially suited to a concentrated
art like poetry. Their frequent lack of precise definition is
an asset rather than a handicap, and the residue of concrete
reality which even the most stylized symbol possesses helps
the poet to keep his work in vital contact with the world of
human experience. It is from this world that he takes his
origin, and it is to this world that he must always return.

8·

Meter

The species of double design treated in the four preceding chapters have a strong family resemblance. Although their individual characteristics differ, their close relationship to one another permits a reader to move among them quite easily without altering his methods or his basic assumptions. Meter, on the other hand, has no apparent relationship to these or to any other species of design, and must therefore be treated as some kind of special case, in a manner which has yet to be determined. As everyone knows, meter is not a design of meaning: it is the arrangement of words into regular patterns of sound, and is addressed primarily to the ear. It has no poetic qualities itself, nor is it necessary to poetry. And yet in spite of this tenuous connection between meter and poetry, meter is without any question the most common poetic device. Not only entire volumes, but bookshelves and even libraries could be filled with examples of its use, and until recent times most poets never considered the possibility of writing without it. In the face of this paradox there is no alternative but to put meter in a class by itself. It is unique.

But these are only the most general and superficial reasons for reaching such a conclusion. As one gets farther into the study of meter, the paradox deepens and the oddity of meter becomes even more remarkable. If a poet observes the rules of metrical arrangement when he is at work transforming words into poetry, the finished product can be called "verse" in recognition of the distinctive whole thus produced. The meter is more than just a vehicle for the poetry: the poetry and the meter interpenetrate to form an indissoluble union. At the same time, we must recognize that the rationale of meter is fundamentally different from that of poetry, beginning with the fact that meter obeys rules and poetry does not. Or, to put it more exactly, meter obeys extrinsic rules. Aside from the one rule that in poetry language shall be an end in itself (if indeed this can be called a rule), the rules of poetry come from the inside, and are generated all over again according to the needs of each particular occasion. Poetry is created, but meter is merely used. And it is used over and over again by all sorts of poets, year after year, as their common property. Meter is a form, a mold, a vessel standing on the shelf waiting to be filled. Yet when it is filled with a particular poem it gives to that poem a shape which the poem thereafter retains for all time and without which we cannot even imagine the poem existing. Can meter be both organic in its function and mechanical in its nature? Whatever the answer, the general public long ago made up its mind, as Chapter 1 indicated, that poetry and verse are identical—a confusion which the best efforts of critics will probably never succeed in dispelling.

In addition to this ambiguity as a poetic device (and no doubt in part because of it), meter has eluded the consensus that literary critics maintain, within certain limits, upon other technical topics, being the subject of a perennial controversy which seems only to grow in intensity every time someone applies himself to the task of resolving it. This controversy affects the "how" as well as the "why"—both the way in which specific metrical passages should be read and the theoretical basis of meter in general. Thus an obstacle almost as serious as the inherent difficulty of meter itself stands in the way of a reader who attempts to get more than a superficial understanding of this device. Just because he lacks the technical background for making an independent investigation of meter, he is at a loss in judging the relative soundness of the theories advanced by professional critics.

This chapter will proceed on the assumption that it is still possible to make a kind of basic sense out of the metrical problem, using a few undeniable facts about meter as points of reference and taking care not to push the search into the great terra incognita which lies around. In the process a number of potentially interesting complications, sub-topics, and nuances of analysis will have to be ignored. The main object, after all, is to ascertain what the ordinary reader needs to know; the professional critic can fend for himself.

"Meter" means "measure." In poetry no less than in anything else the object of measurement is some kind of abstraction from the whole, and the system of measurement assumes the existence of repeatable units having equal value. Practically speaking, there are only three such systems, all of them based on the syllable. One system measures the accent or stress of syllables, one their duration, and one their number; hence they are called the accentual, the quantitative, and the syllabic. After an initial period of experimentation and uncertainty, English poetry settled upon the accentual system, which has prevailed overwhelmingly ever since. Nevertheless, the principle that a line should have a certain fixed number of syllables—the cardinal point of the syllabic system—has remained in force as a concomitant of accentual metrics in most English poetry even down to the present time. Now poets are aware of their freedom to put into effect what a strictly accentual system implies, namely, that the length of a line is determined by the number of stressed syllables only, but in practice they commonly observe the syllabic principle as well.

The object of measurement is provided by the language itself. The words we use are divided into syllables by the act of speaking, and these syllables bear differing degrees of stress. Out of the complex whole which is speech only these two elements have been selected as the basis for English meter. But what is a syllable and what is stress? The syllable is some kind of minimum unit of utterance, and stress has something to do with loudness (real or imaginary); any definition that attempts to go beyond this point runs into difficulty. For poetic meter, however, this point is far enough, and fortunately the ear can tell us without any trouble what the definition on paper cannot. Although they permit a system of great flexibility and resourcefulness, these constituent objects are themselves remarkably fixed. We cannot alter at will the way in which English words are divided into syllables and stressed. The dictionary reminds us of how we must stress words of more than one syllable; the stress of monosyllabic words is not recorded, since it depends upon the nature of the utterances in which they occur, but within any particular utterance the grammatical construction employed, together with the requirements of meaning and rhetoric, leaves very little leeway in the placement of stress.

All this is in a sense given to us, but meter itself is not. That is, the conventional patterns of stress already existing in speech are not organized so as to provide anything that the ear can recognize as regular. (Indeed, the accidental occurrence in prose of a metrically regular passage is felt to be a serious defect.) When modern English, the language we speak, was coming into prominence for the first time as a literary language, poets labored under the disadvantage of not having a metrical tradition. The language itself did not spontaneously tell them what to do. The process of trial and error by which they worked out an accentual metrical system under these handicaps cannot be detailed here, but even a brief look at the poetry of the early sixteenth century (before Sir Philip Sidney) will reveal why it had to be undertaken.

Yet the contribution of these early poets was discovered, not devised. If meter as such did not exist in English speech to furnish them with a pattern for their system, still the nature of the language largely determined which features could be selected as metrically useful. A number of experiments in quantitative meter on the classical model were tried; they failed because the ear of an English-speaking person simply cannot discriminate with any dependability the relative duration of syllabic sounds, and the reason why it cannot is that duration, or quantity, is not a significant element in English speech. To use linguists' terminology, it is phonetic but not phonemic. Quantity is an acoustical phenomenon, the existence of which can be demonstrated by instruments that analyze sound, but since it is not employed as a device to convey meaning, the ear ignores it; the ear is trained to analyze sound in a different way. The ear does recognize syllables, of course, and therefore it would seem that syllabic meter in English is possible. But the difficulties here are formidable, and they spring from the same cause. While the ear recognizes the syllable as a discrete unit in ordinary speech, it is never required to recognize how many syllables a given utterance contains. The length of an utterance in number of syllables, like the quantity of a single syllable, is not significant. On the other hand, the degree of stress given to syllables is always significant, and it is immediately perceptible—it does not wait to be counted. In a syllabic metrical system the ear is asked to ignore what it normally perceives and to perceive what it normally ignores. Its inability to do so makes a poem written according to this system seem metrically amorphous and not obviously different from free verse, except for being divided into lines in a rather arbitrary way. Such is the penalty that a poet incurs for disregarding the natural bias of the English language.

The marking of syllable stress in English verse is called "scansion," and its purpose is to make metrical patterns evident to the eye. Two marks are conventionally used: / for a stressed syllable and ∪ for an unstressed one. Like the dots and dashes of the Morse code, these marks can be combined into repeatable units. Only certain elementary combinations, however, have become established in English verse. These units, known as "feet," are illustrated below, along with the names that have been borrowed from Greek prosody and applied to them. The more frequently used adjectival forms are given on the left; the noun forms are in parentheses.

iambic	∪ /	(iamb)
trochaic	/ ∪	(trochee)
anapestic	∪ ∪ /	(anapest)
dactylic	/ ∪ ∪	(dactyl)
spondaic	/ /	(spondee)

The foot is composed of one stressed syllable and one or more unstressed syllables, except for the spondee. But this last is exceptional for other reasons as well: the only true spondees in English are a small number of compound words (e.g., "make-work"), and the spondee cannot be repeated so as to form a line of verse. Some other theoretically possible combinations of stress turn out in practice to be feet only to the eye. When they are assembled into a line, the ear automatically dissolves them into the simpler feet which they most nearly resemble.

The metrical length of a line of verse is determined by the number of feet it contains. Since this number is almost always the same as the number of stressed syllables in the line, counting the latter is a quick way of measuring line length. The line lengths most commonly used in English verse are these:

> 2—dimeter
> 3—trimeter
> 4—tetrameter
> 5—pentameter
> 6—hexameter
> 7—heptameter

The standard metrical description of a line of verse is made by adding the name of its constituent foot to the designation of its length. The one description that almost everybody knows is "iambic pentameter," for the very good reason that this is the commonest of all English meters (blank verse is unrimed iambic pentameter). It may be illuminating to ask why.

The answer that tradition has made iambic pentameter so common begs the question. Still, it is true that poets learn how to write verse by reading other poets; the precedent which is most readily available to them is likely to be the one they will follow, other things being equal, and the process feeds upon itself as they in turn add their works to the rest. Thus iambic meter comes to seem "natural." It is also possible that this meter seems natural because it really is so—because it conforms to some innate bias of the English language, comparable to that bias which determined the choice of an accentual system of meter. However this theory might be tested, at least we have the evidence of our own ears, to which long passages of the other meters sound artificial. In anapestic and dactylic verse we sense too much immediacy; the verse itself makes so much noise, as it were, that we are distracted from the meaning of the poem. This bravura technique is suitable only to certain kinds of poems: sober thoughts do not move comfortably in tripping or galumphing lines. Trochaic verse tends to sound monotonous and heavy-handed, as anyone who has been exposed to the tedium of Longfellow's *Hiawatha* will agree. But the best explanation for the dominance of iambic meter might be that it is the most flexible and adaptable of all. Some of the quotations later in this chapter will help illustrate the range of variation possible within the limits of this foot. The crucial point (as we shall see) is that the variations, even extreme ones, do not destroy the over-all sense of a single metrical pattern. For example, the commonest of all variations occurs in the initial foot:

$$/ \ \cup \ \cup \ / \ \cup \ / \ \cup \ \cup \ / \ /$$

When in disgrace with fortune and men's eyes.

The initial foot here is not understood as a dactyl nor as a trochee followed by four iambs, but simply as the inversion of an iamb. The next to last foot is likewise irregular, since the accent which is supposed to fall upon "and" is given instead to the following syllable, but "men's eyes" is not a spondee nor is "-tune and men's" an anapest. The ear readily interprets this variation so as to maintain the prevailing metrical pattern.

The dimeter and trimeter lines do not lend themselves to extended use because they force too many breaks upon the flow of thought, especially when rimed. At the opposite extreme, the long line tends to break down into a series of short ones, because the ear instinctively attempts to reduce what it hears to the smallest integral units possible. No doubt in any system there would develop a line which read-

ers felt to be just right—neither too short nor too long—
and the pentameter line in English meets this requirement.
And like the iambic foot, it is flexible. The "caesura," or
rhetorical break, in a five-foot line tends to divide the line
unequally into groups of three-plus-two feet or two-plus-
three. Because the structure of the line, with its odd number
of feet, does not encourage putting the caesura in the middle, the poet can use it to add variety, and because the
reader cannot anticipate where it will fall, his attention is
more actively engaged. The following passage from Milton
shows how:

       4   1
High on a throne of royal state, || which far

     2   3
Outshone the wealth || of Ormus and of Ind,

      3   2
Or where the gorgeous East || with richest hand

     2   3
Showers on her Kings || barbaric pearl and gold,

    3   2
Satan exalted sat, || by merit raised

     3   2
To that bad eminence; || and from despair

     4   1
Thus high uplifted beyond hope, || aspires

   2   3
Beyond thus high, || insatiate to pursue

   2   3
Vain war with Heaven, || and by success untaught

   3   2
His proud imaginations || thus displayed.

    Iambic pentameter has also proved itself to be adaptable
to different kinds of poetry; satiric, elegiac, epic, meditative, didactic, and many others have all found congenial expression in this meter. This could not have happened if
iambic pentameter itself had possessed any strong character.

It is adaptable because it is neutral. And of course its being put to these varied uses helps to maintain its neutrality. This phenomenon raises an interesting question about the function of meter in poetry, because if a metrical form can be shared so indiscriminately, then it cannot have (one supposes) any intimate relationship with the language it accompanies, and one begins to suspect that meter serves only as a kind of extrinsic ornament to poetry. This question, already foreshadowed at the beginning of the chapter, will have to wait a little for answer.

In the meantime we must look at some other problems, the first of which concerns what seem to be deficiencies in the system of scansion. Linguists have determined that there are four degrees of stress in English speech, but in scanning verse these are arbitrarily reduced to two. Furthermore, the system takes no notice at all of two other important elements, pitch and juncture, both of which are constantly used in the process of communicating meaning. We need not go into the definition of these technical terms; the main thing is that our scansion disregards everything but two degrees of stress (often called "strong" and "weak" as well as "stressed" and "unstressed"). Would it not be better to have a system of scansion that recognized all these features of speech and that could be used as a real guide to show how a line of verse should be spoken? Paradoxically, the answer is "No." The supposed deficiencies of our system are actually its greatest advantages. Any pattern or design depends upon the selecting of some features and the ignoring of others, that is, upon abstraction. What we are looking for in scanning a line of verse are the *metrically significant* features: not everything that affects the way it is spoken, but only what determines its metrical pattern. To include other features merely for the sake of completeness would be to obscure those which alone are relevant. In some respects the ideal rendering of verse would be what appears on the face of a cathode-ray oscilloscope when someone speaks it into the instrument—a furiously squiggling line, responding to every acoustical nuance. But how could one put this abundant information to practical use? It defeats its own purpose. As long as one must abstract, one might as well get right down to the bare essentials, for it is these and only these which determine whether a line of verse has a metrical pattern and what that pattern is. The system of English meter is based upon a simple differential of stress. Our scansion is not a set of directions for performance; it tells us how to read the meter, not how to read the poem. From the merely practical point of view, this is a helpful situation, since no two persons would read a poem out loud in exactly the same way, and the fact that most of the differences in these readings cannot be formally symbolized means that no one can take his own personal interpretation and make it into a standard for others.

The use of the two marks in scanning a poem can be shown by means of the Wordsworth sonnet quoted in Chapter 6:

> ⏑ / ⏑ / ⏑ / ⏑ / ⏑ /
> Earth has not anything to show more fair:
> ⏑ / ⏑ / ⏑ / ⏑ / ⏑ /
> Dull would he be of soul who could pass by
> ⏑ / ⏑ / ⏑ / ⏑ / ⏑ /
> A sight so touching in its majesty. . . .

By this point, if the reader has been pronouncing the verse to himself according to the scansion indicated, he senses something terribly wrong. Could the poem ever have been meant to *sound* like that? Certainly English is not normally pronounced that way, and it would be odd if Wordsworth had really intended such an inane sing-song. Yet the poem is a sonnet, and sonnets are written in iambic pentameter. What we have here is a dramatic example of the difference between the way a poem is scanned for the purpose of determining its basic metrical pattern and the way it is marked for the purpose of indicating how that pattern should be rendered in speech. The basic pattern that a scanning like the one above brings out is what may be called the "nominal" meter of the poem. We discover that the nominal meter of Wordsworth's sonnet is iambic pentameter, as we had expected. But we must understand that a proper reading of the sonnet will bring out a pattern somewhat at variance with this nominal one. Let it be called the "actual" meter. Scanning this sonnet according to its actual meter produces the following result:

/ ◡ ◡ /◡ ◡ ◡ /   / /
Earth has not anything to show more fair:

/   ◡   ◡ /◡ /   ◡   ◡   ◡   / /
Dull would he be of soul who could pass by

◡ / /   /◡   ◡ ◡ ◡ /◡ ◡
A sight so touching in its majesty:

/   /◡ /   ◡   /◡ / ◡   /
This City now doth, like a garment, wear

◡   /◡ ◡ ◡ / ◡   /◡ /
The beauty of the morning; silent, bare,

/   /   /   /◡◡ ◡ / ◡ /
Ships, towers, domes, theatres, and temples lie

/◡ /◡ ◡ /   ◡   ◡◡ /
Open unto the fields and to the sky;

◡   / ◡   /◡◡ ◡ ◡ /   ◡ /
All bright and glittering in the smokeless air.

/◡ ◡ /   /   /◡◡ ◡◡   /
Never did sun more beautifully steep

◡ ◡ / / ◡   /◡ / ◡ /
In his first splendour, valley, rock, or hill;

◡   /◡ /◡ / ◡ / / /
Ne'er saw I, never felt, a calm so deep!

◡   /◡ / ◡ ◡ ◡ / /   /
The river glideth at his own sweet will:

/   /   ◡ /◡ /◡   / ◡/
Dear God! the very houses seem asleep;

◡ / ◡ /◡   / ◡ /◡ /
And all that mighty heart is lying still!

Some of these markings are open to question (for example, in line four the accents on "doth" and "like" might be changed around), but on the whole they would be accepted by all careful readers. What they show is a quite remarkable degree of irregularity; only the last line of the poem is completely regular. There is no recommended method for determining, in the face of such irregularity, what the nominal meter of a poem is. The last line of Wordsworth's sonnet gives us a good clue, but if that were the only clue, before he reached it the reader would have been subjected to thirteen lines of chaos which he would have been powerless to deal with, and surely this is not how it happens. If he feels the need for doing so, the reader can scan the whole poem mechanically, as the first three lines were scanned above, paying no attention to the aesthetic aspects of his reading. This will tell him what the nominal meter is, and with that information he can then go back and read the poem properly in its actual meter. But most readers of any experience find it unnecessary to go through such a process; they develop an instinct for meter that tells them almost at once what they are dealing with. They can hear the nominal and the actual meter simultaneously, and can thus check the one against the other—for deviations must have a base to deviate from, and if there is none they cease to be deviations and become simply meaningless: all meter disappears.

The function of nominal meter goes beyond providing a base for deviations. Even in the most irregular poems, perhaps especially in the most irregular poems, it persists to furnish a kind of counterpoint to the actual meter—not on paper, of course, but in the background of the reader's consciousness. The ability to hear both meters at once, like the ability to hear two simultaneous melodies in music, is something that develops with practice. The analogy with musical counterpoint is not exact, since in music both melodies are presumably of equal importance, while in poetry the nominal meter is definitely meant to be a subdued undercurrent to the actual meter—a mere ghost of a pattern. A better musical analogy might be with what happens in modern jazz performances, where the whole trick, rhythmically, is to depart as far as possible from the unvarying four-square beat of the music without destroying that beat altogether. The beat, the basic rhythm, may never be heard as such, but it is constantly implied by the music, and the listener who does not have it firmly somewhere in his consciousness cannot make sense out of the performance. For the performer or composer it is a kind of game he plays with his medium, and it can be the same thing for the poet, too. Here is how Wallace Stevens begins his great blank-verse poem, "Sunday Morning":

> Complacencies of the peignoir, and late
>
> Coffee and oranges in a sunny chair,
>
> And the green freedom of a cockatoo
>
> Upon a rug mingle to dissipate
>
> The holy hush of ancient sacrifice.

The extraordinary series of five unaccented syllables in the first line comes near to destroying the meter at the very outset. But it does not. The next line is a little more regular, the next more so still, until with the fifth line Stevens places the whole thing on an even keel. What he is doing here in a way is testing the reader's qualifications for reading the poem. Some readers might be mystified by this hide-and-seek, thrown off their stride, even annoyed. Experienced readers, having divined what was going on from the start, are able to appreciate the gradual movement toward regularity in the verse and to perceive how in the opening of the poem the verse parallels the casual disorder and self-indulgence of the breakfast scene which it accompanies. They will also perceive that the strictness of meter in the fifth line is no accident, coming with the mention of an event sacred to formal religion.

While it is true that marking scansion is a good discipline for inexperienced readers, like any other kind of artificial help it should be discarded as soon as possible. It is certainly not a part of the aesthetic design of the poem. All one need do to test this is to open a book of poems that some predecessor has sprinkled with accent marks that he did not bother to erase; whether correct or not, they make the poems virtually unreadable.

The need for teaching, or at least learning, scansion is nevertheless very real. Meter is artificial—we are not born knowing how to read verse, nor do we automatically learn how as we acquire our language. Repeated acquaintance with verse will accomplish this end for many persons, those who have what is called a "good ear"; others will make mistakes that they do not even recognize as such until they are told. The line from Shakespeare quoted above ("When in disgrace with fortune and men's eyes") was once scanned in eleven different ways by a class of college students, each one of whom turned in his version marked on paper with (apparently) the conviction that it was correct. To be sure, these versions were polarized around two or three favorite readings, but still the occurrence of so wide a range is very revealing, especially when it turns out that some of the scansions were not only metrically wrong but literally unpronounceable as English.

There is room for suspicion that some of these students might have been able to read the line correctly, and were thrown off when they tried to apply an unfamiliar system of abstract symbols to what they heard or thought they heard in their minds' ears. Perhaps they were straining to be ingenious because they knew they were being tested, and in doing so did not listen critically enough. The results of the experiment do not prove that a little knowledge of meter is a dangerous thing, but they do suggest that of itself this knowledge will do little good. It must be backed up by a considerable first-hand experience in reading verse; there is no way of eliminating the process of trial and error. An incidental but not unimportant result of the experiment is to show that the metrical foot has no real existence outside of the line. It is the line which brings the foot into being, rather than vice versa. The line is not an assembly of small unitary parts, but a whole which can only be *analyzed* into parts, and the nature of the whole determines the nature of these parts. The poet does not compose a line of iambic pentameter by finding five iambs and stringing them together, and the reader, in order to mark the scansion of the line, must first read the line in its entirety and then determine its metrical pattern, which may or (as in this instance) may not conform to a regular succession of identical feet. Hence it was that students who knew what an iambic foot is were at no real advantage when confronted with a nominally iambic line.

The experienced reader carries around in his head a kind of paradigm of the iambic pentameter line, which he has derived from his reading. (The same thing is true of other common metrical forms, but this discussion will be limited, for convenience, to the one form.) This paradigm combines both the regular nominal iambic pentameter pattern and a number of the permissible actual variations from it. Thus he has a way of instantly measuring any line that he encounters; if it is unique in his experience, he may add it to his mental list of variations, or he may reject it as being too wide of the mark. But he does not work only from line to line, either. He surveys the poem as a whole, allowing the poem itself to operate as a determinant on its own individual parts. He respects the *Gestalt,* as psychologists call it.

The problem is at bottom a psychological one and can be discussed and largely explained by using the phenomenon of expectation. The beginning reader is at sea either because he does not know what to expect, or because he arbitrarily sets up an expectation which he has neither reason to hold nor means to modify. The experienced reader, however, brings to the poem a rich and sensitive expectation which he enlists in the process of reading as an active ingredient. Sometimes a poet will draw upon this phenomenon for creating an especially dramatic effect, as Housman does in the first stanza of "Fancy's Knell." The stanza-pattern calls for eight lines of iambic trimeter, with the seventh line of each stanza shortened to iambic dimeter. This shortened seventh line is very effective. Since the expectation of three feet has already been set up by a very strict iambic trimeter, when the line with only two feet is encountered it breaks the pattern abruptly. The mind tries to make two feet fit the space already reserved (as it were) for three feet. The disparity, of course, is evident, but it is partly overcome by mentally stretching the two feet out beyond their normal length, making a rough equivalence in time between two and three. (This much is clear; we can side-step the inconclusive controversy as to the exact role of time in meter.) But the extra immediacy given to the short line by this very act of accommodating it to the pattern causes it to stand out all the more—which is just what the poet wanted. Here is how the first stanza might be scanned:

> ˘ / ˘ / ˘ / ˘
> When lads were home from labour
> ˘ / ˘ /˘ /
> At Abdon under Clee,
> ˘ / ˘ / ˘ / ˘
> A man would call his neighbour
> ˘ / ˘ / ˘ /
> And both would send for me.
> ˘ / ˘ / ˘ /˘
> And where the light in lances
> ˘ /˘ / ˘ /
> Across the mead was laid,
> / ˘ ˘ /˘
> There to the dances
> ˘ / ˘ / ˘ /
> I fetched my flute and played.

This description, accurate according to the usual system of scansion, omits one very important detail. What the reader should hear in the seventh line is more like

> [˘] / [˘ /] ˘ ˘ / ˘
> There   to the dances. . . .

The first foot is elliptical and the second foot missing altogether; this is indicated by brackets. The third foot is extended by an additional weak stress, though still understood as equivalent to an iamb. In reading, the time indicated by the second pair of brackets is occupied by a pause: "There [*pause*] to the dances. . . ." The pause is where an accent is needed (i.e., expected) in order to give this line the three strong accents that every line has had so far. The accent does not occur, and the pause, the gap where it should have been, is more emphatic than the accent itself. It is like what happens when one goes upstairs in the dark and, having expected one more step than there really is, comes down heavily on nothing. The specific expectations at work in the poem are created within this one context, but a proper response to them involves acquaintance with a much larger body of work. Without a good deal of additional experience in reading verse, very few persons would be able to hear more than "There to the dances," supposing that they at least escaped the blunder of reading it as a regular iambic line. One must not only be able to detect the missing foot, but also be able to tell what part of the line it is missing from.

Irregularities in meter are produced by design rather than by accident. Though intrinsically interesting, they also have real functions to perform. These may be classified as (1) avoiding monotony, (2) lending emphasis to meaning, and (3) adding metrical symbolism. The first function is the most obvious one and probably the one of least value, since what is not monotonous is not therefore automatically interesting. We should also beware of concluding too easily that a regular meter *is* monotonous: what theory suggests as plausible might not turn out to be true in practice. In any case the verdict would have to take into account the existence of variations in poems that are much too short to be monotonous—for example, Herrick's "Upon Julia Weeping."

Metrical emphasis occurs when a strong accent accompanies a strong word. In irregular lines this accent is usually displaced, i.e., taken away from another syllable to which the nominal pattern of the meter would have given it, but sometimes it is an extra accent, required by the linguistic construction without any reference to the meter. Examples of the reinforcement of meaning by metrical irregularities abound. The process can be well enough illustrated here by referring again to Wordsworth's "Westminster Bridge," which contains both kinds. In the first line, "more fair" carries two strong accents (the accent on "more" having been borrowed from the last syllable of "anything"), and the

metrical stress coincides very helpfully with the meaning,
since the bulk of the sonnet is devoted to a comparison between nature and the city on the basis of their beauty. "A
sight so touching" and "a calm so deep" each contain three
successive strong accents. Their common import has to do
with this central comparison, but we note that they also develop it significantly. "So touching" tells us that the sight
affects the spectator in an intimate way rather than superficially, and "calm so deep" is yet another step further in
bringing together and relating to each other the realms of
external appearance and inward being or essence. Other instances of reinforcement can be found in "pass by," "more
beautifully," "first splendour," "own sweet will," and of
course in the exclamation "Dear God!" But the most strikingly irregular line cannot be explained at all as a case of
metrical borrowing. Here the nominal metrical pattern is
not so much shifted around as it is abandoned, and the
words tumble pell-mell over one another as they crowd into
the line: "Ships, towers, domes, theatres, and temples
lie. . . ." This crowded effect, which owes so much to the
four strong accents in a row (actually five if one counts the
preceding "bare"), is exactly right for Wordsworth's purpose in describing the crowded city. The words in the
poem huddle together just as the buildings do in the mind's-
eye picture, not differentiated except by the largest of outlines, each receiving one bold stroke of the artist's pen.

We can see in this last example how the second and
third applications of metrical irregularity, for emphasis and
for symbolism, tend to merge. To the extent that the structure of the line resembles the structure of its subject, the
city, it is a device of imitative symbolism. If metrical irregularity is not used as often for symbolism as it is for emphasis, it is nevertheless common enough to provide an abundance of examples. The quotations from "The Rime of the
Ancient Mariner" in the preceding chapter were as typical
as any. To these can be added a number more:

Batter my heart, three-person'd God, for you
As yet but knock, breathe, shine, and seek to mend;

That I may rise and stand, o'erthrow me, and bend
Your force to break, blow, burn and make me new.

(Donne)

Only, from the long line of spray
Where the sea meets the moon-blanch'd land,
Listen! you hear the grating roar
Of pebbles which the waves draw back, and fling,
At their return, up the high strand,
Begin, and cease, and then again begin,
With tremulous cadence slow, and bring
The eternal note of sadness in.

(Arnold)

Generations have trod, have trod, have trod.

(Hopkins)

After the first powerful, plain manifesto
The black statement of pistons, without more fuss
But gliding like a queen, she leaves the station.

(Spender)

Break, break, break,
  On thy cold gray stones, O Sea!

(Tennyson)

I the Trinity illustrate,
  Drinking watered orange-pulp—
In three sips the Arian frustrate;
  While he drains his at one gulp.

(Browning)

Sky lowr'd, and muttering thunder, some sad drops
Wept at completing of the mortal Sin
Original . . .

(Milton)

'Tis not enough no harshness gives offence,
The sound must seem an echo to the sense.

Soft is the strain when Zephyr gently blows,
And the smooth stream in smoother numbers flows;
But when loud surges lash the sounding shore,
The hoarse, rough verse should like the torrent roar.
When Ajax strives, some rock's vast weight to throw,
The line too labours, and the words move slow;
Not so, when swift Camilla scours the plain,
Flies o'er th'unbending corn, and skims along the main.

(Pope)

The last example, a well-known passage of advice from the "Essay on Criticism," draws also upon the resources of sound-symbolism. Samuel Johnson (who very acutely attacked the claims of the sound-symbolists) pointed out that Pope's achievement here was a good deal less than the poet himself imagined. If the meter is kept and the words changed, the imitative effects tend to disappear. Again, it is the sense of the language that does most of the work. There was a limit, of course, to what Pope could do, writing within the close confines of the heroic couplet and burdened with neoclassical standards of poetic decorum. There are not many passages in his poetry outside of this one where the sound really echoes the sense.

Indeed, the striking fact about metrical symbolism is that it is so seldom used. The sound *may* echo the sense, but the practice of poets hardly supports the idea that it "must." Before we conclude that poets have been negligent in taking advantage of this resource, we might consider what would happen if they regularly did so. The writing of verse would be immensely more difficult than it now is, because of the technical problems involved. As a result, there would be a tendency to limit the subjects of poetry to those most easily treated in symbolic meter. And worst of all, the value that occasional metrical symbolism now has would disappear. Its value chiefly depends upon its immediacy, its contrast with the larger context of non-symbolic meter surrounding it. If all meter were symbolic and there were thus no contrast, we would come to take it for granted. It would be automatized. As things now are, special metrical effects are possible because meter is basically neutral; it does not regularly and systematically participate in meaning.

But if meter has only an occasional relationship with meaning, through reinforcement or through symbolism, what is its usual function? This is the crucial question which has been waiting for an answer since the beginning of the present chapter. The first major poet to ask himself the question and to attempt an answer in public was Wordsworth, who inserted a lengthy defense of meter into his preface to the 1800 edition of his and Coleridge's *Lyrical Ballads*. Uncongenial though the role of theoretical critic was to him and awkward as were some of his efforts to perform in it, he still managed to touch upon most of the real issues concerning the function of meter, and in a way that is genuinely thought-provoking. Some years later, Coleridge (for whom theoretical criticism was meat and drink) got around to refuting him in his *Biographia Literaria*. While the two men did not perhaps exhaust the possibilities of this subject, between them they marked out an area within which the modern reader may usefully search for his own answer.

Wordsworth's conception of poetry is basically a genetic one: poetry is what results when a certain sort of man responds to his experiences in a certain way. It is, as everyone remembers, "the spontaneous overflow of powerful feelings." The characteristics of poetry are all traceable to its origin in the poet. As for what a poem is, aside from being a certain amount of poetry, Wordsworth has no concept to offer at all—or none that is in any way consistent with the rest of his theory. This causes him visible embarrassment, for he had, after all, written poems, and poems distinguished moreover by the artificial characteristic of meter. The logic of his position forces him to assert that meter is "superadded" to poetry. The poet selects his language and then versifies it. But Wordsworth had already rejected the devices of poetic diction, such as the personification of abstract ideas, as being artificial; how could he avoid rejecting meter on the same ground? The answer is ingenious. Although he does not put it in so many words, he suggests that meter is defensible because, unlike poetic diction, it does not *pretend* to be natural. The reader is never asked to believe that people really talk in meter, whereas in the neoclassical poetry which Wordsworth disliked, the reader is asked to believe that all the tricks of style sprang naturally from human feeling and might actually have been used by real men. Without being any less artificial, meter is a great deal more honest. Wordsworth's censure of poetic diction is a moral one, falling upon the motives of the author more than upon the objective nature of what he writes. The one objective difference between meter and poetic diction is that the former is regular and uniform, obeying certain laws to which both poets and readers submit, while the latter is arbitrary and capricious, depending on the whim of the poet. From Wordsworth's point of view this is a strong argument in favor of the superiority of meter.

Because meter is regular and artificial, it acts to temper and (as we would say) to "distance" a poetic composition. Poetry is the expression of powerful feelings, and there is always the danger that these feelings, especially if connected with painful objects, may exceed their proper bounds and make the poem unbearable. The presence of meter in such a poem tends, according to Wordsworth, "to divest language, in a certain degree, of its reality, and thus to throw a sort of half-consciousness of unsubstantial existence over the whole composition. . . ." In effect, meter is telling us that we are *not* meeting real life in the poem after all.

Not only does meter act to lower an emotional temperature that threatens to rise too high, it also acts to raise one that is too low. If the poet's language is inadequate to the demands of his subject, the meter will go far toward making up the difference by adding to the poem the pleasure that readers derive from meter of any kind, along with whatever specific associations the particular kind of meter may bring from the reader's previous experience of it. Why, exactly, meter is intrinsically pleasurable Wordsworth does not say, beyond a few suggestive remarks about "the perception of similitude in dissimilitude." He rests his argument finally on the very Johnsonian ground that people in fact are pleased by meter: ". . . of two descriptions . . . each of them equally well executed, the one in prose and the other in verse, the verse will be read a hundred times where the prose is read once." This alone is sufficient to justify the superaddition of meter to the language of poetry.

But the intrinsic value of meter should not be too readily assumed. Do readers derive pleasure from meter simply per se, apart from the other qualities of language with which it is associated? The assumption looks more dubious the longer one examines it. Unfortunately Wordsworth did not really examine it, as Coleridge points out in his reply. And the argument that verse compositions are always preferred over compositions in prose is easily demolished by citing a few examples. If Wordsworth had wanted to antagonize Coleridge, he could not have done so better than by accounting for the value of meter in terms of the pleasure it brings to a poem from the outside, for everything that Coleridge wrote about poetry is founded on his concept of the poem as an integral and organic whole, "the parts of which mutually support and explain each other." The reason why a poem is written in meter must be contained within the poem itself; whatever value meter has, it has because the meter is in the poem, i.e., because it is functional. According to Coleridge, meter has two main functions: to stimulate, and to normalize or unify. His statement of the first deserves to be quoted in its entirety: "As far as metre acts in and for itself, it tends to increase the vivacity and susceptibility both of the general feelings and of the attention. This effect it produces by the continued excitement of surprise, and by the quick reciprocations of curiosity still gratified and still re-excited, which are too slight indeed to be at any one moment objects of distinct consciousness, yet become considerable in their aggregate influence. As a medicated atmosphere, or as wine during animated conversation; they act powerfully, though themselves unnoticed." In regard to the second function of meter, Coleridge is not so very far from Wordsworth. Coleridge is enough of a romantic to believe that poetry is a matter of special concentration or intensity in language, and thus that a poem of any length cannot be all on the same level. The danger is that in reading such a poem a reader will hit the high spots only, rapidly extracting the general meaning and paying relatively little attention to the rest. The relationship between the whole and its parts will be disrupted, and the organic unity of the work will disappear. Meter acts to raise these less inspired passages up to the level of the others by giving them the same outward form. Meter does not make them into poetry, but it is an unmistakable sign to us that they are not prose, and we therefore read them with the kind and degree of attention that poetry requires. All parts of the poem are brought into balance, and the integrity of the whole is maintained as well as—and because of—the equal immediacy of its parts. "Immediacy" is not a term that Coleridge uses, but it is clearly what he has in mind. Here is the important difference between Wordsworth and Coleridge: immediacy is a quality that meter contributes only in the context of the poem, as a result of its marriage with language, whereas the pleasure that Wordsworth speaks about is meant to be an intrinsic quality, one that meter has always and anywhere. Immediacy is a functional attribute, a unifying force; pleasure is a value in itself.

For most modern readers, Coleridge has all the better of the argument. Whatever difficulty they have with his reasoning is counterbalanced by the eloquence of his style and the attractiveness of his notion about organic unity. It would be well in that case to remind ourselves that Wordsworth's ideas are still worth debating. The bias or main direction of Wordsworth's theory is toward emphasizing the "otherness" of meter. If poetry is natural and spontaneous, meter is artificial and voluntary. Even Coleridge agreed to this. Where Wordsworth came to grief was in trying to justify this difference on functional grounds without a concept of what a poem is such as Coleridge later supplied. The bias or main direction of Coleridge's theory is toward emphasizing the "sameness" of meter, in the sense that meter functions harmoniously with other elements in a poem toward a unified goal, and does not impress itself as such on the consciousness of the reader.

Sameness and otherness—these terms are merely ways to condense and rephrase what was said in the opening paragraph of this chapter about the peculiarity of meter. It is the final as well as the first issue. What we get from a close reading of the debate between Wordsworth and Coleridge, besides some very helpful hints that will be utilized in the following pages, is a sense that the truth about meter must include both of these opposite characteristics, not in a form that reconciles them or cancels them out, but in a form that preserves, if possible, the tension between them. No meter is so completely assimilated into poetry that we cannot experience it as meter, that is, as something other than poetry (which does not need meter in order to be poetry), and yet no meter is ever so arbitrarily superimposed that it can simply be taken away, leaving the poetry behind. The language, we might say, does not "have" meter: it *is* metrical. But it is *metrical*, and this characteristic can be isolated from the rest. Surely much of our pleasure in reading metrical poetry comes, for the most part unconsciously, from the continued operation of this invigorating paradox.*

The general functions of meter can be ranged under six headings, and these in turn divided equally between the two major characteristics. But let us make certain what they mean. The sameness of meter refers to its virtual identity with, and its inseparability from, the poetry that we read. In the particular poem, the metrical design is unique, integral —or to use Coleridge's concept, organic. It springs into being as a response to the artistic needs of the poem and satisfies them exactly, leaving no surplus of pleasure that can be enjoyed for its own sake. The otherness of meter refers to its independence of the poetry, to the reader's awareness that in a metrical poem he is meeting a combination of essentially different things. The meter has an authentic life

---

* Meter would thus seem to be just another species of double design. But its doubleness, while fundamental and indisputable, is of another order than that of the designs treated earlier, involving as it does the relationship of poetry itself to a non-poetic element with which it is intimately combined. This situation is unique to poetry, while metaphor, symbolism, etc., are not.

of its own, a history; it comes from the outside. What it contributes to the poem is something valuable in its own right, an extra artistic dimension.

This polarity, then, will control the remainder of the discussion. The following list excludes the two special functions of meter, reinforcement of meaning and metrical symbolism, which have already been presented.

SAMENESS

1. A truly general function of meter is that of giving *immediacy* to its context, as the remarks on Coleridge brought out. Ordinary language is not metrical; by choosing and rearranging words so as to form a regular stress-pattern with them, the poet sets his work apart from ordinary language. It has higher claims on our attention. Whether the content is trivial or not, whether or not our attention is adequately repaid, we still read verse with a special set of attitudes and expectations, and a specially heightened awareness. But the immediacy, though contributed by meter, is a quality possessed by the language as a whole. This is true, however, only where the metrical pattern either reinforces the meaning or is unobtrusively subordinated to it. If the meter is "unnatural" or difficult, then its otherness comes to the fore; it becomes immediate in its own right, asserting an independent claim to attention.

2. Because it gives immediacy to the whole context, meter acts to *normalize and equalize*. The poem may in fact contain prosaic interludes, lapses of inspiration, passages of connective tissue, but since they are not less metrical than the rest of the poem, they tend to be read with the same degree of care as everything else, and their functional value within the poem has an opportunity to redeem whatever intrinsic shortcomings they may have as poetry.

3. Meter also aids in giving a poem a *distinctive personal accent*, very like that of an individual speaker's voice. "Accent" here has nothing to do with pronunciation; it is a matter of rhythm alone. But speech-rhythm can be distinctive, just as sentence-structure and diction can, and when it is it works in unison with them to create the image of one

particular person speaking. Because the unison is so complete, it is hard to isolate what the metrical component of the effect is, but the ear tells us immediately that the voice we hear speaking in *Paradise Lost* is not the same voice that we hear speaking in the blank verse of Robert Frost. Each poet succeeded in placing his own distinctive stamp upon what is basically a common meter. For dramatic purposes, of course, a poet may assume several speaking voices, modifying his meter as best he can to assist the illusion.

OTHERNESS

4. When the metrical pattern is not regularly subordinated to meaning and becomes immediate in its own right, we have something that may be called *metrical play*. A kind of struggle is carried on between the poetry and the meter: the poetry wants to go its own way, but the meter forces it into this essentially alien pattern of regular stresses, a pattern that has in itself no poetic quality whatever. Some poets have taken especial care to hide the struggle and to make the copresence of these unrelated elements seem natural and harmonious, and yet in their works no less than in those of other poets an artificial set of obstacles has been placed in the path, and their skill in leaping them does not mean that the obstacles are unimportant. Robert Frost was fond of saying, "Writing free verse is like playing tennis with the net down." He was wrong: what the writer of free verse really does is to substitute another kind of obstacle for that of meter, and a rather more difficult one because it is variable and self-imposed. Nor is it by any means so easy, in free verse, to tell success from failure, since the criteria are not precise or objective. Free verse is not "free" at all; it is just restrained in a different way. If two players undertook to play tennis seriously with the net down, almost the first thing they would do would be to invent another obstacle, another arbitrary rule, to take its place—perhaps they would decree that every ball had to be played on the second bounce. Otherwise they would soon lose interest and stop playing altogether. But although wrong on this count, Frost was very correctly pointing to one reason for using meter.

It poses an interesting challenge to the writer, and quite a different challenge from that posed by the necessity of writing poetry. Wordsworth listed "the sense of difficulty overcome" as one of the sources of our pleasure in meter, thus undermining his own argument, since our pleasure does not derive from the meter as such, from the mere *dum-de-dum-de-dum* of regular stresses, but from the normal resistance of language to such treatment. A non-metrical component is required. Yet the meter is a superaddition or superimposition—it comes from the outside, and by the voluntary decision of the poet to assume this unnecessary obligation.

5. Being imposed from without, meter functions as a means of *distancing*. Wordsworth's statement of the process is worth remembering. His phrase, "a sort of half-consciousness of unsubstantial existence," is more apt by a good deal than Coleridge's famous "willing suspension of disbelief for the moment," because what needs explaining is not why we do have poetic faith but why we don't have it. If there is any innate or unlearned tendency to react to a work of art in a certain way, it is a tendency to confuse it with real life. The intense and uncritical participation of children in all kinds of dramatic presentations is well known; they have great difficulty at first in convincing themselves that drama is not real. The tendency is perhaps never entirely mastered, nor should it be, for empathy or vicarious participation is a legitimate goal of art and one of the values it has to offer. Still, there are pathological extremes: witness the grown persons who identify famous actors and actresses with the wholly fictional parts that they play. When a character in a television soap opera has a birthday or an anniversary, it is not unusual for the station to receive presents in the mail, addressed to the character and not to the actor, from loyal followers of the series whose dim grasp of reality is unable to cope with a plausible fiction. In truth, the popular audience does not want art, it wants manageable life: plastic geraniums, color slides of the Grand Canyon, wax-museum sculpture, a reconstructed Williamsburg pretending to live in the eighteenth century. Our civilization marches toward the future under a banner

that reads, "You can't tell it from the real thing." Because meter is not natural to language, and hence not "realistic," it acts in poetry to oppose this confusion between life and art. If the function of meter (in number 2, above) is to normalize and equalize the content of the poem in respect to itself, making it internally homogeneous, the function of meter is also to insist that the poem is heterogeneous in respect to the real life surrounding it. This is not to say that the reader is in any actual danger, for example, of mistaking "The Rime of the Ancient Mariner" for a true story. On the other hand, this poem did not just happen—someone sat down and wrote it, and it is this aspect of its artificiality that especially needs to be made visible. Meter is the outward sign of art. The rest of the art—the design of the poem—is less apt to be neglected when meter is present. From a poem in meter we get a greater sense of order and purpose than we would from a real-life utterance. "Someone is in charge here," we feel, and it is a kind of guarantee that the effort we expend in reading will not be wasted.

6. Although meter can help give a poem a distinctive personal accent, according to the way it is handled, the meter itself is a device that other poets have used before, and is recognized as such. Consequently it helps to *universalize or depersonalize* the poem. The poem draws a measure of strength from tradition, from its evident community with other works of art. There is a resonance in meter that it acquires from its long and complex associations with poetry. When a poet uses meter, he acknowledges his debt to the past and at the same time enriches the metrical tradition for future poets by the extent of his contribution and the example of his loyalty. When a reader comes to a composition in meter, he is (as Wordsworth noted) already half disposed to give it credit as a poem. Whether it really conforms in other respects to what he demands of poetry can only be determined after more careful reading, but to begin with he is prejudiced in its favor. And again we face a paradox, for though we hear different voices in *Paradise Lost* and "The Death of the Hired Man," both poems are written in blank verse. However different the latter is from

the former, they do use the same meter. Moreover, the subtlety and idiomatic ease of Frost's blank verse would not have been possible without the long process of adaptation which this meter received at the hands of poets, Milton among them, who preceded Frost in using it. This is not to deny Frost's unique skill, but only to place his skill in its true relationship with the history of English verse.

The whole truth about meter is no doubt less tidy than this table of functions makes it appear. If there are indeed only six general functions of meter, and they do pull in opposite directions as indicated, at least in any given single poem their proportions are not likely to be so equal. Nevertheless, the binary structure of the table is supported by everything we know about meter, and most suggestively by the very structure of meter itself. Meter is made up of an interaction between two opposed but complementary elements, the strong and the weak stress, neither of which is capable of existing without the other, since degrees of stress are always relative. The tension between them is likewise, and fortunately, irreconcilable. But why does the tension exist in verse when it does not exist in ordinary language, which also contains differences of stress? The reason lies in the artificial sequence which meter imposes on these stresses. By regularizing their occurrence, the poet gives to these linguistically significant elements the further characteristic of meter. The result is a completely new significance and a new set of functions. A stress pattern in ordinary language is not the same thing as a stress pattern in verse, even if the two should be objectively identical, simply because the latter is in verse. As the determination to use language as an end in itself produces poetry, so the determination to use syllable stresses for their own sake produces meter. The difficulties or tensions created in either case are also the necessary conditions for success. Meter, like poetry, is a game that we play with language.

9.

Traditional

Forms

When a poet begins the act of composition, he does not always have a clear idea of what the finished poem will be like. He may start with nothing more definite than an image, a word or phrase, or an evocative rhythm. Sensing potentialities in this fragmentary material, he may decide not to interfere with its development by imposing a form on it from without and, instead, will allow it to grow and mature in its own way and by its own momentum. One image suggests a related image; one word attracts another; the rhythm compels a certain arrangement of words and is harmonious with only one of many tones or moods . . . bit by bit the direction which the poem should take begins to emerge, and though the poet is actively engaged at every moment of the process, his role is rather to encourage it than to bend it to his will. In this he is like the sculptor who liberates the statue implicit in a block of wood or stone by letting his chisel follow the grain of the substance. For both of them the act is a kind of discovery, and the result is in every formal sense unique.

On the other hand, the poet may equally well begin with a definite idea of what the poem has to be. He may not be able to visualize every step of the way, but he knows the goal he wants to reach, and he has some notion of how to get there. In particular he may have in mind a certain form that he wants the poem to take—let us say, the form of a sonnet. Whatever his motives for choosing it are, and they could be nothing more than the fact that he feels like writing a sonnet, one important aspect of his job is already taken care of: he can write only fourteen lines, and they will be in iambic pentameter, probably terminating in rimes according to a pattern that other poets have used before him. He has availed himself of a poetic tradition, and the poem which results will be immediately recognizable as a sonnet, sharing a common form with the other poems in this tradition.

The two cases described above are extreme. It is very likely that most poems are written by a process that lies somewhere in between. In either case, the finished poem must justify the form given it: the form must not seem to have been arbitrarily superimposed or, at the other extreme, to be only a fortuitous outgrowth of the pressures of material which the poet did not have under real control. Chapter 3 pointed out that a "good" sonnet could be a bad poem, but in a good sonnet that is also a good poem—which is the only kind worth consideration here—the traditional sonnet form and the original poetic content are fitted together so skillfully that no gaps between them can be discerned. It would be wrong to conclude from this, however, that the traditional form has no characteristics of its own. Some of these characteristics spring directly from the manner in which it circumscribes the poet's freedom (for example, by its length the sonnet is very ill adapted to epigrams and to verse narrative), and some spring indirectly from the uses to which other poets have put it. Hence these characteristics, although absorbed into and made functional elements of the poet's own design, do exist independently, and the poet who chooses the sonnet form certainly chooses it in the full knowledge of what they are and with the deliberate intention of putting them to work for him. In order to appreciate his success, if he does succeed, we have to understand what he was up against; in other words, we have to consider the traditional forms as such. This subject will be best understood if approached indirectly via the device of rime, which is also traditional in English poetry.

Rime is not itself poetic, since blank verse and free

verse do very well without it, but its association with poetry is both widespread and of long standing. Basically, rime is *repetition with difference:* there is enough sameness to establish and make recognizable what it is that is being repeated and enough difference to establish the sense of an achievement or a progress in design. Rime is made possible, as we know, by peculiarities of our language; the poet merely takes advantage of something that already exists, waiting to be used. Both in its combination of sameness with difference and in the fact that it is a device provided by the language we speak, rime very much resembles meter. Their principal difference is that rime does not function phonemically, as the constituents of English meter do. Although meter itself is not found in ordinary speech, the stresses out of which meter is made are omnipresent, and the placement of these stresses is one of the ways by which we normally convey meaning; rimes, on the other hand, are infrequent and accidental features of ordinary speech, and when they do occur they have no effect at all on meaning. In poetry, further, rime is a localized device; when meter is used, it is pervasive, co-extensive with the language, woven into the very texture of the whole. It is true that rime can be indicated by an abstract paradigm (the "rime scheme") as meter can, and that marking a rime scheme is much like scanning a metrical pattern, but the resemblance between these two processes is only superficial. Scanning a poem provides insight into the life and movement of the poet's design, whereas marking a rime scheme simply makes evident in one way what was already evident in another.

The formula for rime in English is as follows. (1) The riming syllable must be one which bears a strong stress. (2) The vowel sound of this syllable is repeated identically. (3) Whatever follows the vowel is also repeated identically, including other syllables if the word is polysyllabic. (4) Whatever precedes the vowel is changed. This means changing consonants, when the syllable is introduced by a consonant (*cold-bold*), or using a pair in which one of the syllables lacks an introductory consonant (*old-bold*). When the riming syllable is terminal, the rime is called "masculine"; when it is followed by one or more further syllables, "feminine" (*older-colder, truthfully-youthfully*). English no longer favors the so-called "rime riche" or identical rime, in which the only difference is one of spelling (*bold-bowled*). What is or is not acceptable is a matter of habit and convention anyhow; modern readers balk at a device that was used without apology in the nineteenth century and earlier, as Wordsworth's sonnet "Composed Upon Westminster Bridge" illustrates when it rimes "by" and "majesty." This is an eye rime or courtesy rime, since it makes use of a normally unstressed syllable, the vowel of which must be altered in its pronunciation before the rime can register on the ear.

In addition to the standard form of rime, there are some variants that follow slightly different rules. "Consonance" requires the change rather than the repetition of vowel sound (*cold-called*); "assonance" requires the change of the terminal consonants (*cold-coat*) or alternatively of both consonants (*cold-boat*); and one of the varieties of slant rime or near rime requires the repetition of the final consonants only (*cold-tilled*). None of these is really common; they exist at all because the paucity of true rimes in English has driven poets to look for substitute or supplementary devices. (Poets can abandon rime altogether, and many have done so. For not only are rimes of the *love-dove trees-breeze* variety unacceptable on the grounds of triteness, but they also act to inhibit the poet's freedom in developing his design: he will think twice before ending a line with "love," even if this word is called for, because he would then have to accommodate a later portion of his poem to the very small range of possibilities that this word leaves open to him, an investment of effort for which he can expect no comparable artistic reward.) Another peculiarity of our language is that complicated or unusual rimes tend to have a humorous effect (as in Browning's *fabric-dab brick*). No doubt the reason has something to do with the degree of immediacy that they create. Limericks, which are meant to be humorous, depend heavily on this device to produce their effect, so much so that often their only excuse for existing is to provide a vehicle for a set of improbable rimes that the author has discovered.

The device which parallels rime, in that it has to do with the repetition of consonant sounds rather than vowel sounds, is called "alliteration." Typically, though not invariably, the initial consonant of a word is the one repeated. In Anglo-Saxon poetry and for a while thereafter alliteration was a major structural device; it went out of fashion in the fourteenth century, lost this function, and rapidly became nothing more than an occasional ornament. Since it is an ornament which contributes no qualities of its own to a poetic context, perhaps it would be better thought of as a kind of seasoning, added to bring out the inherent qualities of the dish without actually changing its taste. It is certainly adaptable to very different styles and subjects, as the following examples demonstrate, the first from Swinburne and the second from Eliot:

> When the hounds of spring are on winter's traces,
>   The mother of months in meadow or plain
> Fills the shadows and windy places
>   With lisp of leaves and ripple of rain. . . .

> Webster was much possessed by death
> And saw the skull beneath the skin;
> And breastless creatures under ground
> Leaned backward with a lipless grin.

The dominant pattern in the first example is that of *pl-lp*, with the assistance of *w, s,* and *m;* in the second the repetition mainly involves *p, b, l, g,* and *s.* A careful analysis will also reveal consonant patterns of the sort that are often overlooked in marking alliteration, such as Eliot's "*Webster-backward.*" The strange thing is that this device furthers equally well the breathless, excited movement of Swinburne's lines and the cold deliberateness of Eliot's. It does so by heightening the immediacy of whatever qualities the context already possesses. And because the alliteration is obviously intentional rather than accidental, it communicates as much sense of design as the other elements in the poem and has a similar claim on our interest. But like all seasonings, if over-used it calls undue attention to itself. For Swinburne alliteration became a habit, and thus by its very profusion, following the psychological law of diminishing returns, it was reduced in his compositions to the status of a mechanical trick of style, more annoying to the reader than enhancing to the poetry.

As usual, technical information of the sort outlined above is only preliminary to the main question, which has to do with function. We want to ask what it is that poets gain by using rime. The answer can be divided into four parts: rime in poetry functions to provide a rationale for the line, to bind lines into groups, to give immediacy, and to distance. Whenever rime is used, it contributes to poetry in these ways.

(1) Traditionally, English poetry has been written in lines. One might go so far as to say that the line is the basic unit of poetry, or at any rate the basic unit of metrical poetry. On the printed page the line is easily enough identified by typographical arrangement, but the typography does nothing more than make this identification possible; typography does not tell us why the line had to exist in the form that it does, or even why it had to be a line at all. The line may be set apart from its context by containing a distinct unit of subject matter or by being part of a clearly marked rhetorical or grammatical pattern, but these conditions are not invariably met, and when they are met they seldom have enough authority to settle the question before it has a chance to arise—and this is what we need. Why should the line have stopped at five feet, or four, or three? No one wants to spend any time debating this, if he can help it, but if no answer is apparent the question begins to take on importance. With short lines the problem becomes all the more acute, since their shortness tends to seem more arbitrary. A rime at the end of a line obviates the problem by functioning as a sort of goal; that is what the line was leading up to, and once having reached it the line should indeed stop. Together they make an integral unit, and the

rime, having immediacy, answers by itself the reader's demand for an artistic rationale. The means of satisfying this legitimate demand is something of a trick, because in fact the rime is not the goal of the line; it is only in bad poetry that the rimes take charge and subordinate other elements to themselves. Our minds know this, but our ears are gratefully deceived by the gesture toward formal integrity.

The one great exception to all this is the blank verse line, which has a rationale of its own. It has evolved in response to the need for a metrical form more plastic than the traditional rimed line and better adaptable to large-scale effects. It not only does not require a special identity for itself, it even tries to avoid one. The worst blank verse is that which marches regularly forward in five-foot lengths, pausing at the end of each unit before returning to commence the next one (i.e., "end-stopped" lines); since it has all the characteristics of rimed verse except the rime, we cannot help feeling, when we read it, that something has been omitted. If it conforms to this extent, why does it not conform altogether? Certainly nothing has been gained by leaving off the rimes. With good blank verse, however, the omission of rimes is a positive advantage. The poet can then go ahead to exploit the opportunities inherent in the pentameter structure (such as were mentioned in Chapter 8). Because he does this, because he creates something for which rime is irrelevant, we do not feel any sense of omission. The tensions and releases, the adjustments of balance, the emphases, the alterations of pace, the weaving together of smaller into larger rhetorical units—all these constitute the poet's main effort and justify his choosing the neutral medium of blank verse.

(2) Rime functions also to bind lines into groups, usually according to a regular pattern. This is a joining function and is opposite to the separating function discussed above. The conventional way of marking these groups is by assigning a different letter of the alphabet to each different rime, in order of occurrence, and then arranging the result in a vertical column, thus providing a quick visual outline of their structure. If the poem is written in stanzas or in any

other way employs regular repetition of rimes, the rime scheme establishes the norm for these groups and gives them a distinctive identity. (But the binding function does not require the lines to have anything in common beyond their rimes.) The binding is a two-fold process. First, there is the objective fact of rime and the pattern that it creates. Second, there is the subjective experience of rime, which is psychological and involves the creation and release of expectations. As soon as the reader identifies the pattern being used, the first appearance of each riming word causes him to anticipate meeting its counterpart; when he reaches the counterpart, his expectation is satisfied. As an artistic achievement, this play of expectation is not itself of high value, but it does reinforce the sense of purpose which every poem ought to communicate, and it gives the poem a forward momentum.

(3) It has already been suggested that rime lends immediacy. The riming words stand out in the reader's consciousness, and in doing so they make possible the results described in the two preceding sections. Basically, they stand out because rimes are not normal in ordinary speech; they may stand out further by being themselves recherché, complicated, or surprising, though at the risk of damage to the poem if it is not designed to accommodate such effects. Nevertheless, rime always communicates a certain sense of surprise: this is the specific quality or tone of its immediacy. Because rime is not phonemic (a fact which we "know" even if we are quite ignorant of linguistics) and because it is not normally found in speech, we are pleasantly surprised to encounter it. Our language has inadvertently provided the raw materials of rime, as it were, but has not provided them with any function; the poet takes advantage of this bit of absentmindedness by turning it to his own ends, and we on our part appreciate his ingenuity.

(4) As the product of ingenuity, rime is a sign of art. It coöperates with meter in distancing the poem, that is, in emphasizing its difference from real life, and what was said about the distancing function of meter in Chapter 8 applies here as well.

The priority or relative value of rime and meter is shown by the existence of much metrical poetry without rime and very little riming poetry without meter. All that we have of the latter is due to one man, Ogden Nash, who perfected a unique parody version of traditional composition, in which amorphous lines totter crazily toward what looks like final collapse, only to be rescued at the last imaginable moment by a desperate lunge at rime. Being thus dependent, rime is even further removed than meter is from anything that we would regard as centrally or essentially poetic. This may be one of the reasons why rime gets so little attention from critics of poetry nowadays. Still, as the preceding analysis tried to show, rime is not simply ornamental, and its continuing use in poetry comes from something more than habit or respect for tradition.

In the history of English poetry, which now goes back some seven centuries, poets have tried almost every verse form conceivable, but only a handful of these innovations survived long enough to gain a place for themselves in the permanent repertory of forms. We call them "traditional," recognizing as we do so that the division is a rather arbitrary one and that there is often no important difference between a traditional form and a non-traditional form except that one has been widely used and the other not. In either case the poet who employs them must submit his design to a set of predetermined rules. What he gains by doing so is a question that has to be answered all over again for each individual poem, but to some extent the potentialities of a form, both as a help and as a hindrance, can be discovered in advance of its specific use. These general characteristics will be our concern here.

The most useful classification of forms is according to the way they are used in making poems. By this standard we may divide them into (1) *undifferentiated* forms, (2) *aggregative* forms, and (3) *integral* forms. An undifferentiated form is one that has no built-in shape other than the minimum and irreducible single line. It is, so to speak, the "yard goods" of verse, a material which can be unrolled to any desired length and cut off at any point the poet chooses.

If it is subdivided at all, the subdivisions accord with requirements of the poetic content rather than with requirements of the form itself, and these subdivisions are of irregular size: verse-paragraphs, not stanzas. An aggregative form, on the other hand, has a definite shape of its own, and it is meant to be repeated without change. It provides a kind of building block for the poem. It too is indeterminate in the sense that any number of these blocks can be added together, making possible structures of all different sizes, but the form itself, the basic unit, is absolutely fixed. Finally, an integral form is just what the term implies: co-extensive with the whole poem. When the end of the form is reached, the poem is over. It is like a vessel which holds only so much and which must be filled completely every time. The disposition of its component parts tends to be prescribed as strictly as the dimensions of the whole, making it determinate both in shape and in size.

The only undifferentiated form of any importance is blank verse—unrimed iambic pentameter. The absence of rime is crucial, for if the lines were rimed they would necessarily be differentiated from one another, even though (as in Milton's "Lycidas") the rimes were placed irregularly and did not make a recurrent pattern. Rime is created by an interplay of similarity with difference, and wherever rime is used it imposes this characteristic on the verse medium. It is the special nature of blank verse to be "pure," meaning either that it is absolutely heterogeneous in texture, with no group of lines resembling one another more particularly than they resemble all the rest, or that it is absolutely homogeneous, with every line formally equivalent to every other line. Blank verse is sufficiently explained by whichever of these points of view one takes, but rimed verse is not so simple: it demands the recognition of both similarity and difference, and of both at the same time, since their copresence and the tension between them is an active ingredient in the metrical form. A poem like "Lycidas," which seems to be an attempt to compromise these opposite techniques for the sake of the best qualities of each, is more correctly understood as having a unique form, like the hypothetical poem described in the first paragraph of this chapter. It does not fit into any of the three categories under discussion now.

The aggregative forms are what we commonly call "stanzas." They are introduced here under the more technical name in order to draw attention to the chief function which they have in the make-up of poems. They are always to be thought of as indefinitely repeatable: nothing in the forms themselves determines how many of them there are in any given poem. The essential characteristic of the stanza is that it establishes a pattern for this repetition in terms of rime scheme, meter, and the number and length of lines in the unit. Inexperienced readers tend to call any typographically distinct unit within a poem a stanza, whether the unit is identical with others or not, but a subordinate unit, obviously patterned (i.e., not a verse-paragraph) and not repeated in the poem, is correctly known as a "strophe." Wordsworth's "Ode on Intimations of Immortality" is made up of strophes. In odes following the Pindaric tradition, like Wordsworth's, the strophe undergoes its most elaborate development. Each strophe, though a part of the whole, has the formal characteristics of an autonomous poem. This high degree of patterning is appropriate to the extraordinary occasion or theme of the ode, and it can also be used for dramatic effect to convey a sense of internal pressures of thought and emotion which cannot, apparently, be contained within the limits of regular stanza form.

The smallest possible stanza, as a unit of lines bound together by rime, is the couplet; the next smallest is the triplet or tercet. The couplet, however, is so close to being no stanza at all that it should not surprise us when we find it being used in a discursive way, where the content runs on from couplet to couplet without a perceptible break, or where at least the individual couplet is not systematically separated within its context to form a discrete unit. This is the pentameter couplet as Chaucer used it:

A povre wydwe, somdeel stape in age
Was whilom dwellyng in a narwe cotage,

Biside a grove, stondynge in a dale.
This wydwe, of which I telle yow my tale,
Syn thilke day that she was last a wyf,
In pacience ladde a ful symple lyf,
For litel was hir catel and hir rente.
By housbondrie of swich as God hire sente
She foond hirself and eek hir doghtren two.

But it is easy enough for the poet to follow the implication
of this form and break the sense with a grammatical pause at
the end of every two lines, producing the closed or "heroic" couplet. This is a true aggregative form, even though
a series of these couplets is conventionally printed in a
block, without space between the individual units. Because
Dryden and Pope made it almost synonymous with their
own poetic styles, the heroic couplet is better known to
modern readers than the open or running couplet. It is, of
course, a more distinctive form. In a long poem the open
couplet provides a relatively undifferentiated texture,
whereas the heroic couplet is always insisting upon its own
identity. The heroic couplet moves forward in small discrete steps; it makes a chain, the separate links of which remain visible no matter how far it is extended. As the most
circumscribed of the aggregative forms, the heroic couplet
can easily become monotonous in long stretches, but it is
just as receptive to variation as any other form if the poet is
skillful enough. Keats's scornful remark about the poets of
the neoclassical period, that "They sway'd about upon a
rocking horse,/And thought it Pegasus," most certainly
does not apply to someone like Pope. "Easy was the task,"
Keats went on to state, forgetting in his youthful impa-
tience that it is always easy to write bad poetry (the work
from which these quotations come, though it uses an open
couplet form, is quite as bad in its own way as anything
written to recipe by the most bigoted neoclassicist). Nevertheless, the heroic couplet is like all the other traditional
forms in that it confines the poet's subject matter within
regular and predetermined boundaries, thus encouraging a
certain ordonnance or disposition of materials and even,

some would claim, a certain manner of thinking. Here the poet is encouraged to mold his subject matter into precisely articulated units and to develop it through coördination, i.e., through setting side by side elements of equal value or function. The two-line stanza is often balanced, with one line parallel to or answering the other, and a similar balance may occur within the line itself by means of parallel words, phrases, or grammatical structures. Again, the balance may be used for antithesis, where the two elements contrast with each other. The rising and falling motion that Keats objected to is quite marked, but whether it is good or bad cannot be decided a priori. The following characteristic passage from Pope's "Essay on Man" illustrates some of these features:

> The bliss of man (could pride that blessing find)
> Is not to act or think beyond mankind;
> No powers of body or of soul to share,
> But what his nature and his state can bear.
> Why has not man a microscopic eye?
> For this plain reason, man is not a fly.
> Say what the use, were finer optics given,
> T' inspect a mite, not comprehend the heaven?
> Or touch, if tremblingly alive all o'er,
> To smart and agonize at every pore?
> Or quick effluvia darting through the brain,
> Die of a rose in aromatic pain?
> If nature thundered in his opening ears,
> And stunned him with the music of the spheres,
> How would he wish that Heaven had left him still
> The whispering zephyr, and the purling rill?
> Who finds not Providence all good and wise,
> Alike in what it gives, and what it denies?

The first couplet announces the proposition that Pope wants to consider; the second couplet parallels the first by restating the proposition in slightly different terms. The third couplet begins the demonstration with a question and answer, each exactly one line in length, and is followed by a couplet which again serves as a restatement, presenting the rationale for human limitation more specifically and concretely. Then in a series of coördinate examples Pope deals with the sense of touch, smell, and hearing, the last one in a unit of four lines with a balanced two-plus-two structure. The cumulative effect of these examples is very strong, but the demonstration has actually not advanced beyond the point where it started, since none of them adds anything new. The final couplet generalizes upon the lesson suggested by the preceding examples and puts the stamp of *Q.E.D.* on the initial proposition. Pope's argument is entirely theoretical, but so vividly is it stated that it seems like an irrefutable appeal to experience.

One notices a good deal of verbal balancing within the separate lines, for instance (reading down the passage) "act-think," "body-soul," "nature-state," "inspect-comprehend," "mite-heaven," "smart-agonize," "whispering-purling," "zephyr-rill," "good-wise," and "gives-denies." Sometimes only the words are coördinate, sometimes whole phrases or clauses; sometimes the words reinforce each other, and then again they are sometimes antithetical. This habit of thinking —if that is what it is—is characteristic of Pope, and there is no doubt that the heroic couplet form encourages it. But to look upon the heroic couplet as artificially limiting and a handicap to free expression is to mistake the whole nature of poetic form. All poets restrict themselves; it is only a question of what particular restriction to adopt. If the poet accepts a certain form, as Pope did, and works successfully within it, there is no point in speculating about what he might have done without it. He very well might have written nothing at all.

The triplet or tercet, a much less common form than the couplet, occurs in two principal versions: one with consistent rimes (*aaa*, *bbb*, *ccc*, etc.) and one with interlocking rimes (*aba*, *bcb*, *cdc*, etc.). The latter is better known as "terza rima," invented and made famous by Dante in *The Divine Comedy*. Terza rima is a brilliant solution to the problem of getting narrative impetus in a small aggregative form and of smoothing out its usual rather choppy motion.

The central line in each triplet, unrimed with respect to its immediate context, looks ahead toward the next triplet, where it will establish the rime for two further lines. Like a man going down a steep hill who must run in order to keep on his feet, by being always a little off balance the terza rima generates a powerful forward momentum. Though it can go on indefinitely, it can easily be stopped at any time by rounding off one triplet into a quatrain, thus: *aba, bcb, cdc, dede*. In his "Ode to the West Wind" Shelley does something like this, making a kind of super-stanza out of regularly grouped triplets. But in spite of its virtues, terza rima has never been extensively used in English poetry, narrative or otherwise.

The four-line stanza, or quatrain, is a more adaptable form because it gives the poet more to work with. Consequently it exists in a number of typical variations, some of which will be illustrated below. It has the further distinction of being less learned or consciously literary than most of the others: it is the old "common measure" of the English hymn and also the chief stanza form of the popular ballad. In these cases it normally has alternating lines of four and three feet, with the second and fourth lines riming:

There lived a wife at Usher's Well,	*x*
And a wealthy wife was she;	*a*
She had three stout and stalwart sons,	*x*
And sent them o'er the sea.	*a*

The quatrain can be nothing more than two couplets added together:

That which her slender waist confined	*a*
Shall now my joyful temples bind;	*a*
No monarch but would give his crown	*h*
His arms might do what this has done.	*b*
(Edmund Waller)	

Its potentialities are somewhat better realized if the couplets blend into each other:

> Come live with me and be my love,   *a*
> And we will all the pleasures prove   *a*
> That valleys, groves, hills and fields,   *b*
> Woods or steepy mountain yields.   *b*
>   (Christopher Marlowe)

As might be expected, the quatrain also appears with an interlocking rime scheme:

> When lovely woman stoops to folly,   *a*
> And finds too late that men betray,   *b*
> What charm can soothe her melancholy,   *a*
> What art can wash her guilt away?   *b*
>   (Oliver Goldsmith)

By extending the tetrameter line to pentameter the poet can slow down the pace of the stanza, giving it a deliberateness and gravity that accord well with certain kinds of subject matter:

> Beneath those rugged elms, that yew-tree's shade,   *a*
> Where heaves the turf in many a mouldering heap,   *b*
> Each in his narrow cell for ever laid,   *a*
> The rude Forefathers of the hamlet sleep.   *b*

This form, which Gray used so successfully in his "Elegy Written in a Country Church-Yard," is often known as the "elegiac" stanza. Whatever its intrinsic appropriateness to the elegy may be, there is no question that our feeling for this stanza has been permanently affected by its association with Gray's poem, and for that reason a poet who used it now would discover that he had, willy-nilly, given his poem a reminiscent air. In this sense it is possible to say that a form has been used up or exhausted; it continues to exist, but no one who values his originality will adopt it. Blank verse has managed to survive obsolescence better than any other traditional form because it is so plastic, allowing a poet like Robert Frost to purge it of its Miltonic associations and, in effect, create a new form adapted to his own genius. But not even blank verse is endlessly variable, and now in the latter part of the twentieth century we seem to have exhausted its last possibility. After Wallace Stevens and Robert Frost, where can it go? This phenomenon is clearly illustrated by the fate of the quatrain that Tennyson adopted for "In Memoriam":

He is not here; but far away	*a*
The noise of life begins again,	*b*
And ghastly thro' the drizzling rain	*b*
On the bald street breaks the blank day.	*a*

The "sandwich" rime scheme of *abba*, coupled with the short tetrameter lines, is distinctive, so that there would be no mistaking this stanza wherever it occurred. What Tennyson did with it (very inadequately represented by a single quotation) he did at such length and with such authority that he left nothing further to do. Above all, the stanza form was so perfectly assimilated into the tone and atmosphere of the poem that if extracted and used elsewhere it would still carry them along with it. However un-Tennysonian the new poem might be, we would continue to hear in the movement of this quatrain echoes of Tennyson's grief, and if the poet tried especially hard to reanimate the form by giving it an application totally unlike Tennyson's, he would succeed only in calling further attention to its basic incongruity for him. Another famous quatrain of which the same thing might be said is Edward FitzGerald's *Rubáiyát* stanza:

The Wordly Hope men set their Hearts upon	*a*
Turns Ashes—or it prospers; and anon,	*a*
Like Snow upon the Desert's dusty Face	*x*
Lighting a little hour or two—is gone.	*a*

Even more than in Tennyson's stanza, the effect here depends upon a hovering or suspended rime: in the fourth line it arrives with heightened emphasis because it has been twice as long in reaching us, the interval having been extended by an unrimed line. (This is analogous to the musical device known as "suspension," which introduces a temporary discord into the path of an expected harmony.) Like the hedonism which FitzGerald's poem recommends in its content, the stanza form is familiar and at the same time gracefully exotic, an amalgam of such specific nature that we would recognize it wherever we encountered it and would immediately refer it to this prototype.

The next stanza in order of length, the quintain, has five lines riming (usually) *ababb*, an example of which is seen in Donne's "Hymn to God My God, in My Sickness." For some reason this is not a very common stanza—perhaps because it is not symmetrical, perhaps because it has neither the conciseness of the quatrain nor the amplitude of the larger forms. At any rate, the six-line stanza riming *ababcc* is much more often found. Since this sexain unmistakably combines the form of a quatrain with that of a terminal couplet, the tendency has been to reserve its couplet for an epigrammatic close or at least to set it apart in terms of content from the other four lines, thus:

My mind to me a kingdom is,	*a*
Such present joys therein I find	*b*
That it excels all other bliss	*a*
That world affords or grows by kind:	*b*
Though much I want which most would have,	*c*
Yet still my mind forbids to crave.	*c*

(Edward Dyer)

The more characteristic version of the sexain uses a pentameter rather than a tetrameter line (e.g., in Shakespeare's "Venus and Adonis"). Another traditional rime scheme is *aabccb*.

Among the larger forms are three famous stanzas of seven, eight, and nine lines respectively—rime royal, ottava rima, and the Spenserian stanza—each of which has a considerable tradition of its own. They are illustrated below by quotations from the works with which they are often identified:

Agayns his wil, sith it mot nedes be,	a
This Troilus up ros, and faste hym cledde,	b
And in his armes took his lady free	a
An hondred tyme, and on his wey hym spedde;	b
And with swiche voys as though his herte bledde,	b
He seyde, "Farewel, dere herte swete,	c
Ther God us graunte sownde and soone to mete!"	c

(Chaucer, Troilus and Criseyde)

When Newton saw an apple fall, he found	a
In that slight startle from his contemplation—	b
'Tis *said* (for I'll not answer above ground	a
For any sage's creed or calculation)—	b
A mode of proving that the earth turn'd round	a
In a most natural whirl, called "gravitation;"	b
And this is the sole mortal who could grapple,	c
Since Adam, with a fall or with an apple.	c

(Byron, Don Juan)

A lovely Ladie rode him faire beside,	*a*
Upon a lowly Asse more white than snow,	*b*
Yet she much whiter, but the same did hide	*a*
Under a veil, that wimpled was full low,	*b*
And over all a blacke stole she did throw,	*b*
As one that inly mournd: so was she sad,	*c*
And heavie sat upon her palfrey slow;	*b*
Seemed in heart some hidden care she had,	*c*
And by her in a line a milke white lambe she lad.	*c*

(Spenser, The Faerie Queene)

Besides its rime scheme, the Spenserian stanza is distinguished by a closing line which is one foot longer than the rest, the "Alexandrine." This ninth line contributes emphasis, much as the final couplet does in other stanza forms, and ends the stanza with a flourish. By being six feet long instead of five, it allows the poet to vary the placement of the caesura, and the line can be balanced (3:3, 2:2:2) or unbalanced (1:5, 2:4, 4:2, 5:1). Our ear picks out the hexameter as much by its different caesura as by its extra length.

Whether the hexameter line slows down the forward motion of a narrative is a subjective question, but without any doubt it does work to isolate each stanza from the rest by indicating, more obviously than a rime scheme alone could do, where the stanza ends. The Spenserian stanza provides the poet with a very large building block; its amplitude and richness demand an appropriately generous area for display. Yet its reputation for being languid—the fit vehicle of stained-glass displays and all that the Romantic movement meant by "faerie"—is unjustified and derives more from James Thomson than from Edmund Spenser. In Spenser's hands it is an instrument for vigorous narrative and swift, realistic scene-painting.

Another structural feature of more traditional poetry is the refrain, usually a line (but sometimes a word or phrase and sometimes more than one line) which is repeated at fixed intervals throughout the poem. It can be varied, though the tendency is toward exact repetition. The refrain is probably as old as poetry itself, coming from a time when the communal and ritual aspects of the art predominated, and one may guess that it was not at first a mere interpolation as it is now but rather was the very basis of the poem, the remainder of which grew out of it by the process of ornamental variation. However that may be, the refrain is no longer in fashion. Where it occurs, it functions to add an extra dimension of artifice, setting the poem apart still more clearly from ordinary uses of language. It also contributes to the thematic or tonal unity of a poem, and its regular occurrence is a way of marking off structural divisions. By remaining unchanged, the refrain acts to keep the poem always circling back upon itself; even a narrative poem like Tennyson's "The Lady of Shalott," which has a varied refrain, derives a certain static, pictorial quality from this repeated element.

With the third major category, that of integral forms, we leave behind the concept of building blocks. An integral form is a group of requirements or directions that apply to the entire poem. It gives the poet, in advance of composition, a precisely drawn outline which he must fill and which he is not supposed to alter. His job is then to make these conditions acceptable to the reader by writing so skillfully that they seem to be not restraints on his freedom but the very outward guise that his freedom demanded to assume. The reader is still conscious of the independent existence of the form as a form, but he cannot find any gap between the form and what it contains nor any evidence that the form abridged or altered what the poet wanted to say. The integral form has something of the nature and the attractiveness of a verbal game, like anagrams, crossword puzzles, palindromes, and word squares. But in these the difficulty is everything; there is no such thing as a better or a worse solution because normally there is only one solution possible. The difficulty of an integral form, on the other hand, is an invitation to the poet to transcend it if he can; if he responds well to his opportunity, the form shrinks in importance, valuable now not for itself but for what it challenged —and allowed—him to do.

One group of integral forms in English verse was borrowed from the French and includes such things as the rondeau, triolet, ballade, villanelle, and sestina. The French forms have never been widely adopted by English poets, however, and with a few exceptions their use has been restricted to that special genre known as *vers de société*. Another group is comprised of eccentric minor forms like the clerihew and the cinquain. What remains are two integral forms that have nothing at all in common except their popularity, the limerick and the sonnet. It would be hard to find a more thorough contrast: the limerick— humorous, objective, irreverent, often bawdy, a true folk poetry with an almost exclusively oral tradition (though confined to the educated ranks of society), and the sonnet —serious, personal, high-minded, deeply conservative in its attitudes, and from its origins to the present day a self-consciously literary form, flourishing in the court, the bower, and the study. Of these the limerick poses the more challenging technical problems, but its content is negligible. Sonnet techniques have in general followed two parallel traditions, the so-called "Shakespearian" and the Petrarchan or

Italian. These forms organize the 14 lines of the sonnet in distinctive ways, as the following examples show:

Let me not to the marriage of true minds	*a*
Admit impediments. Love is not love	*b*
Which alters when it alteration finds,	*a*
Or bends with the remover to remove.	*b*
O no, it is an ever-fixèd mark	*c*
That looks on tempests and is never shaken;	*d*
It is the star to every wandering bark,	*c*
Whose worth's unknown, although his height be taken.	*d*
Love's not Time's fool, though rosy lips and cheeks	*e*
Within his bending sickle's compass come;	*f*
Love alters not with his brief hours and weeks,	*e*
But bears it out even to the edge of doom.	*f*
If this be error and upon me proved,	*g*
I never writ, nor no man ever loved.	*g*

Much have I travell'd in the realms of gold,	*a*
And many goodly states and kingdoms seen;	*b*
Round many western islands have I been	*b*
Which bards in fealty to Apollo hold.	*a*
Oft of one wide expanse had I been told	*a*
That deep-brow'd Homer ruled as his demesne;	*b*
Yet did I never breathe its pure serene	*b*
Till I heard Chapman speak out loud and bold:	*a*
Then felt I like some watcher of the skies	*c*
When a new planet swims into his ken;	*d*
Or like stout Cortez when with eagle eyes	*c*
He star'd at the Pacific—and all his men	*d*
Look'd at each other with a wild surmise—	*c*
Silent, upon a peak in Darien.	*d*

The Shakespearean form is essentially three quatrains with a concluding couplet, and it encourages the poet to organize his material accordingly. In the example here, Shakespeare announces his theme with the first quatrain, using generalized and rather abstract language. The key ideas of altering and removing are then embodied concretely in two meta-phors, each of which occupies exactly four lines. The couplet which ends the sonnet is another general statement; it refers to all that has been said above, but is formally distinct, almost epigrammatic. The Petrarchan form has a two-part structure, with the break or turn coming just a little past the middle point. Keats's discovery of Chapman is presented through an allegory in one unified section of eight lines (the octave). The sensation of discovery, which for Keats is a more remarkable thing even than the fact of discovery, is then developed in a climactic section of six lines (the sestet). Keats uses one of the two alternative rime schemes for the Petrarchan sestet; the other is *cdecde.* In the Shakespearean form the final couplet stands apart from the rest of the sonnet, but since it is only two lines long, it has to assert itself with more than ordinary force if it is to justify its separation. Hence the tendency to epigram. In the Petrarchan form the concluding sestet is neither so isolated nor so restricted in its content; having six lines instead of two, the poet can afford to be somewhat expansive. Since the octave often presents a problem or asks a question to which the sestet responds, the two sections are related as the rise and fall of a wave or the complication and denouement of a story. Hence the measured, almost deliberate movement. Because it uses fewer rimes and weaves them together in a more complex manner than the Shakespearean sonnet does, the Petrarchan impresses an English reader as being rather studied. However literary its true origins may be, the Shakespearean smells less of the lamp. It often conveys the air (for better or worse) of having been improvised; there is a happiness in its success that cannot altogether be separated from its potential for failure. It is a monument to the English habit of making-do, so baffling to the more punctilious and systematic European mind.

Such is the common view of these sonnet forms, and within limits it is sound enough. Unfortunately it does not throw much light on the great diversity which one encounters in looking back through the history of the sonnet. The two forms illustrated here are more in the nature of

ideal models than of predominant types, since poets have
constantly played variations on them ever since the sonnet
was domesticated in England. Shakespeare himself, while he
used the rime scheme that bears his name, by no means always developed his material to accord with the grouping of
three quatrains plus a couplet. Sidney used a Petrarchan
octave with a Shakespearean sestet; Spenser invented his
own rime scheme of *ababbcbccdcdee;* and Milton shifted
the balance of the form by breaking the sestet from the
octave within the ninth line, instead of at the end of the
eighth. There have been "sonnets" with more than 14 lines,
sonnets using only two rimes, sonnets linked with sonnets to
form continuous poems, and a great many idiosyncratic
rime schemes, of which Shelley's "Ozymandias" is a good
example. It seems almost as though poets were as eager to
escape from the tradition as they were to accept it and draw
upon it.

Indeed, in the latter part of the twentieth century they
have escaped—largely by ceasing to write sonnets. When
one asks what this apparently isolated event means, one begins to see that it is connected on the most fundamental
level with the whole question of form in poetry, which, in
spite of the attention given it earlier in this chapter, is still
far from being either settled or exhausted. There is not
space now for more than a brief general review, but perhaps
that will be of some help as a way of getting the question
into focus again.

It is axiomatic that there is no such thing as a poem
without its form. That form, as the opening paragraph of
this chapter attempted to show, may evolve out of the process of composition itself, subject only to pressures inherent
within that particular set of circumstances. Its resemblance
then to the form of any other poem would be a mere coincidence, and an unlikely one. Many poems are written in
just this way (for example, Theodore Roethke's "A Light
Breather," quoted in Chapter 7). We are pleased to see, in
analyzing such a poem, that its form plays an organic role in
the over-all design and that we find nothing arbitrary or inexplicable. Yet there are many poems written in such a way as

to suggest that the exact opposite of this process occurred: the poet chose a form in advance and then filled it as appropriately as he could. We know that something like this must have happened, because we can see the same form in poems by other poets; it has an independent existence as part of a tradition. The borrowing must have been deliberate.

On the face of it, it seems strange that any poet would willingly barter away his artistic freedom for the sake of a ready-made solution to the problem of form. Artistic freedom, however, is not a simple thing. The poet who devises his own stanza form—is he not just as restricted as the poet who adopts a traditional one? Does he not confront the same essential task, which is that of making this form, wherever derived, completely functional? How much real freedom did Keats gain for himself when he devised his own stanza form for the "Ode to a Nightingale"? Everything said about traditional stanza forms applies also here, except perhaps that the *first* stanza composed in the new form may be (though it does not have to) a kind of unique outgrowth of internal pressures. But once externalized and set up as a rule to be followed, the new form serves as a "tradition" for the rest of the poem, which has to live up to it as best it can. We may also question whether there is any consistent difference in coerciveness among the various traditional forms. Blank verse appears to offer the greatest latitude to a poet, but it is easy to imagine that a poet writing in blank verse would find himself more inhibited by the ghost of Milton than another poet, writing a sonnet, by the ghosts of Petrarch and Shakespeare. The history of Keats's struggle with blank verse suggests this. We are naturally attracted by the picture of a poet hammering out his own form on the anvil of his artistic conscience, but this may derive from nothing more than our romantic interest in self-expression, the real facts being quite otherwise. In the functional sense, certainly, all good poetic forms are integral. They begin and end with the poem itself, and they are tested by their "fit." The tailor-made and the ready-made do the same kind of job.

Nevertheless, the traditional forms do have a special

role: they serve to bind poets together in a common enterprise. Like hereditary titles, they are means by which individuals can, while still preserving their individuality, both accept and assert their affiliation with a time-honored structure that transcends the merely individual. And as it is a structure of values, so too is the act of affiliation a value judgment. Nobody forces a poet to write a sonnet; he does it because he wants to, and he wants to because he finds in the sonnet form and its tradition something that attracts him. "I place my vote *here*," he says. The reader who recognizes that the form he sees is a traditional one completes the process by calling to his mind the relevant associations with Petrarch, Shakespeare, Sidney, Milton, Wordsworth, or whatever specific portion of the sonnet tradition is involved. In a sense this poet is competing with the older ones, but he is also joining them: they are in it together. Such is one of the means by which the enormous diversity of English poetry is brought into order.

"The spirit moves, / Yet stays. . . ." Neither traditional order nor individual genius is a value unto itself. They are reciprocal, interdependent. We cannot even imagine the act by which the first poem in human history was written. Though each particular poem contains within it the whole art of poetry (the intention to use language as an end in itself) and thus in a sense creates that art all over again by what it does, every such poem silently acknowledges the prior existence of *poetry* as embodied in the poetic tradition. Its originality has meaning only through implicit reference to tradition. Poets may abandon a certain form because it is so encrusted with precedent that they feel themselves unable to say anything new with it; it has become merely traditional and nothing more. It is not now, as we say, a "living" tradition. But this only means that the form is not at the forward, growing edge of the body of poetry. What it could add to the tradition, it has added. Its value has not diminished in the least with time, and it contributes still to the life of this art—indirectly, now—by its example. The solid achievement of the past is the best guarantee of the future.

10·
The Art of
Interpretation

In 1929 the English psychologist and aesthetician
I. A. Richards published a book called *Practical Criticism*, in
which he described a series of experiments he had been con-
ducting among his students at Cambridge University. What
he had done was to give them each week a group of poems,
unidentified by author or title, and ask that their written
comments on this material be brought to the next class
meeting and handed in. Neither background information on
the poems nor directions on how to treat them were provided, because the object was to obtain as far as possible a
direct and uncontaminated response from the students, who
were, however, given ample time to read as carefully as
they wished. The results were shocking. Richards' experiment proved that even fairly sophisticated readers—most of
his subjects were undergraduate English majors—could not
be trusted to read poetry intelligently when left to their
own devices. Not only did they produce widely varying interpretations and judgments of value, which was perhaps to
be expected, but all too often they failed to make ordinary
prose sense out of what they read. In other circumstances
they might have concealed their trouble by repeating conventional opinions borrowed from textbooks or lecture
notes; here they could not, and so they floundered.

Many critics have pointed out that Richards' experimental conditions were abnormal, since knowledge of the

title, author, and historical context of a poem is a standard ingredient of the reader's experience—and, what is more, a legitimate one. It might also be said that he discovered nothing really new; there have always been at least a few teachers who took the pains to find out how poorly their students read what was assigned to them and whose academic careers were devoted to fostering the better understanding of literary texts. But *Practical Criticism* remains an impressive and sobering work. And it is a classic of its kind, one of the documents that helped define the twentieth-century attitude toward poetry. Thanks in some measure to Richards, we take it for granted that poems need to be analyzed and that every aspect of the reader's response to a poem should be referable to specific features in its text. The emphasis is on meaning; "close reading," or explication, is now the standard approach to poetry. So ingrained has all this become that we have to make an effort of imagination to realize how new it is, relatively speaking. In earlier periods it never occurred to anyone that there might be a regular problem in understanding poetry and that even simple poems might require interpretation before they could be properly appreciated. For many centuries a characteristic document was some form or other of the *ars poetica*, advising poets how to write; now of course it is the textbook, teaching readers how to read. Whether the abilities of readers have actually changed between the two periods is not certain; the evidence is scanty and ambiguous. There is no doubt, though, that conceptions of the nature of poetry have changed radically, and that the modern emphasis on analytical reading is in part an outgrowth of this change—in other words, what we think a poem is determines how we think it should be handled. Even if readers were generally more proficient than they seem to be, we would insist on the importance of training in the art of interpretation.

This chapter uses the somewhat old-fashioned term "interpretation" instead of the more current "explication" because an explication is properly a formal written exercise, meant to be read by others. While the writing of explications is a good academic discipline (long before it became popular in this country the French had adopted it on a national scale for their schools), it is surely not the end for which poems are composed. Our culture is not yet so institutionalized that we can afford to forget the person who reads by himself for his own enjoyment and who has no need to write anything in order to ratify his claim to understanding. Furthermore, inasmuch as an explication is a complete and organized whole, it tends to approach the status of a work of art, with an independent claim to value and with demands on our attention that sometimes have little to do with its ostensible subject. More than one poor poem has given rise to a brilliant explication. Because it is less formalized, interpretation is less likely to become an autonomous activity. If it is an art (as the title of this chapter suggests) it is a very special kind of art, since its aim is directed outward toward the poem. Self-effacing and utilitarian, it exists to shed light upon the work of someone else. But it is not a science: its rules are approximate and unsystematic, they vary according to circumstances, and they are not capable of general proof.

Where do the rules of interpretation come from? Certainly they do not come from any single authority, like a chief critic or a senate of letters or a national academy. The English-speaking world has never recognized such a function, and even in places where it has been tried, it has seldom prevailed for long over the natural anarchy of human opinion. Rather, the rules are developed through trial and error by ordinary intelligent readers as they confront typical problems of interpretation in their reading. Whatever method produces valid results is duly recognized as worthy of adoption for future use, but it takes a great many successful applications of a given method to turn it into anything like a rule. The law of art, it has been said, is all case law: it is a composite of decisions reached through the judgment of particular issues by persons whose immediate intention was nothing more than to resolve what they saw before them. By combining a large number of these cases according to the features they have in common, we can see a pattern of judgment at work, and this pattern can then be used as a guide for future decisions. In this sense alone can we speak of "laws" and "rules." At any moment, however, a case may arise which demands the creation of a new solution—hence precedent cannot be absolutely relied upon. Interpretation is an authentic art in being indeterminate or open-ended, never excluding the possibility of a fresh creation.

A list of basic rules is given below. It will be noted that they are not all of a kind: some of them are, so to speak, primary, having to do with the status or nature of the material which the reader works upon, and some are secondary—practical rules or rules of thumb, having to do with the way a reader proceeds in his job of interpretation. That concepts about the nature of poetry and procedures of treating it are intimately related has already been pointed out.

1. *A good poem stands on its own feet.* Or in the words of Coleridge quoted in Chapter 3, "nothing can permanently please, which does not contain in itself the reason why it is so, and not otherwise." Consequently the poem is both the object and the source of the reader's interpretation. To say that the poem is the "source" of the reader's interpretation does not mean that everything he needs to know is in the poem itself. This is sometimes the case, but often it is not, especially when the poetry is full of allusions or takes for granted some external system of thought with which the reader may not be familiar. Sometimes he may have to do a good deal of research merely to bring himself up to the point where he can begin his interpretation, having found it necessary to determine first and in its most literal sense what the poet is saying, line by line. For this purpose, every help that he can get is legitimate. Where the poem as the source of his interpretation comes in is when this information is tested—as it must be—for relevance. The only possible standard here is the poem itself. During the earlier stages of this testing it may happen that the poem itself, for the particular reader, is not well enough defined to give him an answer; he must then suspend judgment until more evidence has accumulated (this process is further de-

cribed in number 5, below). In the end, however, his understanding of what the poem is provides the standard by
which he reviews and judges his evidence. The intrinsic
value of a piece of information means nothing if it is determined that the information has no role in the design of the
poem. The design of a good poem will make its integrity
abundantly clear.

2. *A good poem is internally consistent.* In effect, this
rule is saying that the design of a poem should not conflict
with itself. If the poem contains antithetical or divergent
elements, they should be subordinated to a single over-all
design, and the reader's job is to discover their function
within this design and hence their excuse for being. In all
cases, the reader must assume that the poem has *one* main
purpose or point, something which transforms the normally
centrifugal force of its various parts and holds them to its
center. It may turn out in the end that the poem has a defective design, but he cannot discover this unless he first begins his interpretation with the contrary assumption (see
number 5, below).

3. *The whole poem means more than any of its parts.*
This rule may look superfluous, but it is still violated all too
often by readers who seize upon a phrase or a line that strikes
their fancy and then proceed to interpret the whole poem
in that light, regardless of the damage which they cause to
the rest of it.

4. *The whole poem means more than all of its parts.*
This rule, a further development of the one above, could also
be stated thus: the whole poem makes the parts of the poem,
rather than the parts the whole. A "part" is simply non-
existent, artistically speaking, without a larger context to
give it a function. The part both contributes value to and
draws value from the whole, so that their relationship is reciprocal, and yet the relationship is not exactly a *quid pro
quo*, for the values exchanged are somewhat different.
What an arm gives to a body is not the same thing as what
the body gives to an arm; without its arm a body would be
maimed, but without its body an arm would be nothing.
The sum of many nothings is still nothing. If this seems too

metaphysical, we can think of the familiar story about the blind men and the elephant, the nature of which they attempted to guess by feeling its parts. The man who felt a leg, for instance, and reasoned that the elephant is like a tree, not only misconceived the nature of the beast but also that of the part he was feeling. In order to understand what the leg really was, he would have had to know about the elephant as an integral whole—manifestly an impossible goal for him. But we may wonder how the reader of a poem is expected to understand the whole poem first, in order to understand its parts. This seems no less impossible. The answer is given under the next rule.

5. *The reader should judge the parts of a poem on the basis of hypotheses about the whole.* Practically speaking, this means that he should sit down and read the poem all the way through at first, without stopping to puzzle over things that he does not understand. Unless the poem is totally enigmatic, he will get a general notion of its meaning. This notion he can frame as a hypothesis, to be tested against the parts of the poem. If it fails to account satisfactorily for the parts, it must be discarded and replaced by another. In the course of doing this, the reader will begin to accumulate insights into the over-all design of the poem, assisted by—and assisting—his better understanding of the parts. What he is looking for is the best possible explanation: one that accounts for everything in the most economical manner (see number 6, below). But at no point prior to his final interpretation is the reader dealing with anything other than hypotheses. If he remembers this fact he will be less reluctant to stop and discard an interpretation that is losing its momentum or running into difficulty. The process is something like building a footbridge across a chasm, if we can imagine that the builder puts one plank down, steps upon it, puts another down, steps upon it, and so forth until he reaches the other side, building the bridge underneath himself at the same time as he uses the bridge—or using the bridge at the same time as he builds it. He performs a bit of magic, an act of levitation, very much like that which the poet performs in order to write the poem.

6. *The easiest interpretation is usually the best.* Scientists, mathematicians, and chess players (they are often represented in the same person) place a high value on what is called an "elegant" solution to a problem. Within the range of possible solutions there is one which stands out above the rest because it uses resources imaginatively, avoids complications, goes straight to the heart of the problem, and above all does so with the least amount of effort. It has a kind of flair or grace, a real aesthetic quality, which is almost as important as the fact that it works. Surely the interpretation of poetry is no less an art than a game of chess or the proof of a theorem. Since it is an art, however, there is no absolute objective standard of elegance. The closest thing to such a standard is the length of an interpretation (here we must think of it as being written down). Of two interpretations which reach the same conclusion, the shorter is almost always the better, assuming that the length of the other one is due mainly to its uneconomical use of means and not to simple wordiness. But interpretations which differ significantly in their methods seldom reach the "same" conclusion, nor is a reader often able to survey two or more complete interpretations at leisure and pick the one which pleases him most. The situation which is more likely to confront him is that of two alternatives leading in apparently different directions toward goals that he cannot yet foresee. Somehow he must choose between them before going ahead. By choosing the easier of these he stands a better chance of staying on a straight course, for complications at early stages tend to produce even more complications at later ones; simplicity, once abandoned, it hard to recover. When the interpretation begins to labor and its parts to proliferate like the epicycles of Ptolemaic cosmology, this is a danger signal—he should stop where he is and consider revising his whole approach while he still can do so. Hence simplicity or elegance, an aesthetic quality in itself, often serves as a kind of touchstone for other qualities, and though its presence does not guarantee correctness in an interpretation, its absence creates the suspicion, often justified, that something very fundamental has gone wrong.

7. *A poem and its interpretation are different things*. No one, of course, would make the primitive error of mistaking an interpretation for the poem it refers to. But a great many readers assume that an interpretation ought somehow to be congruent with the poem, imitating its formal characteristics in the medium of discursive prose. Thus an interpretation is made to begin where and as the poem begins, and to follow the poem in the arrangement and proportions of its own content. At worst, this produces a myopic, line-by-line reading which is almost useless as a means of understanding what the poet was up to, since it surrounds his design with a thicket of separate unevaluated facts, no one of which is manifestly more significant than any other one. Even though he must give the strictest possible attention to the poet's design, the reader must accept and discharge the responsibilities of his own job, which are of a very different kind. He may choose to omit certain details; he may repeat where the poem does not; he may expand or contract; he may skip back and forth; he may separate what the poem has joined and join what the poem has separated. All of this is not with the object of fashioning his own work of art to compete with the poem, however much he hopes to achieve a certain elegance in his results, but with the object of doing justice to the poem in the only way he can. He has no thought of substituting the interpretation for the poem. Nor is the interpretation the "meaning" of the poem in the usual sense of this term, where a word refers to an object or stands for an idea that can be adequately represented by other words. The poet did not mean to say what the reader says in his interpretation: he meant to say what *he* said. Ultimately there is no substitute for the exact words of the poem.

8. *A good poem cannot be exhausted*. An ambitious reader will attempt to get everything out of a poem that he can. This aim is entirely proper and worth emulating. But the reader should bear in mind that a poem is not a container, or if it is one, it is a container that is bigger on the inside than it is on the outside. There never is a point at which a reader can safely claim that a poem has been com-

pletely interpreted, leaving nothing further to be said about it. If at the moment he has nothing more to say, someone else may, and even he himself, coming back to the poem after an interval during which he has substantially forgotten it, may very well discover new insights that had escaped him before. Such is the life of poetry, such its value. Inasmuch as real completeness is an unattainable illusion, the reader ought to consider the desirability of stopping short of even what he knows can be achieved, deliberately omitting from his interpretation things which might be included. He will thus avoid the danger of obscuring his main points and at the same time enhance the elegance of his work. The modern architectural rule, "less is more," has some relevance to the interpretation of poetry. It is a mark of the reader's skill to know when to stop, granted that he also knows how to continue.

9. *Always read as literally as possible.* Essentially, this rule is contained within number 6, above, but the problem it refers to is important enough to receive special treatment. Acting on the premise that all poems are obscure and contain hidden meanings, many readers will begin an interpretation by virtually ignoring the ordinary prose sense of the words that they see in favor of cumbersome hypotheses involving metaphor, symbolism, allegory, and other devices for complicating poetic design, and they do this without first taking into account whether such a method of attack seems appropriate to the work under consideration, which may indeed be quite simple and straightforward. All a priori notions of poetic design are dangerous, the art of poetry being what it is. One has to feel one's way into the design of a poem, and suspend judgment on it as long as possible. The safest way of doing so is to take words at their face value until there appears to be good reason for taking them otherwise. Nor should one scorn to use so humble an aid as the dictionary. R. P. Blackmur, in a now classic essay on Wallace Stevens, showed how the difficulty of that poet could be systematically reduced when one did the obvious thing and looked up all the unusual or puzzling words that one encountered. In a way Blackmur's discovery is itself less

notable than the fact that it came as such a revelation to the critical world. And, as most teachers of poetry would agree, it continues to need revealing.

10. *Accept all the help that the poet himself offers.* This final rule does not suggest that the poet will very often interpret his own poem, whether formally or in remarks reported by others. Naturally, if he does so, his views must be treated with respect, but they should not automatically be given the weight of authority.* It sometimes happens that a poet will misunderstand the true significance of his own poem; he may also make casual or deliberately misleading statements about it, either because his own attitudes toward it are ambivalent or because he feels that a red herring or two drawn across the trail is no more than most critics deserve. To paraphrase D. H. Lawrence: trust the poem, not the poet. But a good deal of help can be built into a poem —names, dedications, epigraphs, titles, and explanatory notes are some of the devices used. They should all be taken seriously. An epigraph, for example, may look like a bit of harmless pedantry, especially if it is in a foreign language and apparently intended to go over the head of the average reader. Yet the epigraph from Dante's *Inferno* which introduces "The Love Song of J. Alfred Prufrock" is of considerable help in establishing the view that Eliot himself takes toward his hero and that we are supposed to share (this epigraph and the title—partially explicated in Chapter 2—are the only non-dramatic elements in the poem, the only occasions when the author intrudes as such). Among other things, the epigraph functions to reveal that for Eliot, Prufrock is not merely the rather pathetic aging *bon vivant* whom we see and sympathize with, but in some deeper spiritual sense truly a damned soul; his is a voice from hell. If there are disparities between Eliot's hell and Dante's, as between Prufrock himself and Dante's Count Guido da Montefeltro, these too are food for thought. It is well to remem-

---

* There is, of course, a sense in which the *poem* offers help, but this is so much the normal state of affairs that it hardly needs to be commented upon. It has been at least implied on every page of this book so far.

ber, however, that such helps are not necessarily self-interpreting. The dedication "To Christ Our Lord" which Hopkins inserted under the title of "The Windhover" has served to confuse a good many readers, and one wonders whether the sonnet would have generated so much desperate ingenuity if the dedication had silently been left off.

The application of these rules to specific cases depends upon the individual reader, whose ability to apply them is just as important as his knowledge of what they are. His ability, in turn, depends upon intelligence, sensitivity, and experience—which no external help like a book on poetry can hope to provide for him. But there is a third requisite to the art of interpretation, one that may legitimately be urged here, namely, his willingness to use the rules. The best qualified reader will fail as completely as the worst if some prejudice or blindness, some wayward habit of mind, interposes between the rules which he has learned in theory and the poem which he has to interpret in fact. I. A. Richards dealt extensively with these obstacles to interpretation in *Practical Criticism*. Much of what he said is still of great value and ought to be read in the original context; this chapter will therefore take a different approach by reducing the whole problem to a simple case of divergence from a norm in either of two opposite directions. There are, on the one hand, the people who don't want to read any meaning into a poem, and on the other, the people who want to read too much meaning into a poem. Together they embody the greatest single obstacle to the understanding of poetry; if they themselves are beyond cure, as unhappily they often seem to be, their example can at least be held up for the edification of others.

The first group includes many philistines, but it also includes many otherwise intelligent persons; what they have in common is an inability to believe that poetry has anything of value to say. They are often willing to concede its value on other grounds, however. One of their characteristic statements runs like this: "I don't think it's right to tear a poem all apart and analyze the beauty out of it; a poem isn't a puzzle, it's supposed to have *sound* and *feeling*; I enjoy a poem by listening to the sound of it—it carries me away." The obvious answer to this is that sound, purely as sound, can be furnished better by nursery rimes and nonsense verses than by serious poems, since they have less meaning to interfere with it. For that matter, why should it have to be the sound of words? Why not the sound of raindrops or of bird song? In what respect is poetry any different from them? As for the consoling or removing power of poetry, the best comment on that was made by a poet himself:

> Oh many a peer of England brews
> Livelier liquor than the Muse,
> And malt does more than Milton can
> To justify God's ways to man.
> Ale, man, ale's the stuff to drink
> For fellows whom it hurts to think. . . .

Housman saw the essential point, which is that the value of poetry must be something peculiar to it, something unobtainable in any other way. The first obligation of a person who holds the view described above is to show on what grounds he can discriminate between the sensory pleasure afforded by poetry and that afforded by other causes—ale, perfume, sunsets, a kiss, the taste of apple pie, the gleam of polished silver—the potentialities are enormous and the dangers equally so. It is hard to see how such a discrimination could be made without invoking the power of poetry to carry meaning (although Housman tried to do so in his published criticism). This is not to say that the meaning, abstracted from the poem and paraphrased, is itself the value; the value is the meaning *in* the words, and the words cannot be disregarded. But it is futile, if tempting, to demolish the "pure sound" argument in this way, since it is not rational to begin with. The prejudice against meaning is best treated by therapy, not debate. The reader who is thus prejudiced must be induced to broaden and deepen his experience of poetry, and must be allowed to see what meaning others get out of poetry. If this does not open his eyes, then nothing else is likely to.

Another group is composed of the persons who believe that every reader's interpretation of a poem is equally correct. "That's the way it seems to me," they will say, "and who has the authority to tell me I'm wrong? Isn't it all just a matter of opinion anyway?" Whether they realize it or not, these anarchists of opinion are in the same camp with the advocates of "pure sound," except that they have gone a step further by denying the basis of meaning altogether. Meaning is a social phenomenon, made possible by a tacit understanding among the speakers of a language that linguistic signs will be used in limited ways. These uses have a coercive force: when two persons agree on a meaning, it is not merely a matter of politeness or an accidental coincidence of opinion, but a matter of their jointly recognizing an obligation which language, so constituted, places upon them. If words can be put to any kind of use that a person chooses, then meaning as we know it disappears. But again we are dealing with a prejudice, not a reasoned attitude. Without exception these persons are quite hard-headed about their own everyday speech, and it is only poetry which brings out the other side of their nature. The prejudice has complex roots, and they are not always the same in every such person. Part of it comes from an assumption that poetry has so little to say in any case that argument about it is irrelevant; part from resentment against professional critics and other such authorities for attempting to impose sophisticated interpretations on what is felt to be clear and simple material; part from a notion that poetry uses a special language which is inherently not susceptible of firm definition; part from a quasi-religious belief in an "inner voice" which tells one what is true and what not; and part from an obscure sense of the genuine aesthetic predicament which is summarized in the old statement that there is no arguing about tastes. Only the last of these merits serious attention here. As Immanuel Kant pointed out long ago, people may say that there is no arguing about tastes, but they continue arguing nevertheless, and this fact is surely significant. Their behavior testifies to their assumption that arguing is not, after all, pointless—there is *something* to argue about, a core of meaning which is accessible to agreement. An anarchist of opinion is no less eager than anyone else to bring others around to his own way of thinking, and why should he want to do so unless he felt that somehow, in an objective and not a private sense, he is right? Hence in answer to him one would first show that his own practice contradicts his theory. Then one would show that he is falsifying the problem by assuming that the only alternatives are critical anarchy and critical tyranny. His opponents do not claim either that conclusions about poetry can be proved in a logical sense or that meaning in poetry can be determined without ambiguity. But they do not see in this fact any warrant for rushing to the extreme of saying that no rational discussion of poetry is possible and that meaning in poetry is not determinable at all. The conditions that apply to the interpretation of poetry may be uncomfortable to live with and incapable of allowing final satisfaction; they do, however, permit a great deal of free activity of just the sort which the anarchist would find valuable if he could bring himself to abandon his rigid critical posture.

At the opposite extreme from these two closely related groups are the persons who joyfully accept what they take to be the conditions of interpretation and proceed to read far more meaning into everything than it will comfortably bear. They can be termed "allegorizers," since the usual outcome of their efforts is to convert all poems into allegories. This they do by assuming that all meaning in poetry is "deep," i.e., the words of a poem never mean what they seem to mean on the surface, literally, but serve only to point toward something hidden which the reader is supposed to divine if he can. Nothing is merely itself; everything stands for something. Although the allegorizers sincerely intend to do justice to poetry, their effect on it is disastrous, for they obliterate the very differences between poems which the poets themselves labored so hard to achieve. As a result, there are many kinds of subject matter but only one design. And this leveling is no compliment to allegory—if "Mary Had a Little Lamb" gets the same treatment as *The Divine Comedy*, Dante is the loser. It is only fair to add that the allegorizers take their cue from other persons; they do not form the habit spontaneously. Teachers, fellow students, or professional critics set the example, either by actually committing these excesses themselves or by failing to make clear enough the difference between a reading that is out-and-out allegorical and one that is only subtle and deeply probing.

A class of college students was once asked, apropos of Hardy's "The Missed Train," to answer in writing the simple question, "What happened?" (Simple questions are usually the most diagnostic kind.) Among the numerous inaccurate answers was the following:

> "Once this man was young and gay, living a life of happiness and fascination with the woman he loved. Quite unexpectedly, she died, and he found himself at a sort of stopping point—a junction—in life. He had never really been aware that such gloom and despair existed. For years [afterward] he lived in the past with his memories of her, and in his dreams he found his consolation. Now he has forgotten many of the details of his lover and their life together because of a great span of years."

The text of the poem (pp. 107–8) shows clearly enough what happened: a man, returning from a rendezvous with the woman he loved, missed his train and was forced to stay over at an inn, where he spent the night dreaming of her. But for the student "train" meant only one thing: the journey of life. Everything else followed consistently from the allegorical reading, although a more perceptive student might still have salvaged some relevant meaning from the conclusion of the poem.

When challenged on his mistake, such a person will often change sides and take the anarchist position that his interpretation is just as good as anyone else's because a poem means only what the reader wants it to mean. He can best be answered by showing him, in the spirit of rule No. 6, that his interpretation is unnecessarily complex and that the poem works better without the allegory.

Some non-allegorical poems invite this treatment more than others do, especially those which contain imagery with familiar allegorical associations. It is easy to guess how a certain kind of reader would react to the ballad of Sir Patrick Spence:

> The king sits in Dumferling toune,
>   Drinking the blude-reid wine:
> "O whar will I get guid sailor,
>   To sail this schip of mine?"

> Up and spak an eldern knicht,
>   Sat at the kings richt kne:
> "Sir Patrick Spence is the best sailor
>   That sails upon the se."

> The king has written a braid letter,
>   And signd it wi his hand,
> And sent it to Sir Patrick Spence,
>   Was walking on the sand.

> The first line that Sir Patrick red,
>   A loud lauch lauched he;
> The next line that Sir Patrick red,
>   The teir blinded his ee.

> "O wha is this has don this deid,
>   This ill deid don to me,
> To send me out this time o' the yeir,
>   To sail upon the se!

> "Mak hast, mak haste, my mirry men all,
>   Our guid schip sails the morne:"
> "O say na sae, my master deir,
>   For I feir a deadlie storme.

"Late late yestreen I saw the new moone,
  Wi the auld moone in hir arme,
And I feir, I feir, my deir master,
  That we will cum to harme."

O our Scots nobles wer richt laith
  To weet their cork-heild schoone;
Bot lang owre a' the play wer playd,
  Thair hats they swam aboone.

O lang, lang may their ladies sit,
  Wi thair fans into their hand,
Or eir they see Sir Patrick Spence
  Cum sailing to the land.

O lang, lang may the ladies stand,
  Wi thair gold kems in their hair,
Waiting for thair ain deir lords,
  For they'll se thame na mair.

Haf owre, haf owre to Aberdour,
  It's fiftie fadom deip,
And thair lies guid Sir Patrick Spence,
  Wi the Scots lords at his feit.

"Blood-red wine? A symbol of sacrifice, of course. The king is a father-figure, a divine surrogate, and Sir Patrick is meant to be understood as Christ his son, who gives his life for others in an adventure known to be doomed from the start. Notice that he is betrayed (by an 'eldern knicht'—Judas) and that he is accompanied by a group of disciples who at the crucial moment are loath to endanger themselves with him." The fact that this reading is inconsistent with the story of Christ and that, additionally, it makes no real sense out of the poem does not bother the bemused interpreter. The most probable explanation of the wine—that "blude-reid" is a conventional epithet like Homer's "wine-dark sea," and that the king was sitting around at his ease drinking wine because, to the anonymous author and his audience, this is what kings are supposed to do—seems too prosaic by far.*

But no poem is immune. We might have thought that William Carlos Williams' "This Is Just to Say," with its matter-of-fact rendering of a domestic situation, would be the least likely candidate imaginable for an allegorical interpretation, and yet this is what a modern critic found to say about it:

> "I have always remembered an extreme example of Dr. Williams' art, the little poem about the plums which he takes from the icebox, and it was not till beginning this essay that I realized that the pristine 'life' of the plums was doubly negated by the refrigeration and the epicurean joy of their destroyer: the poet. The curious irony was that precisely that which preserved them and increased the deliciousness of their perfection (the refrigeration) contained in its essence the sensuous quality most closely associated with death: coldness. So the plums' 'death' (or formal disappearance and disintegration) was symbolically anticipated in the icy charm of their living flesh. This is, I believe, the exact pathos of this brief poem, and rudimentarily illustrates Williams' poetic materialism. Assuredly, this materialism is typical of a 'man of science,' someone whose sensibility must be frozen, as food itself is frozen, to preserve it. Can we not call Williams' poetry a kind of antidote to his human sensibility as a doctor: an inoculation conditioning the 'blood heat' of his emotions?" †

* Many readers want to make the king the villain of the piece, and the voyage a deliberate plot to get rid of Sir Patrick. Others will argue that the king is an irresponsible drunkard, and others will ask why, if Sir Patrick is indeed the best sailor in the land, the king does not already know this. All of these hypotheses tend to make the poem psychologically complex in a typically modern way; furthermore, they are not needed—its design can be understood best by following rules No. 2, 5, and 6, which recommend economical explanation that takes account of the poem as a unified whole.

† Parker Tyler, *Briarcliff Quarterly*, October, 1946.

Even without the unwarranted biographical speculation, this reading makes nonsense out of the poem, and what is worse, solemn, pedantic nonsense. It is no wonder that many persons take refuge in "pure sound."

The reader who steers a middle course between the extremes of underinterpretation and overinterpretation is not inhibited to any serious degree. On the other hand, what, exactly, is he to do? The negative prescriptions outlined above do not of themselves suggest anything positive. The rule of rules, not stated as such in this chapter but certainly implied in all the other rules, is "Adapt your approach to the material." No specific a priori set of directions is possible, given the nature of poetry as an art. But the concept of design which this book has largely been occupied with presenting remains as a general guide to method, and the most appropriate use of the space now left would be for reemphasizing and illustrating once more the function of this concept in interpretation. If it cannot be translated easily and automatically into practice, it still contains the best warrant of success for the reader who is willing to apply it.

The ballad of Sir Patrick Spence is as good an example of design in poetry as one could wish for. (Like the other popular ballads, it may have been composed by a series of anonymous folk artists who shaped it in actual performance, responding to the tastes of their audiences, but since it has all the unity and integrity that a work of art needs—more, indeed, than many works of our own day that come from a single pen—we are entitled to view it as if it had one author.) When a class of college students was invited to comment on the question which the king asks at the beginning of this ballad, every student chose to explain why the king asked the question and what must have been on his mind. No one thought to explain why the *poet* had him do so. In other words, the students were treating a work of art as though it had been an occasion in real life. This mistake led to a number of irrelevant theories of the sort criticized in the preceding footnote, and if followed through the whole poem it would have obscured the design almost beyond remedy. One cannot discuss "why" the king asks this question, because there is no king. He is a fictional character. Fictional characters do not have motives, ideas, feelings, intentions, or past histories, any more than they eat, sleep, bleed, get children, or die—except as an author represents them through black marks on white paper. Their solidity is an illusion. This is not said to minimize the skill of the author, but only to remind us of what that skill consists in. The suggested dimensions of his characters are not meant to be explored as though they were actual or could be meaningfully reconstructed. To do so is to take the character out of the work and thus to destroy the work. The author's skill lies in making us feel that there really is more than meets the eye, while at the same time convincing us that nothing would be gained by showing it.

The king needs a sailor to undertake a voyage for him: this much is clear from the question itself. He is represented as asking the question when and as he does because the poet has a design which requires him to do so. The poet wants to introduce the theme of the sea voyage and to indicate that a specific voyage is planned. He also wants to imply that the voyage is not an ordinary one, for the king, who presumably has many sailors under his command, is at a loss for someone to lead it. (However, his being at a loss is not itself a matter of any significance; the poet is interested in the consequences of this decision rather than in its background.) The poet especially wants to delay the entrance of Sir Patrick into the story in order to make his appearance climactic. The qualifications are known ("guid sailor") but not the man, and so the man's name, when it is subsequently put forward, has the effect of a discovery or the solution to a problem. Of all possible sailors, he is the only one qualified for the mission. The choice of Sir Patrick, being not accidental or routine but fully deliberate, helps give the story its tragic dimension. If his name had merely been the next one on the duty roster, we would have had nothing more impressive than a tale of hard luck. The tragic potentialities are heightened later in the poem by Sir Patrick's awareness of the folly and danger of the mission. He knows what he is getting into. They are heightened still further by his loyal decision to obey anyhow, even after the explicit forewarning uttered by one of his own men. He is chosen, and he chooses. Choice is the ethical *sine qua non* of tragedy. Why, in the "real life" sense, the king asked the question, and even what the voyage was all about, are irrelevant in light of the fact that he *did* ask and that, fatefully, the man he needed was available. Thus the king's question is necessary, not because it expresses a state of mind of the king's but because it functions in the poet's design to compose a tragedy. The "eldern knicht" can be accounted for in the same way: he is not an enemy of Sir Patrick's who sees this as his chance to pay off an old score, but quite literally he is the answerer of the king's question. Being "eldern" and sitting "at the kings richt kne," he is a trusted councilor, and his verdict on Sir Patrick's ability is meant to be taken at face value.

In looking at the poem this way we are not substituting arid technicalities for a rich store of human values and meanings. Rather, we are selecting out of all possible human values and meanings those which alone are relevant to the tragedy of Sir Patrick Spence. The tragedy is created by a literary design, by ways of manipulating language so that it has *this* effect rather than *that*. The reader must decide whether he is going to trust the language of the poem. If he does, he is not absolutely prohibited from speculating about motives and underlying events that this language suggests, but at the same time he is obliged to recognize that the poem is directed away from them instead of toward them. By any method of reckoning, the courtly intrigue is a minor aspect of the poem. Significantly, the poet devotes the last four of his eleven stanzas to something else: the disastrous end of the voyage. Both by its climactic position in the poem and by the amount of space given it, this event stands out as his major emphasis. And we note with some surprise that he has much to say here about the "Scots nobles," who have not figured in the plot at all. Why? There can be no other reason than to make the death of Sir Patrick more striking by contrasting it with the death of the effete nobles. To be sure, they were all loath to undertake the voyage, and they are all equally drowned at the end. The crucial difference lies in the degree of their knowledge. Sir Patrick knew that in obeying the king's order he was virtually accepting his own death, but he sailed anyway. If the nobles were anything but normally reluctant to risk their comfort in an adventure that was no part of their way of life, we are not told so. What they "really" knew is in the same category with what the king had on his mind. What Sir Patrick knew, on the other hand, is the subject of four stanzas; the poet's intention is clear. It is the difference between one who goes out to meet death and those who merely suffer it. Sir Patrick's death is the only one which involved free choice, the quality that distinguishes men, on the moral plane, from automatons, and therefore his death alone has meaning. Because we *see* his choice, it is real. Our attitude is further guided by the poet's scornful tone where the nobles are concerned; his emphasis on the exterior symbols of rank (shoes, hats, fans, combs) is an implicit value judgment. Let the nobles be mourned by their families, says the poet: this public and conventional grief, though doubtless justified, changes nothing in the final audit. Sir Patrick, for whom, ironically, no one mourns, is worth them all.

The term "tragic" does not define the meaning of Sir Patrick's death very precisely, though it is an indispensable part of such a definition. There are many different kinds of tragedies. The process of arriving at a more precise definition would go more or less as follows. We admire Sir Patrick and feel that what he did was right. Essentially, what did he do? Did he obey orders, did he disregard omens, did he make enemies at court, or perhaps was it all three things that he did? These alternatives, while true to the facts of the poem, seem out of harmony with what we sense as its moral atmosphere. Looking back on the poem, we cannot believe that the poet's design was to present an action as unedifying as that, with so narrow a range of human implications. It would hardly have been worth his trouble. On the assumption that the poet meant to hold his hero up as someone for us all to emulate, we can frame a more generous hypothesis: that what Sir Patrick did was to remain faithful to the law of his own nature, even though in doing so he exposed himself to danger from the weaknesses of other men. For Sir Patrick to have refused the assignment, he would have had to put his personal safety above this law. His tragic stature comes from his recognition of the issue and his acceptance of the consequences. But this action, while broader in its implications than the alternatives mentioned above, still has definite limits. For example, it does not touch at all upon the question of what to do when one is given an order to execute that is immoral rather than just ill-advised. What if Sir Patrick had been ordered to scuttle his ship at sea in the night, drowning his passengers? At the same time as he searches for the interpretation with the widest relevance, the reader is looking for the limits beyond which he cannot legitimately extend it. These limits are set by the poem; they are not simply the farthest reach of his own ingenuity.

The importance of asking "why"—and especially the importance of asking the *right* "why"—can hardly be over-emphasized. Now that modern criticism has succeeded in gaining widespread adoption of the analytical method of reading poetry, asking "why" is more important than ever, since a very plausible analysis can be made without taking this aspect of design into account. In fact the more thorough the analysis the less chance there is of its omission being noticed. Every poem contains enough "what" and "how" to keep a critic busy, and many critics aim at nothing more than busyness. The problem can be illustrated by imagining such a critic at work on the first three stanzas of Keats's "The Eve of Saint Agnes," which are well unified as a group and clearly stand apart from the narrative they introduce. Here are the stanzas, followed by the imaginary critic's comment:

> St. Agnes' Eve—Ah, bitter chill it was!
> The owl, for all his feathers, was a-cold;
> The hare limp'd trembling through the frozen grass,
> And silent was the flock in woolly fold:
> Numb were the Beadsman's fingers, while he told

His rosary, and while his frosted breath,
   Like pious incense from a censer old,
   Seem'd taking flight for heaven, without a death,
Past the sweet Virgin's picture, while his prayer he saith.

His prayer he saith, this patient, holy man;
   Then takes his lamp, and riseth from his knees,
   And back returneth, meagre, barefoot, wan,
   Along the chapel aisle by slow degrees:
   The sculptur'd dead, on each side, seem to freeze,
   Emprison'd in black, purgatorial rails:
   Knights, ladies, praying in dumb orat'ries,
   He passeth by; and his weak spirit fails
To think how they may ache in icy hoods and mails.

Northward he turneth through a little door,
   And scarce three steps, ere Music's golden tongue
   Flatter'd to tears this aged man and poor;
   But no—already had his deathbell rung:
   The joys of all his life were said and sung:
   His was harsh penance on St. Agnes' Eve:
   Another way he went, and soon among
   Rough ashes sat he for his soul's reprieve,
And all night kept awake, for sinners' sake to grieve.

"The poem begins with the setting rather than with the characters or plot; the Beadsman takes no part in the action of the poem and disappears altogether from our view at the end of the third stanza. This opening section is mainly atmospheric and pictorial; the dominant emphasis is upon cold (as the very first line announces). The poet proceeds to show us the intensity of the cold by describing in turn three species of animals which are normally well protected from it, ending with man (the Beadsman). Besides cold, isolation is another important emphasis. The poet makes no attempt to describe the landscape as a whole, but merely isolates certain details in it. Further, the Beadsman is isolated; not only is he shut off from the rest of human society at the moment by being where he is, he is shut off from it permanently by his religious vocation. As he moves out through the chapel aisle, we are shown the sculptured dead, who are also cold—so he imagines—and are shut off from human society by death. All that differentiates him from them even now is the feeble spark of life that he preserves; as the third stanza indicates, he is as good as dead already. Isolation and cold are thus connected with the idea of death. Near the end of this episode there is a sudden dramatic contrast as an opened door permits the music of the ball to be heard, and the ball suggests everything opposite to the Beadsman: society, warmth, and youthful life unclouded by thoughts of sin. The function of these first three stanzas is thus to enhance by contrast the story which follows."

This is not a bad analysis, and may even be a very good analysis of its own kind. But it leaves entirely unanswered the crucial question, "Why did Keats introduce a narrative poem about the elopement of two lovers with this bleak picture of cold, isolation, and death?" Or to put it negatively, "Why didn't Keats begin his story with the story itself?" The analysis mentions the function of enhancing by contrast, and this of course does occur, but we still do not know why Keats felt it to be necessary; the great majority of narratives in prose or poetry get along very well without an initial episode of contrast. The real work remains to be done.

First, as to the emphasis on cold, Keats's purpose is not merely to portray cold but also to make the reader feel the cold through his imagination, to empathize. It is one way of lessening the reader's detachment and involving him more personally in what follows. In this case it is particularly helpful because Keats is about to tell a story set in medieval times (and a story, too, with legendary overtones), something which might otherwise have little more than an antiquarian interest. We note that as the Beadsman looks at the statues, leaving the chapel, he performs this act of imagination himself. The statues are praying, as he was praying, but they are permanently fixed—frozen—in their attitudes. Their cold must be far greater than his, since it has accumulated over the years. The distance which the Beadsman's

imagination must cross in order to put him in the statues'
place is roughly the same as that which our imaginations
must cross in order to put us in the Beadsman's place. He is
acting out our role for us. Thus, however remote from our
experience the story may be, the feel of its setting at least
can be made virtually real.

There is a paradox here: the reality that we are asked
to feel is the reality of alienation and loss. The contrast between this reality and the feverish social life at the ball has
the purpose of reminding us that the social life is only temporary, the warmth of love a brief episode before the permanent cold of death. Appropriately, the poem closes as it
began; Angela and the Beadsman are both dead, and the
final word is "cold." Keats also acknowledges the deaths of
Porphyro and Madeline, since their flight took place "ages
long ago." But if this is true, they are dead when the story
begins; they are brought back to life only long enough for
the story to be told. Two separate time-schemes are operating here, as they do in all historical narrative. Whatever the
relative status of the characters in the imagined time-
scheme, in our own, the "real" one, they are all equal. Is this
not part of what Keats is trying to tell us? Keats's honesty
will not permit him the conventional romantic delusion by
which the past is, as we say, brought back to life. The past
can be recreated in art and affectionately re-examined, but
it cannot be made to live in any authentic fashion. The
truth is that these lovers are dead and gone.

In accepting this truth, Keats has transcended it. Our
interest in Porphyro and Madeline is largely conditional on
our sense that their happiness together was only a brief episode. Keats knows better than to follow the lovers off into
the night; any attempt to portray their married life would
have been bathetic. For artistic purposes, death is preferable. The romance of these lovers glows against the background of human mortality; it is surrounded by alienation
and loss. By not only acknowledging the reality of death
but also incorporating it into the fabric of his poem—
vividly incorporating it, so that the reader can feel it—
Keats gives the story its special pathos. This is "why" the

three beginning stanzas establish a contrast with what follows, and this is how they enhance the story.

The magnitude of Keats's achievement in deliberately turning his back upon the "they-lived-happily-ever-after" formula is not that he managed to get along without it but that he took what is in effect its opposite, the felt reality of death, and made it an organic part of his design. Let it be said again that he is doing more than reminding us that the lovers died after all: he is recreating their life within their death. A more extensive analysis of the poem would show how this design is supported by other elements, for Keats does not abandon thoughts of death when he leaves the Beadsman. As we read of the ball, the conspiracy with Angela, and the rendezvous of the lovers itself, we feel now and then the sudden chill of mortality. It is no accident that Angela is one "Whose passing-bell may ere the midnight toll." The central scene in Madeline's bed chamber mingles both cold and warmth, both death and life, through its imagery and its action—for example, Porphyro at the moment of Madeline's awakening from her trancelike slumber sinks to his knees "pale as smooth-sculptured stone," in unconscious imitation of the statues in the chapel. For a brief moment in their meeting, dream and reality become one, but like all consummations it is soon past and they emerge into the world of contingency, imperfection, and—ultimately—death. In fact, even as the lovers quit the stage, and before they are quite out of view, Keats has begun the process of de-materialization by which they are reabsorbed into the realm of legend: "They glide, like phantoms, into the wide hall;/ Like phantoms, to the iron porch, they glide; . . ."

In the minds of some readers the question will again arise, "How do you know that Keats intended this?" The answer is, "In the same way that we know he intended anything at all." He wrote the poem in words that have meanings, and we interpret the poem as an organization of these words. The element of design is not perhaps symbolized as such, but it is implied in and with the meanings by a process that is not fundamentally different from the process by which we communicate intention in our everyday speech. We look for intentions with more care here because it is a poem and not a fragment of conversation; it is made more artfully and aims at a more complex effect. In modern criticism there has been a reaction against the so-called "fallacy" which identifies the poem with the author's intention. The fallacy, however, lies in reading the poem from the wrong direction, that is, from the presumed intention (often discovered through biographical research) to the poem, rather than from the actual poem to the intention that it reveals. As Chapter 3 pointed out, we do not care what the poet, as a historical person, may have thought he was doing; we take what he did and from that we infer the rest. Only enough intention is needed to account for what we see. But that much is vitally important: it is, we should not forget, the author's intention to use language as an end in itself that makes the composition a poem in the first place.

The method of interpretation is determined by the nature of the materials it works upon. If we were called upon to interpret "Thirty Days Has September," we would immediately point out that this composition is supposed to help us remember the length of the months. If we were then asked, "What else?" we would reply, "There is nothing else." If, on the other hand, we are given a composition which has no apparent use or purpose other than to command our interest in the composition itself, we ask more specifically why it exists, and we begin to examine it in detail. Our efforts are guided by what we find in the poem. We want both a conception of its design as a whole and an understanding of how the various parts of the poem work together to support this design. The only alternative is to account for the poem in terms of its purely external causes. No doubt it has them—nothing produced by a human being is unaffected by aspects of personality and of human circumstance—but these causes have no aesthetic status.

What we are looking for may be thought of as a set of implicit rules, valid only for the particular occasion. Their justification lies in the total artistic effect that they make possible. We must, if we can, lay aside our own preconceptions and submit to the direction of the author. Is this not a more genuine tribute to him than any interest we might have in his married life, his political ideas, his relations with publishers, his friends and his enemies? These peripheral areas are worth exploring in due course, but they must be kept subordinate to the true aim of interpretation. We honor the poet as a man, for we know that without him we would have had no poem at all; we are not so misguided, however, as to think that the man himself is more important than what he did. By the act of interpretation we learn to know him as a poet, that is, a man whose characteristic act is to create structures in language that provide their own excuse for being. This use of language is poetry, and poetry is his design.

Index

(Poems printed in full are indicated by reference in boldface numbers.)